Julie-Ann Longman

About the Author

JERE LONGMAN is a reporter for the *New York Times* who has written about sports for a quarter century, including a three-year stint covering the Eagles for the *Philadelphia Inquirer*. His two previous HarperCollins books are the bestselling *Among the Heroes* and *The Girls of Summer*. He has lived in the Philadelphia area for the past twenty-three years.

IF FOOTBALL'S A RELIGION, WHY DON'T WE HAVE A PRAYER?

IF FOOTBALL'S A RELIGION, WHY DON'T WE HAVE A PRAYER?

Philadelphia,
Its Faithful,
and the
Eternal Quest for
Sports Salvation

Jere Longman

HARPER

NEW YORK · LONDON · TORONTO · SYDNEY

HARPER

A hardcover edition of this book was published in 2005 by HarperCollins
Publishers.

IF FOOTBALL'S A RELIGION, WHY DON'T WE HAVE A PRAYER? Copyright © 2005
by Jere Longman. All rights reserved. Printed in the United States of
America. No part of this book may be used or reproduced in any manner
whatsoever without written permission except in the case of brief quota-
tions embodied in critical articles and reviews. For information address
HarperCollins Publishers, 10 East 53rd Street, New York, NY 10022.

HarperCollins books may be purchased for educational, business, or
sales promotional use. For information please write: Special Markets
Department, HarperCollins Publishers, 10 East 53rd Street, New York,
NY 10022.

First Harper paperback published 2006.

Designed by Nancy Singer Olaguera/ISPN Publishing Services

Library of Congress Cataloging-in-Publication Data is available upon
request.

ISBN-10: 0-06-084373-X (pbk.)
ISBN-13: 978-0-06-084373-1 (pbk.)

06 07 08 09 10 ❖/RRD 10 9 8 7 6 5 4 3 2

For Debby and Julie-Ann,
who always throw spirals

Fly Eagles fly, on the road to victory
Fight Eagles fight, score a touchdown 1,2,3
Hit 'em low, hit 'em high, and watch our Eagles fly
Fly Eagles fly, on the road to victory
E-A-G-L-E-S, Eagles!

—*Philadelphia Eagles fight song*

Christ, even that fuckin' Smarty Jones laid down on us.
We were ready to give a parade to a fuckin' horse, that's
how desperate we are.

—The Philly Fan, *a play by Bruce Graham*

Foreword

On September 9, 1990, Bruce Graham, a playwright, watched from home as his Philadelphia Eagles opened the season against the New York Giants. Watching with him that Sunday night was his high school drama teacher, Sandy Stefanowicz, who wore her special helmet earrings. She was the only woman Bruce allowed in his Eagles viewing circle. He was afraid, Sandy said, that someone might talk about fabric or shopping.

Sandy sat in a rocking chair holding Bruce's daughter Kendall, who was eight days old. The baby weighed little more than five pounds and made a perfect fit, like a human football, in Sandy's hands.

The game grew taut, and as the Eagles began a critical drive, Sandy's chair began rocking faster. Bruce turned to her and said, "Give me the baby."

Sandy: "Why?"

Bruce: "I'm afraid you're going to spike her."

On January 14, 1999, three days after Andy Reid was named head coach of the Eagles, a winter storm raked Philadelphia with snow and ice. After experiencing a traveler's nightmare, with a diverted flight and a night spent in the Baltimore train station, Reid worked all day and wanted a decent meal, according to Butch

Buchanico, the team's director of security. So Buchanico took him to an Italian restaurant called Frederick's in South Philly.

A priest walked into the restaurant and recognized Reid. He came over, wished the coach good luck and blessed him. The guys at the next table got curious. They were businessmen who had been drinking something stronger than iced tea and were insulated against the cold and their own social inhibitions.

"Who's that?" one of them asked.

Informed that it was the new coach of the Eagles, a guy stood up and said, "Yo, Coach Reid, welcome to Philadelphia."

Then the whole table booed in unison.

"You know," Buchanico told Reid, "you set a record. You ain't in this town twelve hours, you ain't played a friggin' game and you got booed and blessed at the same time."

I know this obsession. I understand it. Well, not this one exactly. Not the resilient hope and dread of cheering for the Philadelphia Eagles, but something similar and equally intense—a kid's consuming interest in Louisiana State University football.

I grew up in Eunice, Louisiana, population twelve thousand, located eighty miles west of the LSU campus in Baton Rouge. My mother once won season tickets in a Dairy Queen raffle, and we watched LSU game films at Cub Scout meetings. Early on autumn Sunday mornings, I retrieved the newspapers with the eagerness of Christmas presents. With my family still asleep, I returned to bed, pulled the covers over my head and read the sports pages by flashlight.

This boy's fascination became my profession. As I write this, I am fifty and have lived for the past twenty-three years, nearly half my life, in Philadelphia and its suburbs. For the first eleven and a half years, I worked as a sportswriter for the *Philadelphia Inquirer*. For nearly twelve years, I have been with the *New York Times*.

As a beat reporter for the *Inquirer*, I covered the Eagles in 1982, 1983 and 1984, Dick Vermeil's last year, and Marion Campbell's first two years, as head coach. Not exactly the glory days of the franchise. What stuck with me were the characters around the team. Otho Davis, the trainer, used to scare the hell out of rookies by giving them a pill that turned their urine blue. He'd put them in a pool at training camp, hook them to a device that resembled scuba gear and tell them to submerge so he could test their breathing. Only it wasn't scuba gear. It was a hose hooked up to an empty container of mayonnaise.

And there was Jack Edelstein, a guy from a wealthy family that manufactured belts. Nominally, he assisted as a spotter on Eagles' radio broadcasts, but mainly he served as the team's court jester. He'd walk around the locker room talking gibberish, which also made him popular at banquets. But the most interesting thing about Jack was his connection to Hollywood. According to Merrill Reese, the Eagles' longtime radio voice, Jack dated Marilyn Monroe, knew Grace Kelly and Jerry Lewis and served as the best man in Red Buttons's wedding, to which he brought as his date Tina Louise from *Gilligan's Island*. Jack's most notorious prank that Reese loved to recount was to drive up to a tollbooth with a cadaver's arm hidden under his jacket. When the tollbooth operator grabbed the quarter, he came away with the coin and the limb that offered it.

Leonard Tose, the team's self-indulgent owner, got the Eagles to the Super Bowl in 1981 and essentially drank and gambled the franchise away before selling it four years later. During that troubled period, he quite possibly became the first person ever booed in a barbershop. The players went on strike when I began covering the Eagles in 1982, and the later at night you called Leonard for comment, the better the quotes. He could always be found with a drink in his hand and a woman on his arm. He had more wives than quarterbacks. He met one of his wives, Caroline, on a plane. She was a flight attendant in first class, and he greeted her with this immortal pickup line: "Lady, you have a terrific ass."

Unfortunately for the Eagles, the stories have often been more entertaining than the football. Philadelphia won the National Football League championship in 1948, 1949 and 1960, but not since. Through the years, losing became familiar and excruciating. The Eagles improved greatly after Andy Reid became coach, but even their success became a kind of taunt to fans as Philadelphia lost three consecutive times in the National Football Conference championship game. An entire region was buffeted by collective sporting failure. As the autumn of 2004 arrived, no city with teams in the four major professional sports had gone longer without a title—twenty-one years.

Philadelphia's last pro championship had been delivered by the 76ers, who swept the Los Angeles Lakers to win the National Basketball Association in 1983. I met my wife, Debby, for the first time the next day. I had written a story for the *Inquirer* after the decisive game, then taken a red-eye flight from L.A. to await the Sixers' triumphant arrival in Philadelphia. Debby worked for the team at the time, and I bumped into her at the airport.

"You asked me what time the plane was going to land," she recalled.

"Were you excited to see me?"

"I was excited to see the team."

When it came to first impressions, I was no Leonard Tose.

That long-ago championship aside, a dark thought persisted in Philadelphia that something would go wrong with its sports teams. Often, it did. During the 2004 season, the Eagles soared through the NFC, not winning a conference game by fewer than ten points until mid-December. Then, on December 19, the flamboyant receiver Terrell Owens suffered ligament damage in his right ankle and a broken bone in his right leg. He was given only a remote chance of playing if the Eagles reached the Super Bowl seven weeks later.

Now a possible fourth defeat in the NFC title game loomed. No franchise had lost a conference championship that many seasons in a row. The Eagles threatened to become latter-day Buffalo Bills, who had lost four consecutive years in the Super Bowl. Philadelphia became frenzied with doubt. And that's when I got the idea for this book. Sportswriting required a sober concession. To cover sports meant relinquishing the ardor that made them attractive. Surrendering the fan's obsession. Journalism required detachment, impartiality, skepticism. There was no cheering in the press box. And yet, as I neared three decades as a sportswriter, what interested me most about Philadelphia were not the Eagles' players, who remained the same age as I got older, or the games, which could grow dully repetitive. It was the fans and their operatic passion that sustained my attention.

Their faith was unanswered but undying. They were often portrayed as surly, but win or lose, they showed up, year after year, generation after generation, resigned to defeat but fierce and impatient and unshakable in their yearning. Being from Louisiana, I had a high tolerance for their goofy excess. One of my enduring memories of Cajun Mardi Gras was the sight of an equine head and two hooves poking into our den as my mother stood at the door, scolding a neighbor, "Don't you dare come in this house on that horse!"

In many ways, Eagles fans rooted with a collegiate zeal reminiscent of LSU fans. In fact, because big-time college football in Philadelphia was played only by feckless Temple University, the Eagles served double duty. An estimated twenty-five thousand fans showed up one day at training camp before the 2004 season, requiring Reid to use a police escort to and from practice. During the 2003 season, some fifteen thousand Eagles fans took a road trip to Miami, essentially turning it into a home game.

In the 1920s and 1930s, when he was governor of Louisiana and then a U.S. senator, Huey P. Long cowrote one of the LSU fight songs, led the marching band, stalked up and down the sidelines, gave instructions to the head coach and chided the referees. As the current governor of Pennsylvania and former mayor of Philadelphia, Edward G. Rendell spent two hours analyzing each Eagles' game on television and once tried to scuttle the team's attempt to draft quarterback Donovan McNabb.

In another sense, fans of the Eagles and LSU served as American versions of international soccer fans. Not primarily in their hooligan behavior, which was far more muted here than in Europe, but in their roiling, durable ardor and need for civic validation.

In Italy, rabid soccer fans were known as *tifosi*, or those stricken with typhoid fever. I covered the World Cup there in 1990 and saw housewives hanging the national flag on the line with the laundry. I walked into restaurants where waiters refused to leave the kitchen if the *Azzurri*, or the Blues, were playing. In American football, I have witnessed this same devouring enthusiasm in the two places where it is perhaps the most intense: In Louisiana with LSU and in Philadelphia with the Eagles.

Tony Novosel, an academic adviser and history teacher at the University of Pittsburgh, said his city's dedication to the Steelers was the closest thing he had seen to enthusiasm for European soccer.

"They say the national team is like your uncle and the local team is like your immediate family," Novosel said. "The Steelers are like immediate family."

The same soccer analogy applied in Philadelphia with the Eagles. The way fans wore the team colors. And sang the fight song. And embraced affirming victory. And bled with abrasive defeat. They even chanted "T.O." for Owens in the singsong rhythm that soccer fans chanted "Olé, olé, olé."

Soccer rivalries often grew out of differences between religious affiliation or socioeconomic classes, noted Eric Zillmer, the athletic director at Drexel University and a professor of sports psychology. Philadelphia considered itself a blue-collar town in a constraining, shadowed location between New York and Washington, cities with brighter lights and higher-wattage power.

"It seems that Philadelphia has a chip on its shoulder," Zillmer said. In a place with lagging self-esteem, sports became a great leveler, particularly football, and success served "to validate who you are."

In Philadelphia, professional football was consumed in great zealous quantities, just as college football was in Baton Rouge and all over the South, where the sport had aged and seeped in like whiskey in an oaken barrel. People took it personally in these places. It seemed to matter more. There was in the fabric of this fandom pure Sansabelt devotion, something forever elastic, a Dacron-poly triple-stretch gabardine affection. I had come to see a similar football devotion in Philadelphia, one that was almost

Southern gothic, engulfed, tinged with wistful underachievement and a longing for respect.

I became drawn to the game as a boy in Eunice, a randy little town on the Cajun prairie. Eunice was the only place I knew where anybody had ever been arrested for drunken driving on a riding lawnmower. At the Pony Room, a bar outside town, these words of timeless wisdom greeted users of the men's urinal: "Don't throw toothpicks in the trough. Crabs can pole-vault."

Nothing big ever happened in Eunice. "The street lights coming on was a lot of excitement," my father said. Except for the time he sold a Pontiac GTO to Lucy Baines Johnson while her father, Lyndon Baines Johnson, happened to be president of the United States. The godparents of one of Lucy Bird's children lived in Eunice. Lucy Baines bought the car from a dealership owned by my father's stepfather, who was also the mayor and active in Democratic politics. She came to pick up the GTO trailing an escort of Secret Service agents who combed the bathrooms, apparently to make sure no Pine-Sol grenades or Brillo pad trip wires had been set. They seemed tensely officious.

"I reached in my pocket for my cigarette lighter and they took two steps backward," my father said. "They didn't know what I might have in there."

Lucy Baines and her husband attended our Catholic church that weekend, and later, somebody spotted them at the Frostop drive-in. It had a giant root beer mug on the roof and was the place where we celebrated our victories in Little League. Eight of us packed into my mother's car, speeding off in celebrity pursuit. I jumped out and bought an ice-cream cone for camouflage, as if one cone for eight people would make us look any less suspicious as country gawkers.

We had a famous honky-tonk, too, the Purple Peacock, where the dance floor was built from well-oiled lanes of the local bowling alley. Stephen Stills wrote a song about the Peacock, but I met him years later and he got it all wrong, thinking it was a blues joint.

While I was too young to get into the Peacock, Saturday nights for my family in the 1960s were reserved for Lawrence Welk, Jackie Gleason and, in the fall, LSU football. Once a year, maybe twice, my father got tickets and we made the drive to Baton Rouge through speed-trap towns like Krotz Springs and Livonia in the days before Interstate 10 opened, getting stuck behind trucks loaded with sugar cane, smelling acrid smoke from the harvest. Arriving well before kickoff, we formed worshipful lines at the players' entrance to Tiger Stadium. Walking into the concrete bowl, the players seemed heroic and purposeful, and a whole state was captivated by these strapping boys dressed in the purple and gold of Mardi Gras.

Mostly, we listened to games at home on the radio. My brother Tim, my sister Irene and I would place our sleeping bags on the floor of the living room. My father either joined us or lay head to toe with my mother on the sofa. In my youth, LSU players had names that seemed to drip with moss from the bayous: Sammy Grezaffi, Joe Labruzzo, Remi Prudhomme. Years later, I came to wonder whether these players, like *Gatsby*'s Tom Buchanan, were so adored and accomplished by the age of twenty-one that the rest of their lives would "savor of anticlimax."

When LSU lost on Saturday, I felt empty. Once, in the mid-1960s when Steve Spurrier played quarterback at Florida, I listened to the Gators beat LSU as I sat alone in my mother's car in the driveway, the radio on. After the loss I wandered the neighborhood, as vacant and desolate as the weedy field behind our house. It seemed silly now, but football gave us such a sense of ourselves.

We grew up in the rural wide-open, and sports fulfilled a neighborhood full of boys. We built our own baseball field. We played football in the yard until the grass became bald, and once the neighbors lost water pressure when a rough tackle knocked a faucet off the side of their house. We cemented a basketball stanchion in the driveway and folded lawn chairs into hurdles and fashioned vaulting poles out of bamboo. This sense of competition stayed with me, and later I ran the New York City Marathon a few times, although my wife Debby remained skeptical of the health benefits of distance running. As I filled out the entry form for my first race, under "Occupation" she suggested "organ donor."

Then, as now, I liked the travel as much as the games, maybe more. In Eunice, we spent our childhoods watching the Catholic high school play on Thursday nights and the public school on Friday. I preferred road games and loved to fall asleep to the thrum of the tires on the ride home, my father, Jere, and my mother, Ann, riding in the odometer glow of the front seat, my brother and sister and I sprawled in the rear slumbering darkness.

When I played at Eunice High, football provided a comforting, defining ritual, the smell of cigars and peanuts, the peppy exhorting of cheerleaders, the band's brassy geometry and the slap of plastic and leather on a luxuriant field lined and mowed for autumn. There was muscular satisfaction in hitting a running back so hard and clean that you felt his body go slack and yield to your insistence. There was a fleeting sensation of reaching the end zone after an interception, hands shaking, feeling as if you were not quite in the present or the past but in an electric in-between, carried along on an invisible current. There was humiliation in scoring first and losing fifty-six to six and having an assistant coach say, "Go shake their hands, boys, and thank 'em for whippin' your ass."

My high school coach, Joe Nagata, played in the same backfield at LSU in the 1940s with Steve Van Buren, who would later become the Eagles' greatest running back, carrying Philadelphia to NFL titles in 1948 and 1949. As a boy in the early 1940s, my father and his friends caught a train from Eunice to Baton Rouge for LSU night games, returning home as late as three in the morning in those unafraid days. For seventy-five cents, they saw great LSU backs like Alvin Dark, who would make his career as a baseball manager, and Van Buren, who would lead the NFL in rushing four times en route to the Hall of Fame.

A month after my senior football season in high school, my parents let me take my first trip without them. Three friends and I drove twenty-two hours from Eunice to El Paso, Texas, to watch LSU play Iowa State in the 1971 Sun Bowl. We had all the essentials—enough money for cheap hotels and cheaper restaurants, priapic anticipation and the eight-track accompaniment of the Bee Gees and Kenny Rogers and the First Edition.

In college, I would drive with two friends from Baton Rouge to Washington to watch President Nixon resign. As a sportswriter, I would take an elevator a mile below ground at a gold mine in South Africa and jog above twelve thousand feet on an extinct volcano near Mexico City. But there was nothing like the giddiness of a high school kid away for the first time in El Paso, seeing players smoking cigars in the team hotel and traveling across the Mexican border to the souvenir stands and strip clubs of Juarez and watching a sportswriter dance in his boxer shorts in one of these forbidden joints, pants around his ankles. During the game, I poured hot chocolate into my boots to keep my frozen feet warm. At least I think I did. Memory heats and grows dormant, like a volcano, and the dancing sportswriter and the hot chocolate seem so vividly real, but all these years later I cannot guarantee the events were anything more than ashes of false recollection. After the game, we drove home, twenty-two hours in the other direction, setting a world record for times listening to "Just Dropped In (To See What Condition My Condition Was In)." Later, when I worked in Dallas, and drove the state looking for stories, I grew to love West Texas and the brittle cold at night and the diamond-glitter of stars in the vast aloneness.

Baton Rouge held a different attraction. Darkness was a lid that trapped the noise and piquant flavoring of LSU football—the opening drum cadence and cymbal crash of the band and the caped, sequined glamour of the dancing Golden Girls and the roar of Mike, the Bengal tiger mascot. "Everyone is going crazy and the smell of bourbon is in the air," Rohan Davey, a former LSU quarterback, once told me.

In the mid-1970s, I attended LSU and watched games from the boozy haze of the student section. We chanted "Tiger Bait" at the opponents and serenaded them with petty vulgarities: "What comes out of a Chinaman's ass? Rice, Rice, Rice."

In 1975, the Tigers suffered their first losing season in nearly two decades. For April Fool's Day in 1976, one of our editors at the student paper posed on a faux tiger rug, wearing nothing but a pennant borrowed from the campus book store. We superimposed the head of Charlie McClendon, the LSU coach, who took the joke well. Noticing his fig-leaf covering, he exclaimed, "Look at the size of that pennant." The bookstore was not so pleased and refused to accept a return.

LSU had won a national championship in 1958, and Billy Cannon had won the Heisman Trophy in 1959 after beating Ole Miss with a famous trick-or-treat punt return on Halloween. My parents had been in Tiger Stadium that night when Cannon became everybody's all-American. My father sat near Cannon's wife, Dorothy, when she removed her earrings and tossed them into the air as her husband ran eighty-nine yards for the end zone, shedding tacklers the way jockeys shed goggles. Later, Cannon went to jail for counterfeiting, and his legend grew frayed. He remained a hero to some, an embarrassment to others, in sullied affirmation of Louisiana's weakness for rascally misbehavior.

Jake Gibbs, the Ole Miss quarterback and punter that Halloween night, was the last man to make a futile lunge at Cannon. The Eagles considered drafting him after the 1960 season, when Norm Van Brocklin retired, but Gibbs preferred baseball, becoming a catcher for the New York Yankees and, later, head coach at Ole Miss. Every time Gibbs walked to the mound at games in Baton Rouge, LSU fans serenaded him with a boom-box reprise of Cannon's punt return. One heckler chanted ritually, "Catch him, Jake, catch him." Graciously, Gibbs played along until the season of his retirement, when he approached the heckler and said, "Goddamnit, I'm not the only son of a bitch that missed him."

Forty-five years after its first national title, LSU shared the national championship with Southern California in 2003, and football tightened its typhoid grip on the state. The most feverishly stricken lived in purple-and-gold houses and drove purple-and-gold cars and dressed their wedding parties in purple-and-gold gowns. Some rode in purple-and-gold wheelchairs and had purple-and-gold flowers placed on their graves. I knew a woman in

Eunice who had her cat's broken leg set in a purple-and-gold cast.

A few years ago, I met an electrician named Rudy Penton, who even painted his dogs purple and gold during football season and serenaded his grandkids on the drive to school each morning with music from the LSU band. Rudy, who lived in the paper mill town of Bogalusa, Louisiana, had an uncle named Chubby, who used to flock his Christmas tree purple and gold and decorate it with sugar packets when LSU played in the Sugar Bowl. Chubby named one of his sons Mike, after the tiger mascot.

LSU was the primary public university in Louisiana. Its football team enjoyed a uniform allegiance, unlike other places in the South where rivalries between Auburn and Alabama, Florida and Florida State and Ole Miss and Mississippi State dispersed rooting loyalties. LSU football was a staple of the Cajun cultural gumbo, as were politics and hunting and cooking and drinking beer. A rural optimism held that football, like rice and crawfish, would produce a bumper crop each year. That fierce pride was tempered by self-flagellation and mild insecurity, also found in Philadelphia.

As Rudy Penton told me, "When we're number one, it's usually for something bad," ticking off Louisiana's struggles with illiteracy, poverty, chemical dumping, political chicanery. LSU football, along with the bonhomie of the people, the food and the music, became a recommendation for the entire state, just as a portion of Philadelphia's identity was wrapped up in the Eagles.

"It's literally the state of Louisiana taking on [LSU's opponents]," Dr. Mark A. Emmert, the former university chancellor, once told me. "I've been around collegiate athletics all my life. In no place does the psyche of the community soar like when the Tigers win. Conversely, in no place does the psyche crash like when the Tigers lose."

Jim Murray, a former general manager of the Eagles, used to say that you could tell by the sky on Monday whether Philadelphia had won or lost on Sunday, whether the mood of the populace was sunny or sullen. The same might be said about the state of Louisiana.

"More cars are sold on Monday after we win, more clothes are sold at department stores," LSU's athletic director, Skip Bertman, said. "There isn't any question the psyche of the people is wrapped up in the football team. In Louisiana, we are ranked forty-five to fifty in things that are good and in the top ten in things that are bad. But in athletics, we rank very well."

And LSU fans could get every bit as delirious and nasty as Eagles fans. In 1997, when LSU defeated top-ranked Florida, where Spurrier was then coaching his alma mater, Gator coaches and players said they were spat upon and strafed with invective and other hurled objects as Tiger fans stormed the field. The Florida team bus was later encircled by a victorious mob, and Spurrier said it was the only time that his wife, Jerri, ever felt threatened by fans from another school.

"That place is awesome," Jesse Palmer, a Florida quarterback that season, said with lopsided admiration. "The fans were shaking our bus when we drove away. When you drive in, everybody is flipping you the bird—ninety-year-olds, kids, moms. You run into the stadium and even the cheerleaders are yelling at you. It's the essence of college football."

Florida was not the only target. Shawn Andrews, an offensive lineman who was the Eagles' first-round draft pick in 2004 from the University of Arkansas, said that once when several Razorback fans were using portable toilets at Tiger Stadium, LSU fans tipped them over.

"Stuff was flying everywhere," Andrews said. "It was horrible."

In 1967, Louisiana got its own professional team, the New Orleans Saints. A relative gave my family and my cousin's family six tickets to the Saints' inaugural game. Box seats at Tulane Stadium, behind the Los Angeles Rams' bench. We stayed at the Rams' hotel, the Fontainebleau, and ended up on the same floor as some of the players. We had never seen so many big men squeezed into an elevator.

Saturday night before the first game, we took a swim in the

hotel pool. The Rams' trainer shouted from a balcony and told us to hold it down, the players were sleeping. My father took that not as an admonition to keep quiet, but as an invitation to run down the hallway yelling, "Rams are sissies."

Thus unnerved and bereft of sleep, Los Angeles surrendered a ninety-four-yard touchdown run to Saints' rookie John Gilliam on the opening kickoff. There were more than eighty thousand people in that vast metal stadium, jumping and screaming and turning the place into the world's largest tuning fork. It was the loudest noise a kid ever thought he would hear.

George Allen and his Rams recovered quickly enough and put the Saints away, twenty-seven to thirteen. Seven weeks later, on November 5, 1967, New Orleans won its first game, thirty-one to twenty-four, over the hapless Eagles. Two weeks later, Philadelphia returned the favor, forty-eight to twenty-one, and losing began again for New Orleans. Not until twenty years later, in 1987, did the Saints manage a winning season. Games weren't all they lost. At one point, the Saints even lost a consonant and became the Aints. You didn't have to be bad to lose a game, but you had to be awful to lose a consonant.

The nadir came in 1980, a ruinous season of one victory and fifteen defeats. Despondent kicker Russell Erxleben expressed the acute hopelessness felt by everyone who had ever played or rooted for the Saints.

At the University of Texas, Erxleben had set an NCAA record with a sixty-seven-yard field goal. In 1979, the Saints made him their first-round draft choice and the first millionaire kicker. A year later, his confidence was deflated, his concentration destroyed. He blew a field goal that cost the Saints their opening game. After a second mediocre game, Erxleben lost his job to a guy who used to run a clothing boutique.

"I tried to commit suicide twice, but the bullet went wide left," he said.

Even the Saints' greatest moment became a victim of horticultural abandonment. On November 8, 1970, Tom Dempsey kicked a sixty-three-yard field goal that remains tied as the NFL record. A patch of grass from the spot of the kick was unearthed and given to Dempsey as a souvenir. He planted it in his yard. The next year, he joined the Eagles. The grassy patch remained behind.

"I couldn't very well take it with me," Dempsey once told me.

I had several great-aunts, all in their eighties, who still gathered on Sundays to watch the Saints while they laughed and smoked and cursed. On occasion, one aunt wore a football uniform, while another dressed in a cheerleader outfit. But my immediate family had long ago abandoned the Saints, who had one playoff victory in thirty-eight years of miserable existence. The team was now threatening to leave Louisiana. Good, my father said. He'd help them pack.

LSU held a much stronger allure. Still, since graduating in 1976, I had returned only two or three times to cover football games. I had now lived in Philadelphia longer than I ever lived in Louisiana. It was Eagles fans to whom I was drawn affectionately for their manic craving and churning doubt and blissful vulgarity and pliable hearts filled with expectation and terror. I had been on assignment in Berlin during the 2004 NFC championship game, a fourteen-to-three loss to Carolina, watching in the middle of the night in a smoky bar in Potsdamer Platz, where the Berlin Wall once separated East and West, sitting there, nursing a beer, a whole continent away from another raw, throbbing defeat in Philadelphia. I walked back to my hotel in the frozen darkness, feeling oddly guilty and homesick, not because the Eagles had lost, but because I felt dislocated from their suffering fans, whose despair was captured famously by one man leaving the stadium and screaming into a television camera, "Every year they break my heart! I hate them! I hate them! I hate them!"

A season later, Owens unhinged his ankle and broke his leg and fractured a city's beseeching innocence that always lurked beneath a rude bluster. From mid-December through a nervous playoff run to the Super Bowl, I followed a group of Eagles fans to try to better understand this flexible anticipation and fear that enthralled Philadelphia every football season. I did not become a fan—cheering was bleached out of me long ago, like lipstick from a collar—but neither did I try to immunize myself against this annual epidemic of sporting typhoid.

"Eagles fans have an edge like no place else I've ever been," said Al Morganti, a host at WIP, the local sports-talk radio station, and a former colleague at the *Inquirer*. "It's like a ham-and-egg sandwich. The chicken is involved, but the pig is committed. These people are committed."

IF FOOTBALL'S A RELIGION, WHY DON'T WE HAVE A PRAYER?

1

Friday, December 17, 2004

Twelve and one. How was that for a chest-bumping way to open a season? Twelve victories and one freakin' defeat. A city with more confidence and less experience at heartbreak would have felt invincible, not imperiled. Philadelphia was different. Tranquility was a base on the moon, not some cocoon of serenity in which anyone here nestled. Uproar, dispute, that was Philly's natural state. This was the place where Charles Barkley claimed to be misquoted in his own autobiography. The city where David Lynch, the filmmaker, went to art school and found a haunting, exquisite fear. Apprehension. That's what Philadelphia did best. Eagles fans could sense ruin the way a woolly caterpillar could intuit the harshness of winter. They felt a waver in destiny's forecast like an ache in old bones.

"If it's an airplane, it's always going to crash, it's never going to land," Butch Buchanico, the Eagles' director of security, liked to explain about the local sporting mindset.

On Sunday, against the hated and feeble Dallas Cowboys, Philadelphia could run the table for the first time in the National Football Conference's Eastern Division. Home-field advantage could be secured throughout the NFC playoffs. After three consecutive defeats in the NFC championship game, the Super Bowl seemed inevitable. The star receiver Terrell Owens had been acquired in the off-season in a complicated, acrimonious trade involving San Francisco and Baltimore. Owens was audacious and his attitude seemed to bleed over to his teammates with a kind of pleasurable stain, giving the Eagles a relaxed confidence. He appeared to be the final piece of a championship jigsaw, as Pete Rose had been for the Phillies in 1980 and as Moses Malone had been for the 76ers in 1983. Already, Owens had caught fourteen touchdown passes, a club record. One more, and Coach Andy Reid would make good on a promise to squeeze his fleshy physique, sausage-like, into a pair of tights.

But everything had gone too perfectly. Harmony brought boredom, which fostered suspicion. This morning I spoke on the phone with Buzz Bissinger, author of the seminal football book *Friday Night Lights*. He had lived in Philadelphia for two decades. Bissinger listened inveterately to WIP, the local sports-talk radio station, and rooted for the Eagles, but he knew in this city of Independence Hall and the Liberty Bell, that the sporting past haunted the present like bad credit.

Buzz said he worried that Philadelphia was setting itself up again for complete misery. He feared something bizarre would happen. It always did. No city with teams in the four major professional sports had gone longer without a championship—twenty-one years, since the Sixers last won the NBA. The Eagles had not won an NFL title since 1960. Forty-four years. Buzz sensed another strange failure. Maybe Owens would score a touchdown in the upcoming NFC championship game and pull out another Sharpie pen to autograph the ball, only this time his cleats would catch in the grass and he would fall and the Sharpie would puncture his eardrum.

"I swear, I'm just waiting," Bissinger said.

He was a believer that a city's image of itself had an impact on its teams and players. He said he hoped he was wrong.

"Why does it always happen that Philadelphia finds a way to mess it up?" Bissinger asked. "There's a bittersweet fatalism to the place."

Philadelphia was the nation's fifth-largest city, but it seemed to me like the world's biggest small town. It was just like my hometown in Louisiana, but with one and a half million people instead of twelve thousand. Nobody from Philadelphia ever seemed to leave Philadelphia. Of course, they did leave the city for the suburbs, and population drain on the tax base became a chronic problem. But no one ever seemed to want to leave the area. I had never seen another place where people got married and moved in with their parents. My wife, Debby, lived most of her life within a radius of five miles. She always seemed reluctant to visit Louisiana, or anyplace where barbecue was a verb.

One of the things I loved about Philadelphia was its lack of pretense. This was no klieg light hot spot, not a trendy place to be discovered. So insular was it that Pat Croce, then president of the Sixers, declined to give President Bill Clinton a courtside seat during the 2001 NBA Finals. To accommodate the president would have meant displacing a season-ticket holder.

The people here reminded me of the Cajuns I had grown up with. They were more contrary, of course, but you expected that in a rebellious place where the Declaration of Independence was adopted. They were also casually friendly, ribaldly funny and great storytellers, both embracing and suspicious of outsiders. They rooted for the Eagles with a small town's desperate, wonderful fanaticism. They wore the star players' jerseys and flew team flags on their cars and their porches. They wrote shoe polish exhortations on their windshields and bathed houses and buildings in the team colors and knew the words to the fight song and felt the sting of slights that were real or perceived. They both ignored outsiders and cared deeply what outsiders thought of them. They thought they were more passionate and knowledgeable than others and wondered if they measured up.

But just as I was attracted to the small-town embrace of Philadelphia, I was sometimes disappointed by its tepid ambitions. It was a place that too often slumped its shoulders instead of pounding its chest. Philadelphia was the birthplace of the country. The Constitution was drafted and signed here. Philly had been the nation's capital from 1790 to 1800. The nation's first central bank and public library and oldest hospital were located here. The telephone was introduced to the world here at the nation's Centennial Exhibition in 1876. Even the National Football League was based here from 1946 through 1959. But the seat of political power had moved to Washington, and the center of financial power had shifted to New York, as had the offices of the NFL. Philadelphia was left between these two cities as a historical way station, its primacy indeterminate, a place of the past and passed by. Not until the 1980s were ramps added to fully connect Interstate 95 to Center City. Ever watch the national weather? New York and Washington were always mentioned, but Philadelphia was frequently overlooked. Even on place mats at local diners, maps of the eastern seaboard included Boston, New York, Washington and Baltimore but forgot Philly, complained the title character in Bruce Graham's play, *The Philly Fan*:

> *What the hell is that all about?*
> *Baltimore?*
> *Gimme a fuckin' break.*

There seemed to be a comfort here, or a resignation, in being second best. "Scar tissue, so when the scalpel is inserted, it doesn't hurt as much," Graham told me. Until 1987, after a gentleman's agreement expired to build no tower higher than William Penn's statue atop City Hall, Philly had no skyscrapers, that most obvious sign of municipal ambition. Self-destructiveness led the city to bomb a home and burn down a neighborhood in 1985 while evicting the radical group MOVE. For a brief period, the city's slogan was, "Philadelphia: Not as bad as Philadelphians say it is."

"An inferiority complex—you have to fight it every day," Croce once told me.

But the Eagles had raised expectations, especially now with Owens and Jevon Kearse, the sculpted pass rusher, on the team. Kearse had been acquired in free agency from the Tennessee Titans. Fears that his would be a career of chronic injury proved unfounded. No one could challenge the Eagles in the NFC. Here was a Philadelphia civic institution that strived openly to be the best. Perhaps more than anything, the Eagles made a city of the past relevant and vital in the present.

"They have to win the Super Bowl," Bissinger said. "Just getting there is a Philadelphia excuse: we're second best. We need to be the best in something. We need to rid ourselves of sloppy seconds. They have the talent, which means they're destined to do it. In Philadelphia, this means they're destined not to do it."

Bissinger was hardly alone with his awful premonition. The biggest Eagles fan in the state was the governor himself, Edward G. Rendell, a former mayor and district attorney of Philadelphia. A few hours after I spoke with Bissinger, I was on the phone with Rendell.

"Fans love the Eagles fiercely, but always in their hearts they believe something is going to go wrong," he said.

Philadelphia got close, but never crossed the line first, Rendell said. Human athletes couldn't seem to alter this bleak destiny. Neither could a local horse. So much hope had been saddled on Smarty Jones and the 2004 Triple Crown. What did a three-year-old thoroughbred know about decades of futility? A horse would wear blinders to history. Smarty won the Kentucky Derby and the Preakness, and by post time at the Belmont Stakes, Philadelphia awaited with a fervor that was edgy, restless, whipsawed by anguish. People were excited and scared, some too afraid to watch. They feared agonizing deficiency, a conclusion that would be sharp and terrible, and then it unfolded in the worst way. Smarty got caught from behind in the homestretch, confirming Philadelphia's status as a thwarted runner-up.

"Even Smarty let us down," Rendell said, although at least Smarty got a nice parting gift—a life at stud as Wilt Chamberlain of the Bluegrass—while the rest of Philadelphia was left with another cold shower of rebuff.

After each Eagles game, Rendell conducted a postmortem on a raucous cable program called *Post Game Live*. He was just short of his sixty-first birthday, and as part of a *Capital Gang* for sports, he critiqued the performances of players and coaches with the same scrutiny he gave to the latest appropriations bill.

Even as chairman of the Democratic National Committee during a tempestuous presidential election season in 2000, when political instant replay took five weeks to decide whether Al Gore had his feet inbounds or out of bounds as commander-in-chief, Rendell missed only one appearance as an Eagles television analyst.

Lynn Swann, the Republican sports commentator and former Pittsburgh Steelers receiver, was considering a run against Rendell in the 2006 gubernatorial election. Noting this, Larry O'Rourke of the *Allentown Morning Call* told me, "It's the only state where we have a governor who wants to be a sportscaster and a sportscaster who wants to be a governor."

Some thought Rendell's allegiance to the Eagles could cost him political capital. Ernie Clark, an Eagles season-ticket holder since 1961, said Philadelphia fans understood, but "a lot of people must be wondering, 'What the hell is he doing? Isn't there something more productive he could be doing?' If you're not a football fan, you must conclude that."

Rendell had long been known for saying exactly what was on his mind. Sometimes, this raw candor got him in trouble, as it did in 1994 when he wondered aloud while traveling with a reporter from *Philadelphia Magazine* how she would be in bed. And some Democratic poo-bahs took offense when he called for Gore to concede in the 2000 election after a setback in the Supreme Court left the Democrat's chances at fourth and long.

Mostly, Rendell's frankness endeared him to sports fans, who considered him to possess an authenticity that was important in Philadelphia. During his first mayoral administration, Rendell declared that the Phillies would not be swept in the 1993 World Series because he had sized up the Toronto pitching staff and decided that even he could get a hit off Todd Stottlemyre.

As the 2000 presidential election recount went into triple overtime, Ray Didinger, a fellow panelist on the Eagles post-game show, turned to Rendell during a break and said, "Shouldn't you be down in Florida?"

"Naaaah," Rendell answered.

Rendell was hardly the first politician to love sports. Rudolph W. Giuliani, the former New York City mayor, was a rabid Yankees fan. Gerald Ford played center at Michigan. Richard Nixon scripted a pass play for Coach Don Shula before Miami played Dallas in Super Bowl VI. Governor Jesse Ventura of Minnesota served as an announcer for the short-lived XFL football league. Doug Moreau, a former LSU flanker and the most valuable player in the 1965 Sugar Bowl, did color commentary for LSU's radio broadcasts as district attorney of East Baton Rouge Parish.

But perhaps no politician had such a Joe Six-Pack affection as Rendell, who pinch-hit as a host on WIP while he was mayor. He had followed the Eagles for forty years and had been a season-ticket holder for thirty-five. Fast Eddie, he was called, the ultimate frat boy, with flair and vision and a common touch. He had been a fixture at basketball games at the University of Pennsylvania, his alma mater. And he had written the introduction for a book cele-brating a century of Phillies baseball.

As a boy living on Manhattan's Upper West Side, Rendell attended about twenty-five New York Giants baseball games each season. On October 3, 1951, he and his brother Robert listened on the radio as Bobby Thomson hit his shivering home run, the shot heard round the world, and announcer Russ Hodges screamed, "The Giants win the pennant! The Giants win the pennant!" If the Brooklyn Dodgers were stunned, so was Emma Rendell as her two sons began celebrating like "wild Indians." Ed Rendell remem-bered he and his brother scrambling from the bedroom, disrupting his mother's card game and switching on the family's small televi-sion to watch the black-and-white jubilation at the Polo Grounds.

His father, Jesse Rendell, who ran a textile business in Man-hattan's garment district, held a pair of season tickets for New York Giants football games in the 1950s. Ed and Robert shared the second ticket. Both brothers attended the 1958 NFL champi-onship game won by the Baltimore Colts over the Giants at Yankee Stadium. It was the NFL's first title game decided by overtime, a coast-to-coast television broadcast that legitimized professional football and began to elevate it beyond baseball as the national pastime. But it was a bittersweet day for the Rendell brothers. Their father had died less than a month earlier. Otherwise, both sons could not have been at the stadium.

"It was one of the saddest and most poignant moments of my life," Ed Rendell once told me. "I can close my eyes and still remember it."

Fondness for the governor endured in Philadelphia where, as mayor, Rendell expunged a $230 million deficit, built record surpluses, improved services, helped secure the 2000 Republican National Convention and, according to Eagles president Joe Banner, "made it acceptable to have pride in Philadelphia again." He was an ambitious New Yorker, not trapped by Philadelphia's civic diffidence. Sports, for him, represented a social equalizer, "where banker and shoe-shine guy can talk and everyone's on the same level."

One of the men who sat in Rendell's section at Veterans Stadium was a guy everyone knew as Smitty, a retired longshoreman in his late sixties, who still coughed up money for season tickets on his retirement income and showed up every week, good or bad. He came for ten or twelve or thirteen years, part of this fraternity of the hopeful and unfulfilled. And then one day in the early 1990s, Smitty wasn't there. Rendell turned to Cliff Haines, a friend with whom he had season tickets, and said, "Smitty must be dead." A couple of days later, Rendell heard from the family. He had been right.

"That was the only way Smitty would miss a game," Rendell said.

The Vet had been imploded in March 2004. At Lincoln Financial Field, the new stadium nearby, Rendell sat in the club level, near midfield, then walked across the street to participate in the post-game show on Comcast SportsNet. At times, the program drew higher ratings than Flyers hockey games broadcast on the same cable channel.

Afterward, Rendell was known to hightail it back to Harrisburg, the state capital, in a trooper-driven car at speeds above one hundred miles an hour. During one post-game show this season, a fan named Herb e-mailed to ask, if the Eagles made the Super Bowl, would the governor drive or fly to Jacksonville, Florida? Herb suggested that for such a lead-footed chief of state, driving would be faster.

Rendell laughed and said, "Do we have Herb's last name? We want to audit his taxes right now."

His allegiance to the Giants had long dissipated. Now, Rendell got as emotionally involved as any Eagles fan. After Philadelphia escaped Green Bay in overtime during the 2004 playoffs, Rendell turned to the *Post Game Live* host, Michael Barkann, and asked how much longer the show would run.

When Barkann said forty-five minutes, Rendell replied, according to Didinger, "You've got to get us out of here. I'm exhausted. I'm emotionally and physically spent. No way I can do it that long."

As Rendell sat slumped in his chair, Didinger thought to himself, *This is a guy who has sweated through elections for district attorney, mayor, governor and president, and football has wrung him out in a way that an election never had.*

At that moment, Rendell was a fan like every other Eagles fan, having invested a fan's dreams and fears and been rewarded with a fan's fatigued success. To Angelo Cataldi, the WIP personality who interviewed Rendell on his radio and television talk shows numerous times, the governor seemed like the guy on the next stool at the bar, drinking a beer, munching on pretzels, trying to digest news of the latest trade or free-agent signing.

"More than any other politician I've seen, he's totally in step with the mentality of the fan," Cataldi said. "The passion, the craziness, the unpredictability. That's why he's so beloved. Like most Philadelphia fans, once he gets an opinion, he locks onto it. Sometimes the passion of his opinion overwhelms the logic behind it. Some people have gotten the impression that he's loud and unknowledgeable. No. He's loud and knowledgeable."

If he couldn't represent people as a politician, his friends believed, he would be equally satisfied entertaining them as host of a sports talk show.

"Maybe," Rendell once told me. "As much as I love sports on a daily basis, for sure ten times a year I'd be laying in bed thinking, 'You're spending most of your time talking about a game.' I still believe in public life I've had the ability to change the quality of people's lives. In the end, that's the most important thing. For me that would be hard to give up. Although on a day-to-day basis, I would be happy as a clam."

The Eagles have not always felt so happy about Rendell.

Upset that the beleaguered team did not select wide receiver Randy Moss in the 1998 draft, Rendell campaigned stridently in 1999 for running back Ricky Williams, the Heisman Trophy winner from Texas. Before that draft, Rendell ushered Williams into a football banquet in Philadelphia, his arm wrapped around the running back as if they were future in-laws. Meanwhile, Andy Reid, only recently hired as coach, sat at the dais, horrified that a mayor was publicly scheming to influence the team's selection.

"I couldn't go under the table," Reid told *Philadelphia Magazine*. "Believe me, I looked to see if I could."

Reid preferred Donovan McNabb over Williams, but Rendell had doubts that McNabb could become an effective midrange passer. The mayor urged fans to let the Eagles know they favored Williams. They did so with such rapaciousness that it overwhelmed the team's phone system, leaving Eagles officials incensed. This was a team with the sense of humor of a potato famine.

Cataldi, the radio host, gathered a rowdy group called the Dirty Thirty for a bus trip to New York for the NFL draft. They planned to protest Philadelphia's selection if it was not Williams. Cataldi said the protest was Rendell's idea, and Rendell said it was Cataldi's. In either case, the plan ended in spectacular embarrassment. Rendell cautioned the Dirty Thirty to stipulate that they were booing Eagles management, not McNabb. But nuance was not the specialty of a group fueled on a power breakfast of beer and donuts. The drunken chorus of boos pealed on national television and affirmed with tattoo-permanence the hostile, mean-spirited reputation of Philadelphia fans.

"It replaced Santa Claus getting hit by snowballs as the biggest example of idiocy from sports fans," Cataldi said.

Apologies had since been offered, peace had been made. McNabb had become a reliable all-pro, but the debate about him continued. To some, Rendell had showed a justified concern in 1999. To others, he appeared panicked, hysterical. "Obviously, he didn't study that situation as much as he studies politics," Reid told me several years ago. "But I'm glad we had a mayor who was a football fan."

The incident, though, clearly annoyed McNabb. When I asked him early in his career what he thought about Rendell, McNabb said, "Great mayor." Asked what he thought of Rendell as a football analyst, McNabb again said, "Great mayor." I asked him again this season, and he said, "Hey, he's the governor. He can do anything he wants."

For several years, Rendell was not yet ready, like some hagiographers in Philadelphia, to invest McNabb with unqualified praise. He did concede in our conversation today, though, that McNabb had been the right choice over Williams, who was now out of football after failing drug tests for marijuana and possessing a dreadlocked indifference.

"Ricky was a valuable player; his first and second years with the Dolphins, he carried the team," Rendell said. "They were a playoff contender. Ricky's valuable, but I always say a valuable quarterback beats a valuable running back."

As the Eagles won twelve of their first thirteen games this season, however, Rendell sat warily on the bandwagon. "I'm worried," he told me. "The NFC is a weak conference. We beat certain teams just by putting on the uniform. We only played three outstanding games this season. If it's too easy and all of a sudden against top competition it's a tense game, I tend to worry about it. It's like an NCAA basketball team with an easy schedule, and boom, they get beat first time they're tested in the tournament. Where were we challenged? It just worries me."

The good news was, Rendell said, that at least the defensive line was healthy this year, unlike a season ago when it had been depleted by injury for the playoffs. "If McNabb, Owens and Westbrook stay healthy, we're a different team," he said.

In the final game of the 2003 regular season, running back Brian Westbrook had reached down to brace himself upon being tackled. It was a routine play, but for the Eagles nothing ever seemed routine. Westbrook stuck out his arm, hit the ground and tore a triceps tendon. He missed the 2004 playoffs as the Eagles lost a lifeless game to Carolina for their third consecutive defeat in the NFC championship game.

"I'm convinced if Westbrook had been healthy, the Carolina game would have been different," Rendell said.

After that fourteen-to-three loss to Carolina eleven months earlier, Rendell had been caught off guard, believing that *Post Game Live* was in a commercial break when the panel was still on the air. He buried his head in his hands, feeling the same inconsolable hurt that other Eagles fan felt. It was the longest hour and a half of his life, he said. It felt more like eight hours. He could not take one of these defeats again this season.

"If they lose in the championship game, I wouldn't want to go to work on Monday," Rendell said. "I'll stay home and hide out."

2

PRE-GAME

He always had trouble sleeping, but the nights before a game were the worst. Shaun Young awakened at five forty-five and watched a videotape of an Eagles game played three seasons earlier. He had breakfast and pumped iron to get his blood flowing. Then he drove to the stadium. Three hours before Philadelphia was to play Dallas, Shaun had already dressed in his Eagles jersey, shoulder pads, football pants and turf shoes. This might have been unremarkable except that Shaun made a living dumping trash, not quarterbacks.

Each football Sunday, he followed an exacting routine. He painted the right side of his face green, then the left side silver, followed with dabs of eye black. He slid an Eagles earring into the lobe of his left ear and covered his shaved head with a bandanna that flowed down his neck and was emblazoned with a predatory Eagles logo. Shaun, who was thirty-six, worked on a sanitation truck in Springfield, Delaware County, west of Philadelphia, and devoted his life to the grunting men who pushed a ball up and down a field.

His apartment in suburban Media, Pennsylvania, was a wall-to-wall shrine to the team. The sign above the entrance said, "Authorized Personnel Only. Philadelphia Eagles Locker-Room. Pass Required." An Eagles welcome mat greeted visitors, and inside, the apartment was decorated with Eagles jerseys, posters, bobble-head dolls, autographed footballs and photographs of cheerleaders. The ring on his cellular phone sounded the Eagles fight song, and his voice mail urged, "Go Birds." The license plate on his Ford Explorer read IBLDGRN.

He spent his workdays jumping on and off a truck, lifting cans and bags and removing the curbside stink of middle-class discard. The Eagles represented to Young an idealized reflection of himself as possessing a basic, lunch-pail integrity.

These players made extraordinary money to play a boy's game, but Young appreciated them because they put their careers at risk each week in brutal contact. He saw some of himself in them, how they came to work no matter the weather, how they tolerated pain and did their jobs with a gritty honesty.

With its neighborhoods and row homes, Philadelphia did have a working-class feel, but in many ways this blue-collar image was outdated. There might not be a more inhabitable city on the East Coast. It was a place of spectacular beauty and educational purpose. There seemed to be more colleges and universities than water-ice stands. Even after two decades here, I still found it breathtaking on autumn afternoons, with the leaves in riotous color on the Schuylkill River and the sun afire on the water and the rowers and joggers sweating with a chilled, satisfied exhaustion.

A downtown once derided as Filthadelphia had been revitalized as an arts, entertainment and cultural center. Flags of many of the world's countries hung along Benjamin Franklin Parkway, Philly's version of the Champs-Elysées, showing this inward city's reach to the outside. The traditional manufacturing base had long given way to the economies of tourism, education, high technology and health care. The suburbs were moneyed, and even the Eagles themselves, who preferred passing the ball to running under the coaching of Andy Reid, played with a sophisticated finesse known as the West Coast offense. Still, the city reveled in the blue-collar, underdog persona evoked nearly three decades earlier in the movie *Rocky*. For sporting purposes, it preferred to think of itself in high-tops rather than high heels, bounding up the steps of the Art Museum instead of visiting the Dali exhibit inside.

"Football is a hard-hitting, gut-wrenching sport where you put it on the line each day," Shaun Young said.

Just as he put his fidelity to the Eagles on the line each day.

On January 11, 2002, the day before Philadelphia hosted Tampa Bay in a playoff game, Shaun lay on the sofa in his apartment when his appendix burst. He fell to the floor and curled into a ball, remaining in a fetal position for fifteen minutes, understanding what had happened. If he went to the hospital he would miss the game the next day. No way he was missing the game. So he took a shower, then sat in a steaming tub and kept reminding himself that he had a high tolerance for pain. He drove to Veterans Stadium a day later and sat through the game, which the Eagles won, thirty-one to nine. The next morning, he entered the hospital. By then, his white blood cell count was triple what it should have been. He felt such acute discomfort and disorientation that he did not remember driving to the emergency entrance or calling his mother and stepfather to let them know he needed surgery.

He remained in the hospital for a week, and when the hosts at WIP found out, Young became celebrated as the archetypal, steadfast Eagles fan. Strangers visited his hospital room. People he had never met called the hospital and serenaded him with the Eagles fight song and chanted the familiar "E-A-G-L-E-S" cheer in the cadence of a rushed, celebrative scream. The Eagles played another playoff game while he convalesced, against Chicago, and the doctors and nurses told him he could have a small party but cautioned, "No kegs."

It always surprised people to learn that Young did not drink. He might be the only Eagles fan who did not. Not an ounce. Never had. In fact, he lectured school kids on avoiding alcohol and drugs. Sure, he gave himself completely at Eagles games, climbing on railings and screaming so loudly and deliriously that he often could not recall what he said or did, losing himself in a way that felt "like an out-of-body experience."

But he did not understand how fans could appreciate a game when they were too drunk to remember their names, much less savor football's spectacular muscularity. Unfailingly, people seemed stunned to learn that Young was not another nut job, that away from the game he was quiet and inconspicuous. When told this, people reacted with astonished looks, as if they had been handed a wild animal and told it could be petted.

"I don't know who I would be if I did drink," Shaun said. "I don't know if I'd shut down or take it up another notch. It's one of the mystery questions in life. Like why does Fred Flintstone keep going back to that steak shop at the end of the show when he knows he's gonna tip his car over?"

On January 19, 2002, Shaun watched Philadelphia's playoff game against Chicago in his hospital bed, wearing an Eagles jersey over his hospital gown. After the Eagles won, thirty-three to nineteen, a nurse arrived to find him crying. For the first time in twenty-one years, Philadelphia had advanced to the NFC championship game. The nurse thought he needed more medication, until he burbled, "I'm fine, the Birds are going to the championship game."

She started laughing and told him, "You are completely out of your mind."

Earlier that season, Shaun got carried away in his exuberance before a home game against Minnesota. He pounded on his shoulder pads as if he were King Kong, banging so hard that the biceps tendon in his right arm detached at the elbow and rolled up like a measuring tape. The pain was sharp, but he made the game anyway, and struggled to raise his arm in exultation as the Eagles defeated Minnesota forty-eight to seventeen. Almost four years later, the muscle seemed bunched and knotted when he flexed the Eagles tattoo on his arm.

Shaun recalled that Howard Eskin, a local media celebrity, once dismissed him as a "zero trying to become a one, a nobody trying to become a somebody." This did not deter him. The Eagles were his passion and football was a participatory sport in Philadelphia. A guy who sat in the stands in shoulder pads and football pants did not seem so out of place here. At least Shaun remained in the stands. On January 11, 2003, an Eagles fan named Daniel Flagg finally got his chance to meet his heroes and decided to say hello. Unfortunately for him, he did it in the middle of a playoff game against the Atlanta Falcons.

In the second quarter, as a security guard apparently looked the other way, Flagg walked onto the field at the Vet and sat on the Eagles bench, next to running back Duce Staley, then beside quarterback Donovan McNabb. He even grabbed a cup of Gatorade to make it seem as if he belonged on the sideline.

"You from Jersey? I'm from Jersey," Flagg told McNabb before security guards escorted him to a hearing with a municipal court judge. He pleaded guilty to trespassing in a much-publicized case, drew a fine and court costs amounting to $240 and missed the rest of the game as the Eagles prevailed twenty to six.

"I guess I turned into a little kid," a contrite Flagg, who was twenty-nine, told me a few days later. "They were two great players and I wanted to meet them. I guess I could have picked a better time."

Eagles fans felt a membership in, and ownership of, their team and believed they directly affected the outcome of each game. Some did. Earlier this season, Butch Buchanico momentarily forgot that he was the Eagles' director of security, not a blocker on the kickoff team. He ran along the sideline in his enthusiasm, crashed into the side judge and drew a fifteen-yard penalty.

Occasionally, a fan just walked off the streets and joined the team. Vince Papale, a local kid who ran track at St. Joseph's University, which didn't have a football team, made the Eagles at age thirty in an open tryout in 1976, and was embraced as Rocky in cleats. Marvin Hargrove, who had played receiver at the University of Richmond, stopped Coach Buddy Ryan one day in a stadium parking lot after practice, cajoled Ryan into a tryout and played for seven games in the 1990 season. His lone reception went for thirty-four yards and a touchdown.

"In Philly, we don't have seventy-five thousand fans, we've got seventy-five thousand minority owners," Buchanico said. "It's very easy to be successful in town. They want to see a guy, whether he's making a gazillion dollars or a dollar and a half, just put out. 'I'm going to work every day, I'm paying this money for this ticket, just do your job.' That's all they want. They can relate to that. They think it's them. That's their alter ego. 'That's me out there. I can go down on special teams. I got one play left in me.' I used to be one of them. I'm still on the sidelines yelling. They make an emotional investment. They live and die."

Why was that?

"You know, it's controlled violence," Buchanico said. "I mean what's better than that? You go out and knock the shit out of a guy and go back, 'Okay, let's do it again.' You get all your hostilities out and it's controlled. It's a beautiful thing. There's people that kinda live their life through it, you know what I mean? They're bustin' their ass every day and they want to go out there and they want to cheer. Our fans, they live it."

This was not a city of diffuse allegiances. Four generations of fans had grown up consumed with the Eagles, who were born in 1933 and named in honor of the symbol of the New Deal's National Recovery Act. The legend of the team's triumphs and failures had been handed down from father and mother to son and daughter to grandson and granddaughter and great-grandson and great-granddaughter like a first name or a varsity sweater or a hereditary disease.

"I really think people of the city view the team as an extension of the family, that part of the family you see every Sunday," said Ray Didinger, an NFL Hall of Fame sportswriter and native of Philadelphia, who was widely regarded as the foremost authority on the Eagles. "They are like a slightly tipsy uncle who comes over to fix the wiring, and the last five times, he blew every fuse in the house. Maybe this time he'll flip the switch and there won't be a big shower of sparks and the lights will stay on. Given enough chances, they'll get it right. We'll never abandon them because they are family. But it doesn't mean we don't get mad when they screw it up."

Big Daddy Graham, a local comedian and WIP host, had a theory that made sense. Sporting passions were more intense on the East Coast than elsewhere, he believed, because the teams had been around longer and life was more extreme with the daily jostle of people stacked on each other like cans of soup. The routine push and shove of ethnic rivalries between the Irish and Italians and blacks created an edginess, an attitude. Philly was a big city, but worldviews were subdivided by neighborhoods, church parishes, playgrounds and street corners, where turf was to be protected. This accounted for Philadelphia's small-town feel and its agitated relish of football as a symbolic extension of these street-corner turf wars.

"Someone comes in and beats your sports team and it's not so different from a street fight," said Eric Zillmer, the athletic director at Drexel University and a professor of sports psychology. "People take it personally. The thinking in Philadelphia is more provincial than in a lot of cities."

No one could live and die every day through a baseball schedule of 162 games. Same with a protracted NBA season. Hockey was a niche sport. But football, with eight home games in a sixteen-week regular season, was played at an obsessive's perfect rhythm, six days of itchy anticipation rewarded by short, repetitive bursts of regulated antagonism on Sundays.

"It's something you starve for," Shaun Young said.

Pro football owed much of the way it looked and sounded to Philadelphia. The Eagles' first owner, Bert Bell, became NFL commissioner in 1946 and moved the league headquarters from Chicago to the Philly suburb of Bala Cynwyd. He proposed the college draft, implemented television blackout rules and was credited with coining the phrase "on any given Sunday." The portentous voice of the NFL for years belonged to John Facenda, a local news anchor who, it was said, possessed the voice of God. He moonlighted for NFL Films, which was located across the Delaware River in Mount Laurel, New Jersey.

The Eagles won NFL titles in 1948 and 1949, monochromatic years of postwar exuberance when neither the players nor television sets came in color. Philadelphia won again in 1960, defeating Green Bay seventeen to thirteen, handing Vince Lombardi his only playoff defeat. Chuck Bednarik, Concrete Charlie himself, the last of the two-way players at age thirty-five, tackled the Packers' running back Jim Taylor in the final seconds after a threatening swing pass to the Eagles' nine-yard line. Bednarik held down his squirming opponent and counted off the final seconds, then released Taylor, an LSU alum, and said, "You can get up now, Jim, this fucking game is over."

A futile Super Bowl appearance came in 1981, when the Eagles were tight and emotionally spent. They were routed twenty-seven to ten by the Oakland Raiders. This left fans pent up with four decades of unfulfillment, and lately, of piercing, unbearable defeat, three consecutive rebuffs in the NFC championship game, three agonizing stumbles one step away from the Super Bowl.

In this crucible of failure, a peculiar fan identity had been forged. It seemed to me a tumultuous contradiction. This was a city with hopeful, utopian Quaker roots, but fans suffered a Puritan's bleak, vengeful deprivation. They remained forever expectant but believed they were jinxed, cursed, doomed. They cheered with ecstatic release when the Eagles won, but relished sour booing when the Eagles lost. Sometimes, fans appeared to loathe themselves and their team as much as the opponents. They were audaciously confident and grimly insecure. They dismissed rivals as flawed and quaked beneath false bravado. They longed for ultimate victory and feared also-ran defeat. Each season, early triumph brought hope of transcendent achievement and worry of imminent disaster. When failure did not arrive immediately, the city swelled with an irrational ebullience. Like the eye of a hurricane, though, this provided false harbor, and soon came the howling, backhand slap of betrayal.

Philadelphians rooted with a dyspeptic resilience, with a coarse resolve fueled by alcohol and talk radio and ulcered by discontent, with a bottomless craving malnourished by a heartburn diet of misfortune. It was different in other places. Buffalo lost four Super Bowls in the 1990s, but at least the Bills reached football's definitive game. Cleveland hadn't claimed any professional titles since 1964, but it had fewer teams than Philadelphia, and anyway, the Browns' championship that remote season came four years after the Eagles last won. The Chicago Cubs existed as lovable losers. And until the Boston Red Sox won the World Series in 2004, ending a drought that had lasted since 1918, their vain yearning was romanticized and intellectualized, their inadequacy as much a literary failure as an athletic shortcoming. In Philadelphia, defeat was not scholarly or rhapsodized. It was visceral and loud and staggering with too many beers. It was rhythmically screaming "asshole" at anyone dressed in another team's jersey. It was pelting Santa Claus with snowballs. It was getting miserably drunk and angry and ending up in a holding cell with a municipal judge as civic referee. It was leaving the stadium too numb to talk, or swearing that *We shoulda won this goddamn game, we shoulda goddamn won, this is it, no more, fuck it, I have given everything to this team, they owe me, and all they do is lie to me and break my heart and how much of this crap can anyone take.*

The stereotype of the Eagles fan resided like a fly trapped in amber. Angry, unruly, menacing. Sure, the fans could be surly. They embraced this gruffness as a home-field advantage, and sometimes they seemed to behave with a churlish snarl mostly to preserve their reputation. But this surliness had become a cartoon portrait. A wounded passion accompanied this hostility. Retellings of the infamous Santa Claus episode of 1968 had largely shorn the moment of its humor and frustration, lending it instead the easy caricature of rage. Many here felt the pummeling was deserved, or justifiable, during a season of two wins and twelve losses, the venting directed more at an impotent team than a man with a store-bought beard. Even Santa said he understood. He was a fan first, Saint Nick second.

However brusque, Eagles fans possessed a cockeyed faithfulness. They returned every year, seeking renewal, like salmon to their home rivers. They showed up when Marion Campbell would not take their live phone calls for his coaching shows in the early 1980s. They showed up when rain smeared the two-point conversion chart of the bumbling Rich Kotite. They showed up despite wariness that owner after owner seemed to want to win on the cheap. They showed up when Norman Braman gave the all-pro receiver Mike Quick a golf bag with no clubs as a retirement gift. They showed up when Leonard Tose nearly lost the team at the blackjack table and almost moved it to Phoenix in 1984. They showed up when overzealous Jeffrey Lurie called out the food police, fearing fans might be smuggling post-9/11 bombs in their hoagie sandwiches. They showed up as the Eagles united a diverse region from southern New Jersey to northern Delaware and connected a city and its suburbs that were divided by race and money and politics and geography and education and tribal suspicion.

Eagles fans said they would never come back, but they always did, even when their ardor was gut-shot by torment. The league held out the possibility that every team could win every year because of scheduled parity. In Philadelphia, people recognized this as the dangling of a poisoned carrot. Suffering was necessary, unavoidable. Fans expected disappointment and tried to hold back their hearts so the next letdown would not feel so crippling, but they could not hold back and they carried beneath this fear an injured hope that the worst would not happen and things might finally, somehow, turn out for the best.

This sense of camaraderie, of recognition and belonging, is what attracted Shaun Young. He had played sports vigorously as a boy, and even though high school football eluded him, he still kept in shape, lifting weights five or six days a week. His parents divorced when he was six, and his mother remarried. His father lived down in South Carolina, awaiting a kidney and pancreas transplant, Shaun said, having lost much of his eyesight to diabetes. He had a brother who worked in computers and was fifteen months younger. His own job was not glamorous, but it kept him outdoors and so did the Eagles. Some people called Shaun the team's "unofficial official mascot." He saw himself in shoulder pads and grease paint as assuming a role that was both natural and theatrical, just as the Eagles' mild-mannered safety Brian Dawkins viewed himself on Sundays as a fierce, sledgehammering figure called Idiot Man. Emotion took over for both of them, even though one was a teammate, the other a Teamster.

"I'm a Gemini, if that explains anything," Shaun said. "Good and evil twin. Noncrazed and crazed fan. My family is a little concerned with some of the things I've been through. Like when my appendix burst and I blew it off to go to the game and put my life on the line. They're very thankful I survived, but I think they wanted to kick my tail for putting them through it. I remember the first day I came down in this outfit, in '95. My mom had a girlfriend over. She looked at me completely blank. 'I think this is my son, Shaun, but I'm not quite certain.' She shook her head and laughed."

On football Sundays, banker, lawyer, doctor and trash collector were indistinguishable, wearing the same replica jerseys, pulling for the same team, experiencing the same jubilant highs and crashing lows. Shaun wore his shoulder pads and people banged on them and cheered and clapped and hugged and kissed and high-fived and told him that the things he said were the things they wanted to say, that the emotions he felt were the emotions they felt.

"My life has been sports," Shaun said. "Maybe it's the camaraderie, how much fun we have when we win. Maybe even part of the attraction is, 'What would the feeling be like to lose and rebound again?' I didn't think that as a kid. As I got older, maybe subliminally, it might have been, 'What kind of person can I be or will I be, if I go through this, if I put my energy in this, if I put my heart into this and we lose? Where will I be? Will I have enough in me to go back? Will I just say I hate losing, I can't do this anymore, I'm out?' I never gave up, no matter what. I was like that as a kid in sports. I guess that goes hand in hand with being a fan."

Occasionally, his ardor for the team has crossed the line of decorum, most infamously at the 1999 NFL draft in New York, where Young and his loutish Dirty Thirty brethren booed the selection of Donovan McNabb out of Syracuse. Now and for years to come, Young would forever be the guy yelling the loudest, his face painted and contorted in angry response.

Somebody stuck a camera in his face, and Shaun said, "If they pick McNabb, they'll have to deal with me." Now he heard some people calling him a fraud and an idiot. They just didn't want to let it go. It was what it was, Shaun said. He wasn't hiding from it.

"I was out of line," he said. "I said a bunch of stupid things. I acted like an idiot."

But he didn't feel the way he behaved was his true self. When Angelo Cataldi, the morning host on WIP, got people to call the station, feeding the fever against McNabb, Shaun said he wanted to get on the bus to New York, wanted to be part of the Dirty Thirty. He had never been to the draft, and so he told Cataldi what he wanted to hear. That the Eagles should draft Ricky Williams. Then Shaun got caught up in the moment and made a fool of himself. Passion got the best of him. But he apologized to McNabb and his family and the Eagles. What more could he do?

"People think I don't deserve any kind of appreciation and joy because of one day," he said.

On this cold December morning, with the Eagles set to face Dallas and with Young standing in a tent across from Lincoln Financial Field, his devotion to the home team met another boundary, one that he would not trespass. Howard Eskin, the WIP host who was known as the King of Bling and was dressed for his pre-game show in a sheared beaver coat with a raccoon collar, invited fans to eat cockroaches to show their disdain for the Cowboys. A chocolate fondue fountain was available for those gourmands with a sweet tooth for household pests.

"I'd have to be pretty desperate to do something like that," Shaun said, dressed in a black jersey bearing the name of Brian Dawkins, the Eagles' safety.

Others were not so reluctant as a crowd gathered outside the broadcast tent. Jeff Rauchut, twenty-eight, of Chalfont, Pennsylvania, placed three cockroaches inside a hoagie roll with onions and peppers. To the squeamish delight of fans watching from behind a metal barrier, Rauchut bared a roach in his teeth and dipped one in the fondue fountain.

"You let the team know you support them, even if it's eating something disgusting," Rauchut said.

Then Doug Petock, twenty-five, a burly physics student at Villanova, took his turn. It was thirty-four degrees, and Petock, with tussled blonde hair, was dressed in a cape, a T-shirt, shorts and sandals. He did forward rolls on the cold pavement and brandished two *Star Wars* light sabers, banging the toys against the ground. At some point, he cut his leg and blood began to flow.

Even in the middle of a cockroach-eating contest, this appeared singular in its bizarreness to Rhea Hughes, a WIP cohost.

"When was the last time you dated?" she asked Petock.

He bit into a cockroach and screamed something about how the Eagles would chew up the Cowboys. But this wasn't just a tasting, this was an audition. Petock wanted a spot in the upcoming Wing Bowl, sponsored by WIP two days before each Super Bowl. Started twelve years earlier in a hotel lobby, Wing Bowl now drew more than twenty thousand people at six in the morning at the Wachovia Center basketball arena, an event that was both free of charge and restraint.

Essentially, Wing Bowl was an eating contest that melded the delights of exotic dancing and fast food. Semidressed women known as Wingettes fed Buffalo wings to fat, badly dressed men. Most people drank milk at six in the morning. Spectators at Wing Bowl preferred beer, and what they didn't drink, they sometimes threw. The winning contestant got a new car and the favorite Wingette got a free trip to Aruba. If the Eagles ever got to the Super Bowl, this would be the party to end all parties.

For his Wing Bowl tryout, Petock rolled around on the asphalt and ate a cockroach. Well, not one, but eight. He inhaled one off the ground and tossed another into the air as if it were popcorn. Then he swallowed five more in a sushi roll, relishing a tangy confluence of tastes that he described as a squishy crunch.

"Scrumptious," he said later in an odd raspy accent that was part Andre the Giant, part Homer Simpson.

Eskin was suitably impressed and revolted. Petock had made it into Wing Bowl, under the guise of Obi Wing Kanobi.

"Some of the sickest shit I've seen," Eskin told me off the air.

•   •   •

With the game less than an hour away, Shaun Young took a micro-phone and, wearing his jersey and shoulder pads, delivered his customary pre-game harangue on WIP. As always, it sounded like the break in a game of pool. He spoke so loudly and emphatically that his words clacked and collided until they were indistinguish-able in their encouragement of the Eagles and dismissal of the Cowboys.

3

THE GAME

"Dallas sucks" had become such a ritualized admonishment in Philadelphia, WIP's Angelo Cataldi sometimes joked, that when babies learned to say their first ten words, these were two of them. Above all, fans here measured the Eagles' achievement against the historical success of the Cowboys. "Dallas sucks" was both a bitter rebuke and a resentful acknowledgment. Dallas had what the Eagles wanted: not one Super Bowl championship but five.

Philadelphians grew indignant that the Cowboys proclaimed themselves America's Team. Everything about Dallas, from the stars on the helmets to the coat-and-tie rectitude of former Coach Tom Landry, seemed arrogant and condescending. This puzzled Dallas, which considered Washington and San Francisco as its primary rivals. It puzzled me, too, when I moved in 1982 to Philadelphia from Dallas, where I had worked at the *Dallas Times Herald*.

Twice in the five years I lived in Dallas, after the 1977 and 1978 seasons, the Cowboys had reached the Super Bowl. They were winners, unlike the New Orleans Saints of my home state of Louisiana. The Cowboys offered a certain glitz and glamour and can-do innovation during the tectonic shift of the country's economic, demographic and political orientation to the Sun Belt from the oxidized faltering of the Rust Belt. The business of Dallas was bidness, and the Cowboys represented a cool, corporate efficiency. The team was one of the first to use computers, refining the chalkboard strategy of

X's and O's into the electronic gates and switches of the binary code. Even Cowboys fans presented a boardroom demeanor, as if taking a cue from the emotional distance of Landry, the coach. While this suited buttoned-down Dallas, it chafed Philly like jock itch. Any Philadelphia fan who rooted for the Cowboys was reviled as a fraud or a traitor. There could be no more astringent disloyalty.

Eagles fans wore "Dallas sucks" T-shirts and ranted against the Cowboys on the radio and cheered when receiver Michael Irvin lay motionless on the Veterans Stadium turf with a career-ending injury in 1999 and even chased after Dallas icons with power tools.

On September 30, 1996, before a Monday night game against the Cowboys, cousins Steve and Dominic Yanni arrived at Cataldi's pre-game radio show outside the Vet with an inflatable sex doll. The doll was draped in the jersey of Dallas quarterback Troy Aikman. Dominic Yanni had an idea to recreate a scene from *The Texas Chainsaw Massacre*. Wearing a leather mask, Steve Yanni tried to slice and dice Aikman, but these urban Paul Bunyans had not sufficiently contemplated the difference in tensile strength between a sex doll and a pine tree. The doll exploded, the chainsaw caught on the fabric and Dominic's left thumb spurted blood everywhere.

Cataldi offered an ambulance, but Dominic declined. "If I had been sober, I would have gone to the hospital," he said.

Already anesthetized, Dominic instead went to the stadium infirmary.

"Put a fuckin' Band-Aid on it," he said. "I ain't missing kickoff."

Dominic Yanni sat through the game with a bloody shirt and pants as the Eagles lost twenty-three to nineteen. But both medical and financial catastrophes were averted. The cut was not so deep and the chainsaw went back to the store, no questions asked.

"Got a full refund," Dominic said.

Once, Shaun Young bumped into Jerry Jones, the owner of the Cowboys, in a corridor at the Vet. Jones seemed startled at the jersey, shoulder pads and painted face and joked, "I hope it's not going to be like this all day." He stuck out his hand, but Young only slapped at it and kept walking, saying, "Today is not your day."

Not all Dallas fans got off so easily.

Jim Gallagher, a service manager at an automobile dealership and an Eagles season-ticket holder for thirty-three years, watched a wheelchair-bound fan struggling up a ramp at the Vet before a game against Dallas in the 1980s. Two Eagles fans grabbed the chair and began assisting the man, leaving Gallagher to think, *Our fans get a bad rap*. Then the two Samaritans realized that the man was wearing a Dallas jersey under his coat. They turned the wheelchair around, pointed it down the ramp and said, "Take the jersey off or you're going for a ride."

The man removed the jersey, which the two escorts ripped apart. The offensive apparel having been shredded, Gallagher said, the two satisfied Eagles fans resumed their helpful demeanor and wheeled the Dallas fan toward his seat.

Philadelphia finally freed itself from Dallas's smothering grasp on a frigid afternoon at Veterans Stadium on January 11, 1981. Running back Wilbert Montgomery took a handoff through a hole so wide that the entire city seemed to follow him through, liberated, as Montgomery ran forty-two yards for a touchdown in the NFC championship game and Philly defeated the reviled Cowboys twenty to seven.

But it was not until Buddy Ryan became head coach of the Eagles in 1986 that Philadelphia finally gave itself completely over to football. The Phillies had begun to fade after winning the World Series in 1980 and falling to Baltimore in 1983, a big-market team willing for too many years to spend only small-market money on players. Ryan was loud and pugnacious and confrontational, just the way Eagles fans liked it. More important, he not only defeated Dallas in eight of ten meetings, but he relished humiliating the Cowboys.

During the 1987 season, a player's strike occurred. In Philadelphia, union workers roughhoused fans who dared support scab players. A right-to-work place like Texas was different. A number of the Cowboys, including Danny White, Randy White and Tony Dorsett, crossed the picket line and played in a forty-one to twenty-two thrashing of the Eagles in Dallas.

"Buddy didn't forget," Merrill Reese, the longtime radio voice of the Eagles, said. "With Buddy there was always a revenge factor. When the Cowboys came to Philadelphia, if the Eagles were up fifty, Buddy would have wanted them to be up by sixty."

By the rematch two weeks later, the strike had ended. Ryan called for quarterback Randall Cunningham to kneel twice in apparent acknowledgement that the Eagles were finished scoring with a ten-point lead. Then Cunningham faked kneeling and threw a pass toward the end zone for Mike Quick, the Eagles' all-pro receiver. A pass interference penalty was called, and Philadelphia scored on the next play to win thirty-seven to twenty. Landry was infuriated, but Ryan didn't care. "Fuck 'em," he said as he ran up the stadium tunnel to the Eagles' locker-room.

Seventeen years later, when asked about the play, Quick first said, "We shouldn't have run it," then smiled and reconsidered. "Why not rub it in?"

As he usually did on football Sundays, Governor Rendell arrived at Lincoln Financial Field only a few minutes before the Dallas game started. I met him at a souvenir stand, where he bought a Terrell Owens jersey for his son Jesse. The cashier took his credit card and joked about needing to see some identification. After some small talk, Rendell headed to his seat near midfield on the visitor's side.

He had his own Cowboys story that grew in infamy through the years. On December 10, 1989, after city workers failed to remove snow from the Vet, Dallas was barraged by the Eagles in a twenty-to-ten defeat and by a flurry of snowballs tossed from the stands. Some of the snowballs apparently were armored with batteries.

The story had been embroidered through the years, and, depending on which version prevailed, Rendell threw snowballs himself, paid a guy to bean Dallas Coach Jimmy Johnson or con-ceived a clever ruse. The truth was, Rendell said, he bet $20 that a drunken fan couldn't reach the field with a snowball. It was an attempt, he claimed, to trick the annoying man into leaving the area. That subtlety, however, escaped many in Philadelphia. In some cities, this tabloid behavior might have amounted to political suicide. Not here, where the incident was relished as an act of endearing, vote-getting mischief. Two years later, Rendell was elected mayor.

"He paid a guy to throw snowballs and admitted it," former Eagles quarterback Ron Jaworski once told me. "He's salt of the earth. That's why people love him."

Cataldi, the WIP personality, had another take.

"He threw the snowball, and someday in his memoir, he'll admit it," Cataldi said of Rendell. "It was a damn good throw. He hit Jimmy Johnson. He threw the snowball. We know it. It has been confirmed by many people, two or three of whom were actually sober."

At two minutes past one, Philadelphia kicked off to Dallas under a pewter sky at the Linc. The game became as dreary as the afternoon. The Cowboys should not have been a match for the Eagles. Dallas entered the day with five wins and eight losses, while Philadelphia had won twelve of thirteen games. Only Washington among NFC teams had come closer than ten points to the Eagles. Dallas should have provided only meager resistance.

But Philadelphia played indifferently. The Eagles scored first, taking a six-to-zero lead on a two-yard pass from McNabb to tight end Chad Lewis. The extra point was blocked, leaving the Eagles vulnerable, and Dallas scored just before halftime on a seven-yard pass from quarterback Vinny Testaverde to receiver Keyshawn Johnson. The extra point was routinely accurate, and the Cowboys held a seven-to-six lead at the half. Fans were restive, but not panicked. McNabb would pull the Eagles through.

Twenty-six seconds into the third quarter, the season changed. Terrell Owens lined up in the left slot on what was called a "dagger" play, intending to run a deep crossing route. He caught the ball on a slant, pivoted to the outside and gained twenty yards before Dallas safety Roy Williams grabbed Owens from behind and yanked on his shoulder pads, as if shaking the wrinkles out of a shirt. After the season, this horse-collar tackle, as it was called, would be outlawed.

Owens fell awkwardly just across midfield, his right ankle pinned beneath him at a graceless angle. He lay on the field and grabbed the back of his right leg. In the north end zone, fans in Shaun Young's section gasped and began to mutter that the season was finished.

"Jesus Christ," Butch DeLuca, a deli owner up the street from my house in the suburb of Havertown, said in his seat in the south end zone. "Here we go again."

John Kleinstuber, a chef and assistant manager of a golf club, had given his season ticket to his mother-in-law this afternoon. At six feet four inches, and 240 pounds, Kleinstuber still had the sturdy appearance of the high school tight end he had been twenty-three years earlier. He sat with his father-in-law in the living room of his row home in Havertown, wearing an Eagles fleece pullover. For each game, he kept handy a homemade penalty flag that had been fashioned out of a golf ball and a yellow cloth napkin. If he saw an infraction on his big-screen television, he tossed the flag. Mostly, it just scared the cat, named Buddy Ryan.

As Owens limped off the field, it didn't look good.

"He's done," Kleinstuber told his father-in-law.

On the radio, Merrill Reese, the Eagles' announcer said, "He is limping badly as he comes to the bench. This is serious. This is what you fear most in these games, injuries to key players."

Owens needed assistance as he walked up a tunnel to be X-rayed. Sitting on a cart, he curled his tongue and rubbed the leg, as if trying to knead a cramp. Then he threw his head back and his face wrenched in pain.

The play had happened right in front of Governor Rendell. *The curse is back*, he told himself.

From her seat on the west side of the stadium, Jennifer Clark used her cellular phone to contact her brother Chris. The Clark family was in its fourth generation rooting for the Eagles. Ernie Clark, a retired bank vice president, had been present for all of the Eagles' great home triumphs: the 1948 NFL championship game at Shibe Park, the 1960 NFL championship game at Franklin Field and the 1981 NFC championship game at Veterans Stadium. His four children were grown now. Three had families of their own, but their Sundays still revolved around the Eagles. The Clarks held five season tickets. When the team played at home, Ernie and his son, Chris, and his three daughters, Terry, Jennifer and Susan, sat together. For a few hours, the Clarks were as they once had been. No bills to pay or children to attend or emergencies or pressing obligations, just a father out with his kids, experiencing the joy and heartache of an uncomplicated afternoon. Football was a kind of gravity that pulled a scattered family back into the same orbit.

On this afternoon, though, Ernie Clark had decided to skip the game. He and his wife, Anne, had just returned from the Bahamas. He was tired and Dallas did not figure to put up much of a fight. The rivalry had lost some intensity. He would watch this one at home in Warminster, Bucks County.

Chris Clark also decided to sit this one out. The defeats at home to Tampa Bay and Carolina in the previous two NFC championship games had consumed him. Eleven months earlier, in the minutes after the Eagles had played lethargically in a loss to Carolina, Chris had told his sisters he couldn't take it anymore. How much defeat could one fan suffer?

"I can't do it," he said at the time. "I can't come back."

Terry Funk, his sister, had shot back at him, "It's not about you. You don't have a choice. When they stunk in the seventies, your dad did it. Now you're going to do it and then your kids are going to do it and their kids are going to do it."

Eventually, Chris reconsidered and came back again this season. How could he not? But he had tried to sort his priorities. Was this the way he wanted to live his life, yanked up and down on an emotional chain by results on a scoreboard? So he skipped the occasional game now to spend weekends with his wife, Deb, and their three children who were four, three and one year old.

Still, he watched on television from home in North Wales, Pennsylvania. As Owens went down, Chris said to himself, *Oh, no*. He flashed back to 1991, when quarterback Randall Cunningham hurt his knee and was lost for the season in the opener at Green Bay.

Oh, my God, Chris told himself. *The season's over.*

Owens had set an Eagles season record with fourteen touchdown receptions. Football was the ultimate team game, and that's what Chris liked about it best, but sometimes an individual player came along and seemed to make all the difference. Owens was one of those players. But now he was hurt. It looked bad.

"Did you see it?" Chris's sister, Jennifer Clark, said when she called from the stadium.

"Jen, it's bad," Chris said.

"No, he just walked off."

She seemed encouraged. She had spoken with her father. It didn't seem too serious to him.

"He walked off the field," Jen said.

His family considered Chris a pessimist. He considered himself a realist.

"Jen, it's bad," he said. "Those ligaments don't prevent you from walking. I'm not a doctor, but he's hurt."

Chris remembered an injury to linebacker Bill Bergey from the 1970s, and how Bergey also had walked off the field in disguised severity.

"I hope he's okay, Jen, but I watched the replay," Chris said. "His leg wasn't supposed to go in the direction it did."

On the phone, Chris sensed that his sister became deflated with the realization that Owens could be hurt badly.

"Oh, do you think?" she said plaintively.

"I don't know. But it doesn't look good to me."

Chris hoped the injury, if serious, would be a broken bone, not a ligament tear. A bone would heal faster than an unraveled ligament.

As the second half began, Ray Didinger walked from Lincoln Financial Field across the street to the Wachovia Center basketball arena. Inside were the offices of Comcast SportsNet, the cable television network. After each game, Didinger, Governor Rendell and Vaughn Hebron, a former Eagles running back who had won two Super Bowls with the Denver Broncos, analyzed Philadelphia's performance on *Post Game Live.*

As he walked into the Comcast SportsNet office, Didinger noticed people watching the game with shocked looks on their faces.

"What's wrong? What happened?" asked Didinger, who was now a senior producer for NFL Films.

"T.O.'s hurt," someone said.

He watched a replay and saw that Owens had walked off the field.

"It's probably not that bad," Didinger said.

"No, it's the Eagles," someone replied. "It's bad."

It was announced during the game that X-rays of Owens's leg had turned up negative. But that gave little comfort to many Eagles fans. Nervously, they watched in the drizzle until the end, when McNabb retrieved the game with two long scrambling runs and running back Dorsey Levens punched the ball over the goal line from two yards for a twelve-to-seven Philadelphia victory.

Leaving the press box, I got on an elevator packed with fans, none of them yelling "Dallas sucks" or even talking excitedly of having beaten the Cowboys. The Eagles had won yet another title in the NFC East and had clinched home-field advantage throughout the conference playoffs, but no one celebrated. The outcome of the game did not matter nearly as much as the severity of Owens's injury.

"Anybody worried?" I asked the group of fans as we descended to the ground floor.

Several shook their heads. Then, finally, a season-ticket holder named Mary Ann Haggerty nodded. "I'm worried," she said. "I'm an Eagles fan. There's always a reason to worry."

At his post-game news conference, Coach Andy Reid began as usual with the roster of injured players. As always, he spoke in a flat, unrevealing tone. He might have been a teacher calling roll. Owens's name was not even mentioned first. He had a sprained ankle, Reid said. X-rays were negative. A magnetic resonance imaging test would be performed in the morning.

There was a good chance that Owens would not play the following week at St. Louis, even if able, Reid said. The Eagles had reached their first goal of the season, gaining home-field advantage for the conference playoffs. They would not play another meaningful game for a month. That left plenty of time to heal, if necessary. No need to risk further injury.

"We'll see how the MRI goes tomorrow," Reid said. "The positive is that it wasn't broken. The negative is that it did swell up."

Would Owens be 100 percent by the beginning of the playoffs in four weeks? Reid was asked.

"Well, we'll see," he said. "I can tell a little bit better after the MRI what's going on in there. I don't want to say anything."

The Eagles' locker-room was curiously quiet, even somber. Joe Banner, the team president, sat with his shoulders drooped. When I asked the garrulous receiver Freddie Mitchell if he had any indication that Owens's injury was serious, he replied testily, "Think we'd tell you?"

Clearly, this seemed more than a mere sprained ankle. "That's the impression I got," said Ron Jaworski, who now worked for ESPN, as we left the locker-room.

On *Post Game Live,* Governor Rendell noted that, however severe the injury, Owens wouldn't be needed until the playoffs began in a month.

"Wait and see," he said.

Still, the ballooning confidence of a whole season had been deflated by a single injury. The Eagles had now won thirteen of fourteen games, but on one play the fans' swagger had become a limp. In a city where everything that could go wrong often did, the Eagles faithful would spend a nervous night waiting for the results of Owens's MRI. In a place where every sporting fender-bender escalated into the Cuban Missile Crisis, it was time to duck and cover.

"I can't even say it's unbelievable, it happens every year," Shaun Young said when I reached him on his cell phone, his voice reduced as it was each Sunday night to a depleted, scratchy remnant.

McNabb had missed six weeks of the 2002 season with a broken bone in his ankle and had not been fully recovered for the playoffs. Then Brian Westbrook tore a triceps tendon in 2003, forcing him to watch the playoffs from the sideline.

He did not believe in curses, Shaun said, "but it seems that somebody up above is sprinkling us with some nasty dust."

Late tonight, Howard Eskin reported on WCAU-TV, the local NBC affiliate, that Owens heard something pop when he fell. He knew he was in trouble.

And now, perhaps, so were Philadelphia's hopes for the Super Bowl.

4

Monday, December 20

A whole city waited apprehensively for the results of Terrell Owens's MRI. Andy Reid was scheduled to make an announcement at noon. Television stations would go live. The victory over Dallas was forgotten, replaced by a stressful uncertainty.

On WIP, Angelo Cataldi said he felt like a patient waiting on a test result for a bladder infection. He hated waiting. "Basically, a doctor is going to tell us if we have a season," Cataldi said. "If the answer is, he can't play for the rest of the season, it's over."

This city, whose identity was heavily invested in its sports teams, held its collective breath. WIP advised motorists to pull over for Reid's announcement or risk a municipal pileup. In my daughter Julie-Ann's ninth-grade Western Civilization class at suburban Haverford High, Leon Smith told his students that they could draw pictures of Owens crying, "or us crying for him."

Noon arrived and Rick Burkholder, the Eagles' trainer, had something worse than bad news. No news. The results of the MRI were inconclusive, he told reporters at the Eagles' training complex in South Philadelphia. More tests were being done.

"We don't want to get into what the testing is," Burkholder said.

There would be an update in a few hours. It didn't sound good.

Meanwhile, distressed fans wondered whether the Eagles, with their morose fate, had become the new Red Sox. These were the great Philadelphia voices, bruised, full of despair and conspiracy and vowels as messy as onions on a cheesesteak, voices wounded by betrayal in a town that had known far more losing than winning.

Some complained that Owens should not have played in such a meaningless game. Others worried that he might have worsened his injury by walking off the field instead of riding in a cart.

"Are we the whiniest thirteen-and-one team in the nation?" a caller named Jim asked on WIP's early afternoon show.

"That's not whining," Steve Martorano, the host, replied. "That's panic."

Some callers bristled that Eagles fans relished catastrophe, so they didn't have to aspire to victory. Others complained that, without Owens at receiver, the team would have to rely on the uncertain hands of Todd Pinkston, Freddie Mitchell and Greg Lewis. Not a single pass had been caught by an Eagles receiver against Dallas after Owens got hurt. An entire half of football, and not a single catch.

Pinkston, in particular, bore the callers' wrath, given his apparent reluctance to catch balls thrown over the middle. Some called him alligator arms. He had violated a fundamental rule of Philadelphia sport: He did not seem to give maximum effort in a place that demanded exertion and sweat and, through years of losing, had come to prize endeavor over achievement. Another caller joked bitterly that he had just seen results of an MRI taken for Pinkston. The results were alarming. His spine was completely missing.

Three o'clock came and went. A news conference was rescheduled for four. Again the TV stations went live. This time Burkholder had sobering news. Owens would need surgery in two days. He had suffered ligament damage in his right ankle, and tremendous rotational forces had transmitted up his leg, breaking the fibula just below his right knee. The fibula bore little of the body's weight and would repair itself. But screws would have to be placed in Owens's ankle to stabilize the tibia and fibula while the ligaments healed.

"The obvious question is, what does this mean to his season? What does this mean to his career?" Burkholder said, an entire city hanging on his answers.

Three weeks after surgery, Owens would begin training on a stationary bike and running in a pool, Burkholder said. At five weeks, if everything went well, he could begin running on land. The Super Bowl was in seven weeks.

"If things would work out, there is an outside chance that he can be prepared to play in that game in some role," Burkholder said. But, he added, "There are a lot of hurdles that have to be taken on before he can ever get to that point."

Ernie and Anne Clark watched the news conference from their home in suburban Warminster, Bucks County. They had attended the Eagles' 1960 championship game before they married and had become season-ticket holders the next year. Now they sat in the family room, decorated with lithographs of Shibe Park and the various local sports teams. The Clarks had waited more than four decades for another title. This seemed to be the year. Now the very player who would take the Eagles over the top was hurt, a long-shot to play in the Super Bowl. It felt as if the air had been sucked out of the room.

"This isn't fair," Anne Clark said to her husband. *It was like somebody punched you, really. It just didn't seem right.*

I called Butch DeLuca, owner of Butch's Deli, just up the street from my house. He was a rabid fan. His store in Havertown had a neon Eagles helmet in a front window. An Eagles poster decorated the other window, and a life-size cardboard cutout of Donovan McNabb stood inside the front door, which bore an Eagles logo. So did Butch's checkbook. Figurines of Owens and defensive end Jevon Kearse stood on the cash register. A wall of the store was given to Eagles autographed jerseys and photographs and minia-ture helmets. He even had a can opener that played the theme from *Monday Night Football*.

Butch held four season tickets in the south end zone at the Linc. Five months earlier, his daughter, Melissa Kelly, had gotten married at a hotel across from the stadium parking lot. The Eagles pep band played at the reception and Melissa had her wedding photographs taken on the playing field. In one picture, her hus-band, Tim Kelly, bent down in a three-point stance, wearing his tux, while Melissa stood behind him, a bridal quarterback dressed in her wedding gown and veil. Melissa and Tim attended each home game, but Tim sat with his brother and a couple of other buddies. He needed his space. Melissa sat with her parents and her brother Brian, who had worked with the Eagles as an intern during the 2003 season.

This afternoon, Butch was out of the store, running errands. I reached him on his cell phone. He had already heard about Owens. His words came out like an angry moan.

"It's the Philly jinx, unbelievable," Butch said. "Now we have to go with the same mediocre receivers we had last year. Everybody's devastated. Terrible. Terrible."

His son-in-law got the news and thought, *You gotta be joking. This can't be happening again. God is doing it on purpose.*

Owens had traveled to Baltimore to see Dr. Mark Myerson, an orthopedic surgeon who would operate on him. The receiver spoke with reporters on a telephone conference call, saying he had wished for the best news but had gotten the worst news. The one hope was, Owens kept himself in superb condition. He had already moved a portable hyperbaric chamber into his living room. This would help facilitate the flow of oxygen to the injured leg and might speed the healing process. He said the right things about being a quick healer, but Owens sounded guarded about whether he would be able to play anymore this season. He suggested that he would not put the rest of his career at risk.

"I'm going to be smart about the situation," he said, adding, "If I am able to go, God willing, then I am going to give it a shot. If not, I will be the biggest cheerleader on that sideline at the Super Bowl."

On *Daily News Live*, a weekday cable television program featuring sportswriters from the *Philadelphia Daily News*, Dr. John Kelly IV, the vice chairman of orthopedic surgery at Temple University Hospital, said that Owens risked the "rapid onset of arthritis" if he returned too quickly.

"An athlete with even a little bit of ankle arthritis is a retired athlete," Kelly said.

In his opinion, Kelly said, the only way Owens could return in time for the Super Bowl was "that he goes to a faith-healing service."

Now every Philadelphia sports fan seemed damned like Malcolm McDowell in *A Clockwork Orange*, sitting with eyes pried open, forced to relive each brutal sporting occurrence in this city's turbulent history.

The whole aching chronicle began to play out, on the radio, in conversations, in the minds of everyone a certain age, the stories of vinegary disappointment. Fans could rattle off the failure as if it were a grocery list of the forlorn:

The 1961 Phillies lost twenty-three consecutive games, a modern record.

The 1964 Phillies blew a lead of six and a half games with twelve to play, suffering baseball's most ignominious regular-season collapse.

The gravelly voice of Johnny Most cried "Havlicek stole the ball!" as Boston's John Havlicek deflected an inbounds pass from Hal Greer in the final seconds of Game 7 of the 1965 NBA Eastern Conference finals, preserving a one-point victory for the Celtics over the Sixers.

The 1972–1973 Sixers finished with nine wins and seventy-three defeats, the worst record in NBA history.

The Sixers took a lead of two games to none over Portland in the 1977 NBA Finals and lost four straight.

The rookie guard Magic Johnson jumped center for the Los Angeles Lakers in Game 6 of the 1980 NBA Finals, scoring forty-two points and grabbing fifteen rebounds as the Lakers won the title over the Sixers, even though Kareem Abdul-Jabbar sat out with a sprained ankle.

The Sixers took a lead of three games to one over the Celtics in the 1981 NBA Eastern Conference finals and lost three straight games, along with the series.

Curt Schilling wore a towel over his head in Game 6 of the 1993 World Series, unable to watch reliever Mitch "Wild Thing" Williams, who threw a ninth-inning pitch that Joe Carter knocked into the seats for a home run, clinching the Series for Toronto.

The Flyers took a lead of three games to one over New Jersey in the National Hockey League's 2000 Eastern finals, only to be bounced out of the series in Game 7, as Eric Lindros was bounced off the ice and knocked unconscious by a shuddering hit. In 2004, the Flyers again lost in Game 7 of the Eastern finals, to Tampa Bay, where the only ice to be found otherwise was in the bottom of a bourbon glass.

"We lose the World Series to a team from Canada and the hockey playoffs to a team from Florida and football playoffs to a team from Carolina, where they live in trailers and sleep with their sisters," said Russell Lamplugh, a twenty-five-year-old Eagles fan. "Wing Bowl is our Super Bowl. We don't win nothin'."

Once again, hated Dallas had disrupted an Eagles season. Roy Williams had a history of this kind of yanking tackle that he made on Owens, not yet forbidden, but potentially dangerous. Many Eagles fans recalled 1967, when halfback Timmy Brown had been separated from his senses, and some teeth, by a vicious elbow thrown by Cowboys linebacker Lee Roy Jordan. Now a city's self-assurance, like Brown's jaw, had become dislocated.

"It's like a guy who has had his heart broken by seven different girlfriends," Ray Didinger said. "You start going out with the eighth girl, and everyone tells you this one will work out, but all you can do is think how the other seven ended."

Philadelphia had not always felt the stabs of sharp pain over last-second defeat or dire collapse. During the 1980 season, the Eagles, Sixers, Phillies and Flyers all advanced to the championship game or series of their respective sports. And Villanova won the NCAA basketball championship in 1985 with a victory over

Georgetown that verged on perfection. The Phillies had reached the
World Series again in 1983 and 1993, and the Flyers, who won consecutive Stanley Cup titles in 1974 and 1975, had also played in the
NHL finals in 1985, 1987 and 1997. Some believed Philadelphia
fans had irrational expectations for success. In his book about the
Eagles, *Bringing the Heat,* Mark Bowden wrote that fans "love"
their teams "like overbearing parents, who, disappointed with their
own lives, place unrealistic demands on their children—and are,
consequently, forever frustrated."

Yet, success in Philadelphia seemed to be a fractured fairy tale.
Frequently, victory seemed to be nothing more than a gag gift, an
exploding cigar. The Villanova title had been tainted by later
admissions from point guard Gary McLain in *Sports Illustrated*
that he had played some games on cocaine. St. Joseph's University's third-place finish in the 1961 Final Four was stricken from
the books by a point-shaving scandal. Villanova finished second to
UCLA at the Final Four in 1971, only to have its appearance nullified because star player Howard Porter had signed with an agent
during the season, violating collegiate rules.

Lately, it was the Eagles who had enticed hungry fans, only to
trick them with a pie in the face. The 2003 NFC championship
game against Tampa Bay had begun with a quick touchdown and
certain victory in the final game at Veterans Stadium, then faded
into a loss so funereal that fans were too numb to boo or tear the
place apart. Shaun Young could not get out of his seat for thirty
minutes, maybe forty-five, after that game. He watched the clock
kick down to zeroes and sat mute, defeated, as several Tampa Bay
players laughed at him in his jersey and shoulder pads and flipped
him the finger.

Shaun was struck by a nauseating sense of déjà vu when the
Eagles lost the 2004 NFC championship game to Carolina. *I can't
believe this is happening again.* He sat in his seat after the final gun
sounded and felt as if he could not get his legs to move. Other than
a death in the family, it was the worst feeling in his life. He walked
back to his Ford Explorer and sat there for five minutes, ten, fifteen. He turned the radio off, not wanting to listen to recrimina-

tion and heartache. He felt like the walking dead, and it took all of his energy to put his vehicle into drive and leave the parking lot. For a couple of days he didn't answer his phone. He knew others wanted to console him, but he was beyond consolation. So he just let the phone ring and left those who tried to reach him listening to "Go Birds" on his voice mail, which now carried a misplaced, perverse cheerfulness.

"I'd go through the pain of another burst appendix before I'd go through another loss like that," he told me.

This civic depression had ended abruptly on March 4, 2004, when Philadelphia signed Jevon Kearse, a premier pass-rushing defensive end, as a free agent from the Tennessee Titans. Two weeks later, Owens had joined the Eagles. Philadelphia's front office had recognized the urgency of a run at the Super Bowl. All the pieces were in place. But this meant more pressure to succeed, greater expectations, a higher ledge from which to fall. No achievement came unqualified in Philadelphia. When things were at their best, many learned to expect the worst.

Why was that?

Foremost, of course, it was the losing. Defeat held a dreadful prominence here. The Phillies were one of the most futile teams in the history of sports. They lost one hundred or more games twelve times between 1921 and 1945 and managed only forty-six winning seasons in 122 years of existence. The Eagles won the NFL title in 1960 and did not reach the playoffs again for eighteen years.

Phil Sheridan, a columnist for the *Inquirer*, thought that talk radio had discovered how to market ill-tempered behavior over losing back to the city itself, as if to say, "This is now your identity as the most obnoxious sports fans." But he had grown up in Philadelphia, and he also noted a mean streak that predated sports talk radio.

"People take it so much more personally here," Sheridan told me.

Psychologists developed a theory called Basking in Reflected Glory. Essentially, the theory stated that one's self-esteem could be improved by identifying with the success of something or someone else, like a sports team and its players. The team became "we" and fans rushed to swaddle themselves in team colors. In Philadelphia, Sheridan said, the theory should be called Wallowing in Reflected Misery.

"There's not enough glory to bask in," he told me. "When other things are not going well in people's lives, it's much easier to be upset about this than be upset about a job not going well or your company moving or you being downsized. Schools are bad here. There are all kinds of social problems. The tax base is drained out. But it's much easier to get unified behind this negative of sports rather than the negatives that are harder to fix."

During the Phillies' postseason run in 1993, as they were defeating favored Atlanta to win the National League, Sheridan said he knew at least four people who told him, "I hope the Phillies lose to the Braves because I couldn't stand to lose the World Series."

Apparently, the idea of winning the World Series never occurred to them.

In 2001, when the 76ers advanced to the NBA Finals, fans realized they had no chance against the Los Angeles Lakers. So they partied up and down Broad Street the night the Sixers beat Milwaukee to win the Eastern Conference.

"The expectation of failure is so intrinsic, so built in and so wired into the neurons of our brains," Sheridan said. "It's like, 'It's going to happen, we might as well get it over with now.'"

Some believed the bedrock of this sporting fatalism could be found in Philadelphia's Quaker heritage. E. Digby Baltzell, the late, eminent sociologist at the University of Pennsylvania, argued in his book, *Puritan Boston and Quaker Philadelphia*, that the Quaker notions of individualism, tolerance and equality made for disinterested and ineffective civic leadership. Boston had its Puritan sense of community mission, while Philadelphia languished in municipal torpor, fostered by apathy of the rulers and antipathy of the ruled.

In Baltzell's words, Philadelphia was "inoculated with an 'anti-leadership vaccine,'" the bequest of Quaker egalitarianism and anti-intellectualism, the author Stacy Schiff would write in the *New York Times* as Super Bowl XXXIX approached.

"Success is a birthright in Boston," Schiff would write. "It surprises in Philadelphia."

Or, as Dominic Yanni, cousin of Chainsaw, owner of a limousine service that once ferried former Eagles coach Ray Rhodes, told me in a less academic but more pungent fashion: "We have no life in Philly. The government sucks. We're taxed to death. We have the highest city-wage tax in the world, the highest insurance rates in the United States, the highest number of lawyers of any city on the face of the earth. And it's a union-featherbedded city."

The Eagles, representing the city's tough-guy, working-class image, served as a kind of thread that stitched the holes in people's daily lives, Yanni suggested.

"It's a blue-collar town," Yanni said. "These people feel entitlements. Football is our life, our pastime, our dream thing. Nothing excites Philadelphia more than Eagles football. Deep down we want them to win, but the masochist in us begs them to lose. It's a two-faced thing. Part of us wants them to win, part wants them to lose so we can complain. They are the hope and frustration of our lives."

5

Tuesday, December 21

The front-page headline of the *Philadelphia Inquirer* mourned, "Oh, the Pain," which perfectly captured the dour mood of the city and the prospects of Owens's return to the field.

Dr. Mark Myerson, the Baltimore orthopedic surgeon who operated on Owens, told the *Inquirer* that "it doesn't make sense to say" the receiver could be back to play in the Super Bowl. That was about as straightforward and glum as it could be. T.O. seemed to be history. Apparently, the Eagles would have to try to win the Super Bowl without him. "Screwed," said a headline in the *Philadelphia Daily News*.

I had witnessed at least one episode of even greater consuming grief over the health of an athlete. This time, it involved an entire country, not just a city. I happened to be in England in April 2002, when the British national team captain and former Manchester United soccer star, David Beckham, suffered a fractured foot.

On talk shows, on trains, in pubs, Beckham became the most urgent topic of conversation amid fear that he might miss the 2002 World Cup, which was approaching in less than two months in Japan and South Korea.

Tony Blair, the British prime minister, even interrupted a cabinet meeting on the budget and the Middle East to remark on Beckham's injury. The Queen Mother had died only three days earlier, but this did not seem to be any less of a loss.

"Our Worst Nightmare," screamed the front-page headline in the *Mirror* tabloid.

"Beckham Faces End of the World," blared the *Guardian* broadsheet.

One British tabloid ran a photograph of the actual size of Beckham's foot on the front page. The paper suggested that healing might be accelerated by a communal laying of hands on Beckham's broken metatarsal.

To which Terry Venables, a former coach of the British national team, replied, "Thank God it wasn't a groin injury."

Beckham recovered to play in the World Cup, and England advanced to the quarterfinals before losing to Brazil. That would be insufficient for the Eagles, with or without Owens. Let Eagles fans pour over Owens's X-rays for the next six weeks, as British fans had obsessed over Beckham's. Players didn't have that luxury. They seemed professionally resentful of the suggestion that they couldn't get to the Super Bowl without Owens. They had reached three consecutive NFC championship games without him. Why couldn't they reach the Super Bowl?

"Nobody's crying for us," tight end Chad Lewis said after the Dallas game, "and we're not going to cry for ourselves."

On its front page, the *Daily News* took a more propitious stance with the headline, "The Dream Ain't Dead." Columnist Sam Donnellon, a voice of control amid the stampede of panic, said, Hey, wait a minute. Every other team in the NFC was seriously flawed. The Eagles' defense had allowed fewer points than any team in the league. Philadelphia still had the conference's best quarterback in Donovan McNabb and most resourceful running back in Brian Westbrook.

"'Tis the season to be jolly," Donnellon wrote.

Through the day, it seemed to dawn on the city. Maybe all was not lost after all. Slowly, the initial fright subsided. Tentative hope began to melt frigid disbelief. *One player does not make a team.* Still, many felt they could not stomach a fourth consecutive loss in the NFC championship game.

"You'll have to make reservations to jump off the bridges,"
Shaun Young said.

Wednesday, December 22

In a procedure lasting one hour, Dr. Myerson inserted two screws
and a plate into Owens's right ankle. Two ligaments had been torn,
not simply stretched as first believed. Still, Myerson offered some
qualified hope.

Under normal circumstances, it would take eight to ten weeks of
recovery before a person could resume athletic activity, Dr. Myerson
said at a postoperative news conference, his South African accent
distinctive from the harsher intonations of Philadelphia and Baltimore, where the surgery on Owens had taken place.

Yet, Dr. Myerson continued, "I think there is a reasonable possibility that he will return to play in about six or seven weeks. But
that is not predictable, and a lot will depend on his recovery and
rehabilitation over the next month or two. While it is not unrea-
sonable to hope that he returns, it's not something that we would
expect."

If Owens rushed his recovery, he might break the screws and
plate in his ankle during running and cutting activities, Myerson
continued. He could not "fairly or accurately" say what the conse-
quences would be. Owens was an extraordinarily conditioned athlete, the doctor said. He would begin exercising soon in a pool, his
cast covered like a salad in a vacuum wrap. In two weeks, he could
begin moving the ankle. In four weeks, he could begin riding an
exercise bike. By the time the playoffs started in mid-January, if
things went well, he could begin bearing weight on the ankle.

Myerson's words seemed to swoop and dart like a kite, soaring
in one direction and circling back in contradiction. A "reasonable
possibility" existed that Owens could play, but it was not something to be expected. Each fan would have to sort out this seman-
tic inconsistency.

Merry Christmas.

Monday, December 27

The Eagles played for the first time without Owens. Andy Reid had a choice of providing legitimate entertainment for paying and viewing customers or keeping his remaining players out of the emergency room. Reid chose the latter in this Monday night game, a twenty-to-seven defeat in St. Louis. Brian Westbrook, who missed the playoffs last season with a torn triceps tendon, was not even allowed in uniform, lest Reid be tempted to use him. Instead, Westbrook stood on the sideline, looking fashionable in Bubble Wrap. Donovan McNabb played for one series. I think he wore a crossing-guard bib. So much for getting reacquainted with receivers not named Owens. Instead, Reid shut the whole thing down. He did everything but cordon off the team with police tape.

Bend but don't break used to be a description of the Eagles' defense. Now it was the hope for McNabb's arm and legs. His backups, Koy Detmer and Jeff Blake, were not-ready-for-prime-time players. Now we knew why Reid sat McNabb. If he ever got hurt, this season was history. If I were Reid, I'd protect McNabb with more than blockers at practice. I'd use highway cones. I half expected Reid to tiptoe around the next few weeks with a stethoscope around his neck instead of a whistle.

On *Post Game Live*, Governor Rendell said that Reid's strategy was risky but probably the best of two alternatives.

"I think Andy knows his players better than anybody," Rendell said. "You gotta ride with Andy."

Ray Didinger thought the Eagles could beat any first-round playoff opponent in the NFC, even caked with a little rust. Another panelist, Vaughn Hebron, who had won two Super Bowls with Denver, felt uneasy. His Broncos had shut down for the final weeks of the regular season in 1996, only to lose their divisional playoff game to Jacksonville.

Once a team lost its sense of urgency, Hebron said, "It's smoke and mirrors."

•   •   •

Before the game, a video tribute honored Reggie White, the former all-pro defensive end for the Eagles and Packers. Shockingly,
he had died a day earlier at his home outside of Charlotte, North
Carolina, at the age of forty-three. A preliminary autopsy report
said that White had suffered a heart attack that may have been
related to a respiratory problem and a sleeping disorder known as
sleep apnea.

He had seemed so indestructible as a player, so nimble and
powerful at 300 pounds. When defensive end Hugh Douglas first
came to the Eagles in 1998, after White had moved on to play in
two Super Bowls with Green Bay, he recalled how White had
toyed with Barrett Brooks, a young Eagles tackle.

"Tossed him around like a rag doll," Douglas said.

A devout Christian, White was known as the Minister of
Defense, and he retired with the NFL record for sacks, since broken. One hundred ninety-eight times he dragged a quarterback
down behind the line of scrimmage.

"Jesus is coming," he would sometimes say to those who tried
to block him. "I hope you're ready."

There was no doubting the sincerity of White's beliefs, or his
generosity. Ray Didinger had traveled to the tattered neighborhoods of North Philadelphia with White who, each Friday after
practice, met with former Eagles running back Herb Lusk, a minister at the Greater Exodus Baptist Church. They distributed food
and clothing, and sometimes they brought pizza along as they
walked through the community, preaching and urging people to
take back their streets, to take control of their lives.

"I judge people by what they do rather than what they say,"
Didinger said. "A hell of a lot of people talk a good game and don't
do shit. This guy really helped people."

And yet White also represented for me the complications of
mixing religion and sport. I was uncomfortable with the ostentatious way that religion was displayed on the field. Players seemed
to trivialize, not enhance, their faith when they pointed to the sky
after touchdowns or interceptions. It seemed theatrical, contrived.
A moment of supposed devotion was undermined by showy melo-

drama and made indistinguishable from spiking the ball or pulling out a Sharpie pen or grabbing a cell phone from beneath the padding of the goalpost.

It appeared to me that religion had become a spiritual buffer against the insecurity of pro football, and that it amounted to an abdication for some players, who seemed reluctant to take responsibility for their own performances. This I could understand, given the tenuous hold on their jobs.

The NFL offered the lure of big bucks but often not the stability of guaranteed contracts. Linemen, especially, were made to play with an immense bulk that could prove unhealthy for their hearts and respiratory systems and internal radiators. Pro football was the country's most popular game, but it was also violent and vicious, men crashing into each other with great size and speed, often on artificial surfaces that were glorified parking lots. The next crunching hit could always be a player's last. I had been at the Vet in 1993 when the Chicago receiver Wendell Davis, an LSU alum, dislocated both kneecaps on the same play. Sometimes I wondered, if the public could sit closer to the field, within earshot of mundanely brutal contact, whether some people would call for the end of the NFL the way they called for the end of boxing.

While I sympathized with players, I did not believe that God cared or determined who caught a particular pass, made a tackle, won a game. If we were all just divine marionettes, if self-determination was impossible, what was the point of playing games in the first place? Did God wave a Terrible Towel, have a celestial Dawg Pound or wear a Cheesehead? And if he did play favorites, how come the Saints never made the playoffs?

The idea that God had programmed every outcome undermined the value of sport as the ultimate meritocracy, providing clear results based on preparation, strategy and performance. What was the point of sitting in all those meetings, watching all that film, practicing all those plays in numbing repetition, if the conclusion was already decided?

If it was, Las Vegas made for a helluva practical joke.

In an article that appeared in *Sports Illustrated* as White and

Green Bay faced Denver in the 1998 Super Bowl, some theologians found this idea of athletic predetermination to be blasphemous, anti-Christian.

The dubious notion that God cared who won the Super Bowl, or had a direct involvement in athletic contests, especially in light of war and persecution and genocide, "trivializes the whole notion of God's involvement with the world," Richard J. Wood, dean of Yale Divinity School, told the magazine. "It is a heresy."

Joseph C. Hough, dean of Vanderbilt Divinity School, told *Sports Illustrated* that while he believed God imbued us with dignity and grace to face suffering and tribulation, the suggestion of divine influence on a football game "makes God look immoral and arbitrary. I find that religiously offensive."

But, in the article, White would not be dissuaded from biblical evidence that God interceded directly in daily lives. "God intervened in David's fight with Goliath," he said. "When Jesus died, God intervened in Jesus' victory over death."

Certainly, White was entitled to his views. But I found it troubling that certitude in his fundamentalist beliefs left him intolerant, a purveyor of divisive stereotypes instead of open-minded inclusiveness. In an unfortunate appearance before the Wisconsin Legislature in 1998, he said that African Americans "like to dance," that Hispanics "can put twenty or thirty people in one home," that Native Americans "knew how to sneak up on people," that whites "know how to tap into money" and that Asians "can turn a television into a watch."

He also said that homosexuality had "run rampant" in the United States and added, "I'm offended that homosexuals will say that homosexuals deserve rights."

White was provocative, but also maddening, columnist Bob Ford wrote in the *Inquirer,* saying that "too often, he sacked common sense and threw good judgment for a loss."

Fallout from White's remarks had resulted in harsh rebuke and loss of a possible career as a television football commentator. It had also led to a reassessment of his spiritual beliefs. In the end, White had found enlightenment, not from clarity but from ambiguity and conflict, from deep questioning of what he had done, what he had said, what he believed.

Didinger, a senior producer at NFL Films, had interviewed White a month before he died. Among other things, White admitted he had not been entirely forthright when he said that God's word led him to Green Bay from Philadelphia in 1993 as a free agent. The Packers had also offered the most money.

"There's a lot of things that I said God said, that I realize he didn't say nothing," White told Didinger, reflecting on his life. "It's what Reggie wanted to do."

He had stopped preaching, White told Didinger. He had not abandoned his faith or converted to Judaism, White said, but he had been studying Hebrew for up to ten hours a day, wanting to understand the Old Testament more completely, in its original text. He had relied on what people had told him, on a Cliff Notes version of the Scriptures, he said. He feared that interpretations had been lost or distorted. So he charged after an understanding of Hebrew as he had charged after quarterbacks. It was, he said, the hardest thing he had ever done.

"I've been a preacher for twenty-one years, preaching what somebody wrote or what I heard someone else say," White told Didinger for NFL Films. "I was not a student of Scripture. I came to the realization that I became more of a motivational speaker than a teacher of the Word.

"I was an entertainer. People seem to want to be entertained instead of want to be taught. Really, in many respects, I've been prostituted. Most people who wanted me to speak at their churches only asked because I played football, not because I was this great religious guy or this theologian. I got caught up into some of that until I got older and I got sick of it. And I just sat there, like, 'What should I do?' And I came to the realization, if I'm going to find God, I better go find Him for myself."

Maybe he had been wrong, White said.

"God doesn't need football to proclaim who he is," he said, adding, "I came to the realization that what God needed from me more than anything is a way of life instead of the things I was saying."

On December 8, White phoned Andrea Kremer, a reporter for ESPN. The call came out of the blue. They had not spoken in two years. Kremer happened to be in a pharmacy near her home in Los Angeles. She sat for more than an hour, taking notes while others waited for prescriptions to be filled. White told her, she said, that he had not been in church for four years, that he had stopped celebrating Christmas, which he found to be a manufactured holiday, and that his remarks to the Wisconsin legislature had been "one of the greatest regrets of his life."

"He seemed, I don't want to use the word troubled, because that connotes a lot of different things, but I'd say he was definitely on a journey," Kremer said. "So much of what he had been saying and preaching was what other people had told him. He felt he needed to go and find out for himself. If he could learn Hebrew and read Scripture directly, he could best understand what the Word truly was."

Eighteen days later, White was dead.

6

Friday, December 31

Philadelphia's reputation as a callous, insensitive place suffered a potentially fatal blow today in Bob Ford's heartwarming column in the *Inquirer*. A city could only stand so much of this benevolence. Propriety and decorum could not be far behind. Then what did you have? How many games had a team ever won because of its generosity?

In a story that was impossible to read without a box of Kleenex and a longing for a fight in the Seven Hundred Level at the Vet, Ford wrote of Bob Singleton and his son Robbie. They had driven from upstate New York to Philadelphia to watch the Eagles play Green Bay on December 5. As his eleventh birthday approached, Robbie Singleton had never seen an NFL game in person. He loved Brett Favre, the Packers' quarterback.

Father and son smartly avoided wearing Packers clothing, but they didn't avoid getting fleeced. Outside of Lincoln Financial Field, someone sold the Singletons a pair of counterfeit tickets for $250. Once again in Philadelphia, the milk of human kindness had curdled.

Just when the day seemed lost, Leo Carlin, the Eagles' ticket manager, came up with two tickets for sixty bucks apiece. Favre had a rough go of it as Philadelphia won forty-seven to seventeen, but Robbie Singleton got his birthday wish and even sang the Eagles fight song on the way home.

Later, Eagles fans offered the Singletons use of a home and box-seat tickets for next season's game against Green Bay. On the phone, I told Bob Singleton that his family's story would ruin

Philadelphia's reputation for inhospitable behavior. No, he said, the city had maintained its bristly dignity. Near the end of the game, a father and his ten-year-old son, both with faces painted in Eagles colors, moved near the Singletons and began shouting, "Fuck you" at the Packers' kick returners.

Oh, and one other thing.

"Robbie did get to see his first topless woman in the parking lot," Bob Singleton said of his son. "Well, as far as I know, it was his first topless woman."

Sunday, January 2, 2005

The Eagles closed out the regular season at home with an attitude of safety first, victory second. They lost a charade of a game, thirty-eight to ten, to the Cincinnati Bengals. Andy Reid coached by the Pottery Barn rule that Colin Powell used in international diplomacy: You break it, you own it. Once again, the Eagles' starters spent the game packed in Styrofoam peanuts. The back of Donovan McNabb's jersey said, Fragile, This End Up. When he backed up, he beeped.

The crowd howled, then left early. Bill Lyon wondered in the *Inquirer* whether the slovenly game qualified as consumer fraud.

All would be forgotten, of course, if the Eagles reached the Super Bowl. They had finished with thirteen victories and three defeats, the best record in the NFC. As a reward, they would have a bye in the first round of the playoffs and two weeks of respite. Their opponent in the divisional playoff round would be the St. Louis Rams, Seattle Seahawks or Minnesota Vikings. The Eagles would be rested, but would they be rusty? It was the question on the mind of everyone who followed the team.

I was on assignment in New York, covering a women's college basketball game between Connecticut and St. John's, while the Eagles played Cincinnati. UConn handed St. John's its first defeat of the season, and after his news conference, UConn Coach Geno Auriemma asked about the Eagles.

"They got crushed," I told him.

Auriemma had moved to suburban Philadelphia from Italy when he was a boy. He was voluble and funny, an endearing wiseass. And he could coach as ornately as he could talk, having won five national championships. He did not like Reid's strategy. And, being from Philadelphia, it was his right to express his dissatisfaction.

"This is not a good sign," Auriemma said. "You can't rest all your guys and lose and think you're going to go into the playoffs and turn it on. That's bullshit."

On *Post Game Live*, Ray Didinger had a sobering statistic. Only one NFL team had ever lost its last two regular-season games and reached the Super Bowl—the Green Bay Packers in 1967. Still, he would not question Reid. Neither would Governor Rendell, who said, "I know there's history against it, but I say, 'Trust Andy.'"

To which panelist Vaughn Hebron said: "Trust him up to the [NFC] championship game."

For Reid, this had always been a clumsy endgame, football checkmate.

Tuesday, January 4

The playoff brackets were set. After a bye for the wild-card weekend, the Eagles would open the divisional playoffs on Sunday, January 16. Already, the wait was becoming unbearable. Would the Eagles be ready? Had they lost all their momentum with a counterfeit finish to the regular season? Apprehension seemed as contagious as the flu.

"Bowl or Bust" warned a headline in the *Inquirer*. "Anything else and this has not been a good season," cornerback Sheldon Brown said.

On WIP, Angelo Cataldi used a stark image: "It feels like twelve days before the jury comes back with the verdict. Are we going to the gas chamber?"

Thursday, January 6

Available playoff tickets sold out in ten minutes. Terrell Owens spoke up for the first time since his surgery. His leg was healing, but his feelings were not. In an interview with columnist Stephen A. Smith of the *Inquirer*, Owens said he was confident he would be able to play in the Super Bowl. He was exercising in a pool and felt no pain when he put weight on his leg. But he was not happy with the way the season had gone, not with fourteen touchdown receptions, not with twelve hundred receiving yards.

"I was really frustrated as to how my production had gone down," Owens told Smith. "And it wasn't due to a lot of double coverage. A lot of people may want to say it was double coverage, but if you break down the film and see where the balls are going and where I am, I tended to get frustrated."

He did not have a definitive answer for his lack of production, Owens told Smith.

"And I definitely don't want to seem like the person who's never satisfied," Owens said. "But, dude, I know what I bring to the table. I know what I do when I get out on that field. You can't tell me I'm not open more than half the time when I'm out on that field. I don't care if it is double coverage.

"I think if a lot of people were to watch the actual game film instead of highlights from television, they'll see what I'm talking about."

Would they see Donovan McNabb looking in another direction? Smith asked Owens. Would they see Andy Reid trying to keep Owens from scoring again so the coach would not have to wear a pair of tights to pay off his preseason bet?

Owens bit his lip. He went out of his way to praise McNabb and Reid, Smith wrote, hinting that his perceived lack of production was "probably part of Coach Reid's game plan to prepare others for playoff competition."

If that's what he thought, why did Owens bring up the subject in the first place? That was one problem I had with him. He claimed to be a truth-teller, but he was disingenuous. He was an expert not at the truth but at the dodge.

I liked the theatricality of his touchdown celebrations. I liked it when he pulled out the Sharpie pen and autographed a football after scoring for the 49ers. I liked it when he shook his pompoms with the cheerleaders. I didn't even mind when he stomped on Dallas's star logo at Texas Stadium. Too often the NFL was the No Fun League. But in the guise of truth, Owens often preferred to feint, as if he were trying to evade a cornerback. He seemed to be criticizing McNabb but wouldn't admit it.

I had gone to see the Eagles at training camp in August, on the day an incendiary story broke about Owens and former San Francisco teammate Jeff Garcia, who was now quarterback of the Cleveland Browns. In a Q&A article in *Playboy*, Owens was told by his interviewer that Garcia "has denied rumors that he is gay."

"What do you think?" the magazine asked him.

Owens replied: "Like my boy tells me: If it looks like a rat and smells like a rat, by golly, it is a rat."

Speaking with reporters that day in August, Owens said his interview with *Playboy* had been only a "loose conversation," and that, "Everybody is going to make a big deal out of it, but it wasn't like I came out and said Jeff was gay."

He had said everything but. His remarks were irresponsible, potentially libelous, homophobic. His words could have been construed as comparing gays to rats.

Garcia dismissed Owens's words as "ridiculous, untrue" allegations. Reid punted, saying only that he didn't read *Playboy*, and the Eagles' front office shrank from a public apology. Calling Owens's comments "appalling," Rita Addessa, executive director of the Pennsylvania Lesbian and Gay Task Force, told me, "These comments that equate gay men to some inferior life form do real harm, creating a cultural environment which justifies violence against gay and lesbian people."

Now, in a different context, Owens was at it again, making

inflammable remarks, then backing away in a verbal crabwalk, as if to say, "Who, me?"

Eagles fans went into a snit. Was T.O. up to his old, divisive tricks? Was this the first fissure in a cracking of team solidarity? John Kleinstuber, a season-ticket holder and golf club manager, wondered why Smith had to write the article. *At a time like this?* It was the reporter's job, of course. The reporter's obligation was to inform the reader, not to be concerned about the fallout among fans and Owens's teammates.

Terry Funk, whose family had season tickets since 1961, couldn't believe what she was reading. *You gotta be kidding me. T.O. hasn't been in the spotlight, so now he's gotta get headlines. This is the last thing we need.*

Friday, January 7

An irate fan had been convicted of pirating the e-mail addresses of local sportswriters to express his dissatisfaction with the Phillies. Plenty of people felt the same disgust, but few of them faced three years in prison for venting their anger.

Allan Carlson, forty-one, who had moved from the Philadelphia region to southern California two decades ago, was convicted of seventy-nine charges related to fraud, identity theft and computer hacking. According to the FBI, Carlson hacked into computers in seven states, collected e-mail addresses and fired off anti-Phillies screeds that were purportedly sent from sportswriters at the *Inquirer* and the *Daily News*.

Because many of the e-mail addresses were outdated, the rants were returned in a kind of electronic boomeranging. Sportswriters found their mailboxes clogged with up to forty thousand messages, and one worked for a hundred hours to restore his computer.

Carlson's attorney admitted in court that his client was obsessive, perhaps even psychotic, but was not an intentional lawbreaker, the *Daily News* reported.

He only meant to say the Phillies stunk.

7

Governor Rendell had begun to anticipate an all-Pennsylvania Super Bowl. Pittsburgh had finished the regular season with fifteen victories and one defeat, thrashing the Eagles twenty-seven to three in November. If the state rivals met again, Rendell would root for the Eagles, just as former New York City Mayor Rudolph W. Giuliani had rooted for the Yankees over the Mets in the 2000 subway World Series.

"What type of pandering politician would I be, after rooting for a team for forty years, to say I'm going to be neutral?" Rendell had told me.

Plus, he said, no one in Pittsburgh would believe him anyway.

He did say jokingly—at least I think he was joking—that if the Eagles and Steelers reached the Super Bowl, he would propose that the game be shifted from Alltel Stadium in Jacksonville, Florida, to Beaver Stadium on the campus of Penn State.

"The stadium holds thirty thousand more people," Rendell said. "That's more money for the NFL. I'll try to convince the mayor of Jacksonville that he doesn't want two sets of hard-working, hard-drinking, two-fisted fans tearing up his town for a week."

Apart from their social habits, the governor did sense a difference in anticipation between fans of the Eagles and Steelers. Where disciples of the Eagles always feared defeat, supporters of the Steelers always expected victory. This residual confidence came from four Super Bowl victories between 1975 and 1980.

As the regular season wound down, Rendell had asked a Pittsburgh fan if he worried that the Steelers would squander home-field advantage for the American Football Conference playoffs.

"Nah," the fan replied.

"You'll never get an Eagle fan to talk like that," Rendell said.

Shaun Young told me this about Pittsburgh fans: "They're hardcore. Their hunger is to get another championship. Ours is a more desperate hunger. They want that taste back. They know what that taste is. We want to know."

I decided to take a drive to Pittsburgh to see this difference for myself.

James Carville, the political consultant, once described Pennsylvania as Philadelphia and Pittsburgh with Alabama in between. By this, he neatly divided the state into urban Democrats and rural Republicans. But if Pittsburgh had similar political leanings, it was also suspicious of Philadelphia as a big-city bully. Rendell noted that he was the first Philadelphian elected governor since 1910.

The two cities did find similar rooting interest in 1943, when personnel shortages during World War II led the Eagles and Steelers to combine under the Frankenstein name of the Steagles. The team was composed of stateside military personnel, players who came out of retirement and those declared 4F and thus unfit for service.

Dan Rooney, chairman of the Steelers and son of their founder, Art Rooney, was a kid of ten or eleven at the time. He used to ride the train with the team and players helped him with his homework.

"We had this one guy, Tony Bova, who was almost blind in one eye and the other eye was questionable," Rooney said. "But he was a legitimate receiver. I guess he could hear the ball coming."

Vic Sears, a tackle who would later play for the great Eagles teams of the late 1940s, had stomach ulcers. According to the Associated Press, guard Eddie Michaels was nearly deaf and center Ray Graves had only one ear.

"Let's face it, there was a war going on," Sears told me. "If you were healthy, you were in it."

Even though the teams were combined, the Eagles and their coach, Earle "Greasy" Neale, played a domineering role. The Steagles wore the Eagles' green and white, not the Steelers' black and gold. Of the six home games, four were played at Shibe Park in Philadelphia, and two at Forbes Field in Pittsburgh. Neale of Philadelphia and Walt Kiesling of Pittsburgh nominally shared coaching duties. But Neale had the stronger personality. He was a dexterous man who was an accomplished bridge player and had been an outfielder who batted .357 for Cincinnati during the infamous "Black Sox" scandal of the 1919 World Series. His elaborate T formation offense prevailed over Kiesling's single wing.

There was tension among the players, too. Al Wistert, a rookie tackle from Michigan, said he signed for three thousand eight hundred dollars, while none of the veterans made more than four grand. Some thought he made up to forty-five hundred bucks and gave him the cold shoulder. One teammate even turned his back on him at training camp.

"It was a miserable year," Wistert remembered. "No one would talk to me."

In one game, the Steagles set an NFL record by committing ten fumbles. Still, the team finished with five victories, four defeats and a tie and gave the Eagles their first winning season.

By the end of the decade, the Eagles would be the NFL's dominant team, winning consecutive titles in 1948 and 1949. Wistert's teammates finally began talking to him, and he became an all-pro, although Neale did continue to bust his wise-guy chops.

During the 1948 season, Wistert came limping to the sideline, and told his coach, "I think I broke my leg."

Neale looked at him and said, "Get back in until you're sure."

I had the radio tuned to WIP as I left for Pittsburgh in early afternoon. The hosts, Glen Macnow and Ray Didinger, were imagining the frenzy of a Super Bowl parade. At moments like this, Eagles fans possessed the acute and incurable hopefulness of people who left their Christmas trees up year around.

Macnow, coauthor of the *Great Philadelphia Fan Book*, recalled the Flyers' first championship parade in 1974. There would be a second Stanley Cup title and another parade in 1975, but this first one was orgiastic. Two million people showed up on South Broad Street for the celebration. "There are grown men in this town who can't remember their wife's birthday, but can still point out the tree they hung from as the Flyers' first parade passed by," Macnow and coauthor Anthony Gargano wrote in the fan book.

On the radio, Macnow remembered that Bernie Parent, the Flyers' goalie, halted the entire parade because he had to pee. Just stopped the procession and ran into a row home to use the bathroom.

"That woman still hasn't flushed that toilet," Macnow said.

Spectators crowded the procession, handing Champagne to the players, kissing them, shaking their hands. In one case, a handshake became a shakedown. One fan, Didinger recalled, grabbed the hand of Flyers' Coach Fred Shero and swiped a championship ring he had won in the American Hockey League.

If the Eagles won the Super Bowl, the crowd wouldn't get anywhere near the players, Macnow surmised. But it wouldn't stop the parade to end all parades, he said. He could imagine the celebration.

"Take a magnum bottle of Champagne, put it on one of those paint shakers at a hardware store, let the machine run for twenty-two years and pop that baby open, letting loose all those pent-up frustrations, hopes and dreams," Macnow said, repeating a scenario he had described to me earlier. "It'll be the most incredible celebration any city ever had."

In Harrisburg, WIP faded out and I was left with Pearl Jam and Talking Heads to get me through the Allegheny Mountains. The Pennsylvania Turnpike was built to confront the Alleghenies. It became the nation's first superhighway, a New Deal and WPA precursor to the Interstate system, an engineering marvel with its gentle grades and parallel tunnels. On this sodden day, the rolling stubble fields and barns and silos gave way to the mountains, blue in the distance, then brown as the back of a bear. The sun shone briefly and turned the sky the color of a bruise. I stopped for a yogurt cone but somehow avoided the siren call of "World of Pigeons."

It was dark when I reached Pittsburgh after nearly five hours, driving along the Monongahela, which flowed north and was once a so-called river of sweat that floated the exertions of the steel industry. It was at night that Pittsburgh had its chance at greatness, with the bulkhead gleam of downtown and shouldering bridges and waterways merging in serpentine reflection.

At my hotel, I met up with Rob Ruck, a history lecturer at the University of Pittsburgh who was cowriting an autobiography of Art Rooney, the Steelers' founder. Sport had replaced steel as the defining aspect of the city, Ruck said. Expectations demanded victory. Both Philadelphia and Pittsburgh saw themselves as work-hard, play-hard, blue-collar cities. But Pittsburgh had toasted recent victory, while Philadelphia had known only defeat for two decades. From 1960 through 1992, the Steelers, Pirates and Penguins won all nine championship games or series in which they participated, while Pitt won a national collegiate football title.

If you included the dozen Negro League championships won by the Pittsburgh Crawfords and the Homestead Grays, if you counted the early-century boxing champions and college football successes, "I would argue that no city of comparable size has this record of achievement in twentieth-century sport," Ruck told me.

Pittsburgh was sliced like a topographical cake, partitioned by hillsides and river valleys, as well as race and class and ethnicity, Ruck noted. What unified the city were sports, especially football and the Steelers, he said.

On one hand, the Steelers represented a diversified Pittsburgh, one that had moved beyond the collapse of steel and remade itself. It had a new convention center, a renowned cancer center at the University of Pittsburgh and the Andy Warhol museum. The Steelers played in a new stadium, Heinz Field, and even had a just-unwrapped quarterback in rookie Ben Roethlisberger.

"What a great allegory for Pittsburgh, a city that was at the end of its glory days right around the time the Steelers last won the Super Bowl, and is now remade into a center of technology, world-class medicine and high-tech education," Rob Reeder, a doctoral candidate in computer science at Carnegie Mellon University, told me in an e-mail message.

Pittsburgh was also a throwback town, tinged with nostalgia for the glory days of the 1970s, when the Steelers won four Super Bowls as the steel industry crumbled, said Wallace Miller, the coroner of Somerset County, Pennsylvania, located eighty miles to the southeast.

"You see people walking around in Jack Lambert and Jack Ham jerseys," Miller said. "And that was thirty years ago."

This wistfulness for better times could be found at bars like Chiodo's Tavern, a local institution once situated near the front gates of the immense Homestead Works of U.S. Steel. The mills along the Monongahela were long shuttered, their smoky commerce replaced by university research buildings and tidy brand-name retail.

Except for the timid naughtiness of brassieres hanging from the ceiling, Chiodo's was as much a museum as a bar. A photograph near the entrance showed Nikita Krushchev, the former Soviet leader, driving by Chiodo's, doffing his hat, on a visit to Pittsburgh on September 24, 1959. A patch of Astroturf hung on a wall, along with photographs of the Steelers dating to 1933, when they were founded as the Pirates.

Pittsburgh represented America both in its headlights and in its rearview mirror. The region lost one hundred fifty-eight thousand manufacturing jobs and two hundred eighty-nine thousand residents between 1970 and 1990, according to Carnegie Mellon University. Its population was nearly halved since the 1950s. Currently, the city faced its worst financial crisis since the steel industry buckled, the Penguins endured a season-ending work stoppage and the Pirates struggled to challenge big-market fences while swinging small-market bats. Even the dominance of area high school football, which had produced such luminous quarterbacks as Johnny Unitas, Joe Namath, Joe Montana and Dan Marino, had waned. While Pittsburgh Central Catholic won Pennsylvania's large-school championship in 2004, teams from the Philadelphia suburbs won six of the previous eight years.

And yet, while other Pittsburgh corporate citizens like West-inghouse, Rockwell International, Gulf Oil, Mesta Machines, J&L Steel and U.S. Steel reduced or ceased operations, the Steelers remained a dependable, resolute touchstone. The team recommended Pittsburgh both for its smokestack past and its stamina at reinvention. The Steelers' headquarters, in fact, were located on the site of the old J&L steel mill.

"They are the city of Pittsburgh," Bob Clark, a hospital purchasing manager, said over a beer at a back table in Chiodo's.

He had sold his tickets this season to a friend because of the disruptive behavior of some fans.

"I decided to take a year off," Clark said. "Bad choice."

Still, he followed the Steelers fervently.

"They're like the identity of the town," Clark said.

Andy Kelly, a retired account executive with CSX railroad, sat at a table with his brother. Pittsburgh was saddled with a billion dollars' worth of debt, and its 2005 budget did not even include money to fix potholes, according to the *Associated Press*. As Kelly saw it, the Steelers provided a black-ink counterweight to red-ink crisis. And so, at the Satin and Lace lingerie shop, the mannequins were decked out in Terrible Towels. And at a Steelers souvenir stand in the revitalized warehouse area known as the Strip District, even the fire hydrant was painted black and gold.

"We were the industrial center of the universe," Kelly said. "Now we're in the dumps. The Steelers show we're alive, a major city, still a force."

Joe Chiodo, the elfin, eighty-six-year-old proprietor of the tavern, once ran buses from the bar to Steelers' games. Tonight, he was in a bad mood. He didn't want to talk about the team.

"I hope they lose every game," he said.

He felt betrayed by what he called the nosebleed shuffle of his seats from near the forty-yard line at Three Rivers Stadium to "peanut heaven" in the end zone of Heinz Field. Chiodo pointed his finger and said, "If the old man was around, they never would have done that to us."

He meant Art Rooney, who purchased the Steelers for two

thousand five hundred dollars in 1933 and dusted them off from the scruffy sandlots of Pittsburgh's north side. The Rooney family still owned the team and ran it in the family's unpretentious image, or as unpretentious as one could be in the prosperous world of the NFL.

Art Rooney wore a tuxedo once in his life. Dan Rooney, his son and the Steelers' chairman, still walked from home to each game. Even cheerleaders were considered too ostentatious. The totemic moment for the Steelers was a Coca-Cola commercial from 1979 when Mean Joe Greene, the star defensive end, tossed his jersey to an adoring fan.

For the Eagles, that defining television moment was less adored, far more controversial, in the wake of Janet Jackson's breast-bearing performance at the 2004 Super Bowl. It had occurred two months ago during a pre-game skit on ABC before *Monday Night Football*. The actress Nicollette Sheridan from *Desperate Housewives* dropped her towel and jumped into the arms of Terrell Owens, asking him to abandon his team for the evening.

Tony Dungy, coach of the Indianapolis Colts, said he found the skit offensive, because it played to stereotypes about athletes as sexual predators and black men having a weakness for white women. Dan Rooney, the Steelers' chairman, was outraged.

"I thought it was disgraceful," he wrote in an op-ed piece in the *New York Times*.

A letter writer to the *Times* chided Rooney for a kind of Norman Rockwell naiveté in the age of half-naked cheerleaders and drunken, profanity-spewing fans. But it was clear Rooney felt that the NFL, and the Steelers in particular, represented traditional values that the Eagles had undermined.

These were the same ideals that made a one-man play about Art Rooney, called *The Chief*, the most popular production in the thirty-year history of Pittsburgh's Public Theater, according to Ted Pappas, the theater's executive director.

"The team and the play triggered what's best in this city—a sense of community, pulling through when the going gets tough, the old values of family, friendship, loyalty," Pappas said of the play, which had ended its second run a month earlier.

Before the NFL liposuctioned its charm and Botoxed its personality, a roguish charisma persisted. Fondness for the Steelers sprung from great affection for Art Rooney, who died in 1988. He patiently stuck by his team even though it needed forty years to win a division title. He had been a semipro football player, an Olympic-caliber boxer, a horseplayer who made his fortune by owning a number of tracks. When he huddled with friends, they were likely to be priests and cops and newspapermen and racketeers. When Pittsburgh reached its first Super Bowl in 1975, Rooney sat in the press box instead of the owner's box.

He loved to attend wakes, said Gene Collier, a columnist at the *Pittsburgh Post-Gazette,* who cowrote *The Chief* along with Rob Zellers. When his wife, Kathleen, died, Rooney took some flowers intended for her and placed them in the viewing room of another man at the same funeral home. The deceased had virtually no family, so Rooney also signed the man's guestbook, as did some of the Steelers.

When a relative of the man arrived, he seemed perplexed, Collier said, asking, "Dad knew Lynn Swann and Franco Harris?'"

Once, Rooney ran for registrar of wills, and said he didn't know anything about the job, but would hire somebody who did. "*Time* magazine ran a short: Finally, an honest politician," Collier said.

Even with the enmity he felt toward the Steelers, Joe Chiodo still revered Art Rooney and covered the walls of his tavern with Steelers memorabilia—photographs, a clock, a trophy from a Rust Belt rivalry with the Cleveland Browns. He also kept a set of miniature NFL helmets on a shelf above the bar.

"I want to show you something," Chiodo said, taking me behind the bar.

He pointed to an Eagles helmet. It was upside down.

"That's because they always lose," he said.

8

Sunday, January 9

A friend picked me up at the hotel for a tour of Pittsburgh. We grew up together in Eunice, Louisiana, but hadn't seen each other in thirty years. Rodney Landreneau's parents were such LSU fans that his father showed us highlight films at our Cub Scout meetings. Rodney was now a thoracic surgeon at the University of Pittsburgh, and his youngest brother, Fraser, a neurosurgeon, was an LSU team doctor.

"Here it's crazier," Rodney told me. "At LSU, it's still sport. Here, it's live or die. The city really bases its identity on the good and bad teams of the Steelers."

Six months after the season, an obsessive Pittsburgh fan names James Henry Smith would not let even death separate him from his favorite team. Wearing black-and-gold silk pajamas, Smith would be laid out in a recliner at the funeral home, facing a television that played an endless loop of Steelers highlights. Another fan would be charged with harassing a woman after allegedly impersonating not one but two of the Steelers' quarterbacks.

Rodney could appreciate the zeal, even though he was a fan of the New Orleans Saints and understood that hope had its limitations. A week earlier, Rodney said he had become depressed when LSU lost to Iowa in the Capital One Bowl. But people here had an intense devotion to the Steelers that LSU fans would struggle to match in Baton Rouge, he said. Rodney knew of a guy with the names of Steelers' greats tattooed on his back.

"They've got that hard-nosed attitude," Rodney said. "It fits that steel industry mentality. People identify with linebackers and offensive linemen. Their passion is knocking somebody out. The Eastern European influence is tremendously large. These folks are tough people."

Several weeks earlier, a patient of his arrived for an appointment dressed in black-and-gold adoration, wearing a Steelers jacket, a Steelers necklace, a Steelers pinkie ring and a Steelers watch.

"I had to tell him he had lung cancer, but all he worried about was whether the Steelers would win the next week," Rodney said.

When his teenage son, Josh, was five years old, Rodney said, he took him to a Steelers game against Dallas. Josh was a Cowboys fan. He wore a blue parka and had his face painted blue, with silver stars around his eyes. Steelers fans cursed and pulled Josh's stocking cap over his eyes when the Cowboys did something spectacular, Rodney said, adding that he nearly got into a fight while protecting his son.

"It's wild," Rodney said. "If the Steelers lose, they go into a state of depression. They don't sleep or they have fights. The stadium's a tough place where I wouldn't want to bring my kids. Wild and rowdy."

We ate lunch in the Strip District at Primanti Brothers. Just as Philly had its cheesesteak, Primanti's had its indigenous creation, a sandwich with meat, coleslaw and French fries mashed between slices of bread. A couple more of those, and I wouldn't have been Rodney's friend. I would have been his patient.

Pittsburgh had a bye this week in the AFC playoffs, but the Indianapolis-Denver wild-card game played on the television at Primanti's, and several fans wore their Steelers jerseys. Next we went to a bar and met Marc Mrvos, a friend of Rodney's and a distributor of medical supplies. At thirty-five, he still had the solid, blocky build of a college lineman.

He pulled out his cell phone, which bore a Steelers logo. At home, Mrvos had the likeness of a goalpost inlaid in the wall of his entertainment room. ("If you hit the plasma screen, you're not allowed to kick anymore.") On game days, he decorated the goalpost with yellow ribbon. For Mrvos, Steelers' Coach Bill Cowher, with his jut-jawed reliance on running the ball and punishing defense, evoked the qualities fans saw in themselves—hardworking, blunt, durable.

"In Pittsburgh, you're either a tough guy or you're not," he said. Cowher provided something else, beyond his coaching. His presence suggested a certain constancy that was no longer dependable in a town that had had to remake itself entirely. "With the Steelers, things remain the same," Mrvos said. "I'm thirty-five. In all my life, they've had two coaches."

For displaced Pittsburghers, who left in pursuit of work no longer available at home, the Steelers held a particular resonance, Vic Ketchman, the senior editor of the Jacksonville Jaguars' website, had told me. He left Pittsburgh at age forty-four, nine years earlier. It was sometimes said there were two kinds of Pittsburghers: those who came back and those who wanted to come back.

"Iron City beer had a slogan, 'It tastes like coming home,'" Ketchman told me. "That's what the Steelers are like, coming home."

An estimated twenty thousand Steelers fans—some said it was thirty thousand—had attended a game earlier in the season in Jacksonville. For the Pittsburgh diaspora, the team represented a kind of sentimental longing for the way things used to be.

"They are the team for all the ones who like the old things," Ketchman told me. "For all of us who don't want fast food, who don't want to live in a new bedroom community and pay association fees, who don't want progress forced upon us. Pittsburgh is an old place. It feels about right."

Beyond the sense of greatness lost when the mills closed, fidelity to the Steelers was a matter of municipal respect, said Jennifer Carnig of the University of Chicago. She had not lived in Pittsburgh since high school, but the longer she was away, the more she held the Steelers dear. She even named her dog Cowher, after the Steelers' coach.

"In the late seventies and early eighties—when more people in

Pittsburgh had work in the fast-food industry than any other business because the mills closed—the one reason we were able to hold our heads up as a collective unit was because of the Steelers," Carnig told me in an e-mail message.

She wrote her thesis in urban history on what the Steelers meant to Pittsburgh in the decline of the steel era.

"Pittsburgh is and was the butt of jokes, and no matter how well we do for ourselves, no matter how beautiful that city is now, we can't stop people from thinking that Pittsburgh is dirty and depressed," Carnig said. "But on any given Sunday, we can let the world know how tough we are and that's something. No matter how hard times get, we have our pride. That's what the Steelers are about."

The people who made less money had a deeper feeling for the Steelers than people who made more money, Mrvos told me. Maybe they avoided paying bills or taking a vacation to save up for season tickets or the Super Bowl. And because they gave so much of themselves to the team, they demanded a great deal in return, Mrvos said.

"If they lose, I'm sick 'til Tuesday or Thursday," Mrvos said.

He was leaving today on a business trip to Minneapolis. He would arrive home next Saturday and go straight from the airport to his tailgating party at Heinz Field. He'd love an all-Pennsylvania Super Bowl, Mrvos said, although he seemed to have a bit of doubt about the Steelers' chances against the Eagles, which I found surprising.

"You'd like to kick your big brother's ass, but you don't want to take a chance of him putting you on the ground," Mrvos said.

In late afternoon, Rodney returned me to the hotel so I could watch the Packers-Vikings game on television. This game would impact the Eagles. St. Louis had defeated Seattle in the other NFC wild-card game. If Minnesota beat Green Bay, it would face the Eagles in the divisional playoffs. Every time I turned away from the screen, the Vikings seemed to score. Brett Favre, whose gunslinger daring had lapsed into recklessness, threw four interceptions, and Minnesota won thirty-one to seventeen. Next stop, Philadelphia.

"I love the Vikings in this game," Sean Salisbury said on ESPN. Eagles fans considered Salisbury and Merril Hoge of ESPN and Cris Collinsworth of Fox as the Three Stooges of commentators. They never seemed to give the Eagles any respect. "With no T.O., the Vikings' defense is playing a little better," Salisbury said. "The Vikings' offense is far more explosive. If they can deal with the Philadelphia blitz, the Vikings are moving on to the NFC championship game."

The big news of the day was Randy Moss celebrating a touchdown reception by pretending to moon Packers fans and doing a bump and grind with the goal post.

"That is a disgusting act by Randy Moss," Fox announcer Joe Buck said as he watched the celebration. "And it's unfortunate that we had that on our air live. That is disgusting by Randy Moss."

A Fox announcer shocked by disgusting behavior? This was the same network that championed reality television and its desire to humiliate as well as entertain. The network that gave us *Temptation Island*, where couples were offered the chance, essentially encouraged, to cheat on each other.

Funny, but Buck didn't find it equally disgusting when Fox left the cameras on Moss and let him "motherfucker" the Packers crowd a couple of times.

As it turned out, Moss's celebration was merely a pantomime of the actual pants-dropping taunt that Green Bay fans traditionally performed in a fleshy farewell to opposing players leaving Lambeau Field in their team buses. Buck himself shilled for a beer company that no doubt contributed to this coarse behavior. In fact, Buck appeared in commercials with a character named Leon, who portrayed the same kind of self-centered, ill-mannered athlete that Buck had criticized Moss for being.

On Fox, the host James Brown called Moss "classless" and embarrassing. Terry Bradshaw said that Moss was "putting his team under tremendous pressure because of his childish behavior."

All of Moss's prior transgressions were trotted out on television tonight, including notice that he had left the field with a few seconds remaining in the final regular-season game. He quit on his team, he quit on plays when he was not going to catch the ball. True, he could be a loathsome teammate. But leaving early was one faux pas about which Eagles fans could not legitimately complain. In 1989, Buddy Ryan let Randall Cunningham and several other players leave an exhibition game at halftime to attend a birthday party for Whitney Houston. The flaky Cunningham had spare rooms built at his house for Houston and the running back Eric Dickerson.

A year earlier, Ryan himself had left a regular-season game against Washington with one second on the clock and the Eagles down twenty to nineteen, instructing his players to improvise with laterals and "use the Stanford-Cal deal." Some of the local sportswriters thought he had to pee.

This latest Moss episode reminded me of a line from Richard Ford's novel, *The Sportswriter*, in which he wrote, "If sportswriting teaches you anything, and there is much truth to it as well as plenty of lies, it is that for your life to be worth anything, you must sooner or later face the possibility of terrible, searing regret. Though you must also manage to avoid it or your life will be ruined."

By searing regret, I think he meant the remorse of spending a career on frivolous games, of reporting in the newspaper toy department. But sportswriting also required a concession, or admission, that some, maybe much, of what it involved was a protection of untruth: That athletes were more than what they did. That they were role models. That sports built character. That hitting a ball or throwing a pass or shooting a basket possessed a moral value. In truth, sports built characters, not character. As for being role models, many athletes, perhaps most, were neither prepared nor accepting of the responsibility. Charles Barkley had it right: Parents, not athletes, should be role models.

Sportswriters had contradictory demands of those who played games. We required that athletes be educated and articulate but willing to say nothing that might provoke or discomfort. We required them to denounce individuality, then we celebrated the necessary selfishness of those who stepped outside the team to score the winning touchdown or hit the decisive jumper. We required them to be untamed on the field and perfect gentlemen off the field. For the self-appointed guardians of sport, Moss was a threat. He did not play along. He would not be shoehorned into narrow, convenient heroism. He provided a mug-shot refutation of bubblegum-card piety, a tart defiance of sugary, Wheaties-box virtue. He had no friends and no interest in what people thought of him, he would tell *Sports Illustrated* upon being traded to Oakland in the off-season, saying, "If you don't care for me, then, oh well."

Perhaps it was our expectations, more than the athletes and their behavior, that were out of bounds. It was time to admit that sporting values taught to kids were ethical fungo drills, for practice only, not to be applied between the lines of 'roid-rage elite sport. Jim Bouton, the former Yankees pitcher and author of the defining book on sporting adolescence, *Ball Four*, once told me, "We ought to be glad more athletes don't speak out on issues, because most of their solutions involve a punch in the nose."

9

Driving back to Philadelphia in the rain, I picked up WIP again in Harrisburg. The afternoon hosts were Steve Martorano and Anthony Gargano. A caller named Matt had a slight problem. His fiancée had roped him into attending the baptism of a friend's baby on Sunday during the upcoming Eagles-Minnesota game.

"I'm trying to get out of it," Matt said.

Trying, but not succeeding.

"She gives me a statement like, 'Football's not everything,'" Matt said, wounded. "I don't know what to do. I said, 'We're gonna have to have a TV there.'"

This was a problem, too, Matt said. The father of the baby to be christened was a Giants fan. He'd probably prohibit a TV out of spite.

"It's up to you," Martorano said. "Some guys wouldn't take one for the team. If you ask me, if you had to take one for the team, this is the game you gotta miss. It's not like it's the NFC championship game, much less the Super Bowl."

"Yeah," Matt said weakly.

"Besides," Martorano said. "You ought to be clever enough to keep track of the game."

"I guess I'll put a little battery TV in the car and run out and look."

"Don't you have an evil twin?" Martorano asked.

"I wish," Matt said.

He hung up.

"That's a tough one," Martorano said. "Christenings. Why don't people check their [football] schedules? These schedules are out years in advance. Seriously."

A caller named Jeff also had a baptismal issue for Sunday's playoff game.

"It's our first-born," Jeff said. "My wife planned it like three months ago. I can't believe it. We were going to have it at a hall. Some didn't have TV accessibility. So I decided to have it at my house. I wired my whole basement so I'm going to have two TVs set up."

"Is your wife okay with all this?" Martorano asked.

She didn't want a hundred people at the house, Jeff said.

"No, no," Martorano said. "I mean is she okay with the fact that you'll be watching [the game]?"

"Yeah," Jeff said. "She knows the priority here."

"Wait, wait, time out," Martorano said. "What's the priority?"

"The Eagles."

"Over wiping original sin from your son?"

"We called the church," Jeff said. "There's only going to be three baptisms. The priest is an Eagles fan, so he's going to rush it as fast as possible. The game starts at one, but we're really thinking it's not going to get kicked off until about one thirty."

"No," Gargano said. "Probably about one-oh-eight."

"One-oh-eight?" Jeff said, crestfallen. "Really?"

"Hey, Jeff," Martorano said.

"Yeah?"

"It may be time to just dump this Christianity thing altogether and concentrate on football," Martorano said. "Come on, tell the truth."

"Talk about football as a religion," Gargano said.

"You know you believe in the Eagles more than you believe in God," Martorano said to Jeff.

"No."

"If you believed in God, would you be messing with one of these sacred rites?"

The NFL set the playoff schedule too early, Jeff said.

"It's their fault."

A caller named Billy said two of his daughters were scheduled to be christened last September. He called his sister and asked her to be the godmother of one of his daughters, Anna. He gave her the date, and she said she couldn't do it. The Eagles were playing.

Not to worry. They rescheduled for Sunday, September 19. The Eagles played on Monday night that week, the twentieth.

"How do you feel about that?" Martorano asked.

"Tell you the truth, it was a big break for me," Billy said. "I didn't want to have it when the Eagles were having a game, either."

"We understand it worked out great for you that your pain-in-the-ass kid didn't interfere with the game," Martorano said. "I'm asking you how you feel about your sister."

"Oh, I thanked her," Billy said.

"Kinda what I thought," Martorano said. "I'm glad it all worked out. You not only saved the tickets to the game, but you saved the eternal soul of your child. That's terrific. You know, I'm praying for you right now. Praying with all my heart. Have I lost my mind?"

I imagined Martorano with cartoon steam shooting out of his ears.

"Why don't you people just give up the notion that you believe in anything but the football team," Martorano said. "Give it up. Somebody told you, you gotta pour water on the kid's head, and you don't care about any of this. God almighty. I don't care what you worship, but be honest with yourself. Drop all the phony-baloney religious crap that none of you believe. You're frauds, hypocrites. You worship at the altar of the Eagles."

Yet another caller, this one named Joe, had a twist on the christening story. A month ago, he had asked the priest who performed his wedding to baptize his daughter.

"When's the date?" the priest asked.

"January 9."

"Can't do it."

"Why not?"

"Depends on what the Eagles do."

"Whaddya mean?"

"If they're playing a playoff game, I can't do it."

"Father, it's my only daughter. It would mean a lot to us."

"Nah, I gotta run a concession stand down at the Linc. If they're playing, I gotta make up that money. I can't do your daughter."

"Father, that's unbelievable."

"Depends on what they do."

Luckily, Joe said, it all worked out. The Eagles had a bye on January 9. The priest came and christened his daughter.

"Wait a minute," Martorano said. "Does the good Father know you've got to render unto Caesar? His first job is to you."

"He's gotta deal with the almighty dollar first," Joe said. "You know how the church goes, know what I mean? Luckily it all worked out. He was able to christen our daughter and it was a beautiful day."

"No thanks to him," Martorano said.

Wednesday, January 12

The Minnesota game was four days away, and Philadelphia was stoked with anxious enthusiasm. The *Daily News* sent a photographer around town with a life-size cardboard cutout of Donovan McNabb. Anyone wanting a picture taken just had to line up. The photographer wouldn't be hard to spot. He was driving around with McNabb's likeness sticking out of a sunroof.

Those most frantic to see the game went, not to the ticket window at the Linc, but to the produce section of the Shop Rite supermarket in northeast Philadelphia. A day before, Angelo Cataldi put out the call of the wild on WIP: "When people get desperate, we try in every way we can to exploit their desperation."

In that sense, Angelo was ringmaster of the Eagles circus, a man who kept the city swinging on its emotional trapeze. By six o'clock on a cold, misty morning, a crowd had arrived at Shop Rite, hoping to win tickets or to see someone else performing stupid tricks to win tickets. That would not prove difficult.

Angelo and I worked together at the *Inquirer* in the 1980s. He followed me on the Eagles beat and became a finalist for the Pulitzer Prize in 1986. He held a master's degree in journalism from Columbia University and became a relentless investigative reporter. Sixteen years ago, he gave up newspapers for the radio. It could not have been a more jarring change, trading serious print journalism for screaming noise on the radio, but the switch provided two things for Angelo. One, it gave him a huge pay increase. He now reportedly made more than $1 million a year. Two, it gave him freedom from editing.

Heavy-handed editing had driven him crazy at the *Inquirer*. Early one morning, while on the Eagles beat, Angelo told me that he drove to the home of the sports editor, incensed that the story under his byline bore insufficient resemblance to what he had written. In his words, Angelo went "berserk" in the sports editor's living room, throwing the paper on the floor and stomping on it.

It was seven thirty in the morning, Angelo recalled, and the bleary-eyed editor "looked at me as if I'd grown a second head."

Radio offered an open mike and an open invitation for Angelo to say whatever he wanted. *Sports Illustrated* named his show one of the top dozen in sports talk radio around the country, once describing it as "Howard Stern visiting *Pee-wee's Playhouse*."

Angelo's ascendancy on the radio came during an incongruous time, when the explosion of technology appeared to give fans greater access to their heroes, when, in truth, they had never been so isolated from them, separated by the velvet rope of money and the revolving door of free agency. WFAN in New York implied, by its call letters, that it bridged the gap between fans and teams in sports talk radio, but it was WIP in Philadelphia that made the fan the star.

This was important, said Angelo's sidekick, Al Morganti, in a city where fandom was a participatory sport. Angelo was as responsible as anyone for the searing butane flame of interest in the Eagles. He was not beholden to coaches or players. Instead, he gave boisterous voice to the fans to complain or savor in their loud, oddball, unruly, clannish and perpetual devotion.

Making regular appearances on his show were a troupe of eccentric characters that he endearingly referred to as "crazies," "my idiots," the "lunatic fringe." One of these characters was Shaun Young.

"He's genuinely nuts," Angelo said. "He's so wrapped up in it. He's always fascinated me because there is nothing there but true feeling for a football team. I swear, there's never a moment when he stands back and says, 'They're running up and down the field with a ball. How real is that?' No, it's like, 'I've decided to define my life by the fortune of these men wearing these uniforms and trying to advance a ball up a field.' I love him. I've always had great admiration for him, because it's genuine."

At age fifty-three, Angelo was a kind of Johnny Carson of the radio. He gave his listeners a sense that they knew him personally. He went through a divorce and remarriage and troubles with his teenage daughter on the air. He deflated the pompous and made the dull more interesting. He didn't mind looking foolish and relished the role of benign lechery. And he was good with animals.

Right there among Shop Rite's fruits and vegetables, Angelo gathered the assorted nuts. Whoever performed the most outrageous stunt this morning would win a pair of Eagles tickets. First up was Ed Lover, who wore an Eagles thong and sneakers. He accessorized with a guy in a Randy Moss jersey and wig. The guy seemed to be a Philadelphia version of the Gimp from *Pulp Fiction*. The Gimp was being led around by an extension cord attached to his neck. He spoke nary a word.

"He don't talk to the media," Ed said.

Ed wore a helmet, not a real football helmet, but a party helmet with attachments and tubes for consuming beer. Which explained the size of his stomach.

"That's not a midriff, that's a third trimester," said Rhea Hughes, a WIP cohost.

"I'm a sexy man, Angelo," Ed said.

"I guess in some societies you would be," Cataldi said.

For his stunt, Ed would have the Gimp pour a gallon of paint on him and cover him with a pillowcase full of feathers.

Then another fat guy showed up, also half-naked and covered in green paint, but with Moss's number eighty-four painted on his butt in Viking purple and gold.

The two fat, half-naked guys began yelling at each other. Ed silenced the argument with a trenchant aesthetic point: "He's got clown paint on and I'm using real MAB paint."

That settled, Ed and the Gimp headed outside to the parking lot. Their stunt would be performed in a parking spot for the handicapped. A piece of plastic was laid down, and Ed did some calisthenics. Heaven forbid he should pull a muscle. Then the Gimp began to pour the paint and shake out the feathers. Ed ran back into the supermarket, dripping and smearing green everywhere, as if some Hershey Kisses holiday experiment had gone horribly awry.

"That's terrible," Angelo said in loopy admiration. "I'm not going to put a microphone near you, because you're ridiculously disgusting. All I can tell you is you have set a very high bar for what it will take to win these tickets. You are clearly in the early lead. Now, if you would, please get the hell out of here. My God, this is revolting."

As if Ed had scored a touchdown, the appreciative crowd chanted, "E-A-G-L-E-S, Eagles!"

Whatever Ed and the Gimp did alone in their private lives, "We don't want any part of," Al Morganti, Cataldi's cohost, said.

"When we came up with this concept," Angelo said, "I didn't realize that we were tapping into an entire culture of mentally ill people."

"I used to spend a lot of money on drugs to see this in my head," Morganti said.

Then a woman named Ginger walked up. She wanted to audition to be a Wingette. Wingettes served chicken wings to the contestants at Wing Bowl. They were sort of like waitresses at Hooters, but without all the clothes.

Ginger approached Angelo carrying two cantaloupes.

"I was just wondering if you would squeeze my melons?" Ginger said.

She passed the audition.

The next contestant for tickets was a woman named Stacy, who wore a miniskirt, stiletto-heeled boots and an Eagles tank top.

It was important to see Sunday's game, Stacy said.

"I bleed green," she said. "I gotta be there."

For her stunt, she would climb a stepladder in her miniskirt, bend over more than was absolutely necessary and stock a rack of potato chips.

"I'd stock anything for Eagles tickets," Stacy said.

"Would it be prying if I asked whether you are wearing a bra?" Angelo asked.

"I am not," Stacy said.

"God bless you," Angelo said. "And let me just state that we are in the produce section, which is slightly refrigerated."

A woman named Ruth called and said she, too, wanted to be a Wingette. She had grown up in New York and was a converted Jets fan. She was forty-two, Hispanic, with long, black curly hair. People told her she looked like Halle Berry.

"I am required by law to ask if, being of Hispanic nature, you have the J. Lo. derriere?" Angelo said.

"Definitely," Ruth said.

That's all Angelo needed to know. Ruth was a Wingette.

Brian Westbrook, the Eagles' running back, phoned WIP, and they patched him right into the supermarket. Westbrook sensed the excitement, and the angst, of local fans. By Sunday, the Eagles would not have played a meaningful game in nearly a month.

"There's a feeling of not knowing," Westbrook said. "Everyone thinks we have a good team, but everybody's kind of doubting us a little bit. It's almost like preseason. They haven't seen our starting unit. They have their fingers crossed. We're here to let everyone know we're gonna go out and have a good showing."

Westbrook said he was chomping at the bit, raring to go. So was Randy Williams, the final ticket contestant at Shop Rite, in a weirdly unassuming way.

"If you don't mind my saying so, you seem a little odd," Angelo said to Randy.

He was dressed in a winter cap and a green shirt. Later, off the air, Morganti would say that Randy seemed like the guy "who the CIA looks around and says, 'We better go after this guy before he shoots the president.'"

Randy explained that he hadn't had breakfast yet, so he would sing the Eagles fight song while licking the wheels of a shopping cart.

"I don't know if this is safe," Angelo said in feigned apprehension. "You have signed all the proper legal waivers, correct?"

Why was it so important to get tickets that Randy was willing to lick the wheels of a shopping cart? Angelo wanted to know.

"Because I love the Eagles, I love Philadelphia, I love the Philadelphia fans," Randy said. "I gotta do this."

He had a plan. He would sing *Fly Eagles Fly* while he licked and slurped.

"I can't watch," Angelo said.

Randy turned the cart over, sat astride it and began his breakfast.

"Aaaargh," Angelo said. "He's licking. He slurped."

Fight Eagles fight, score a touchdown 1, 2, 3, Randy sang as he licked, warbling in a soft, unhurried voice.

"Tastes like chicken," Randy said.

Hit 'em low, hit 'em high, and watch our Eagles fly, Randy sang. Now he was spinning the wheel and sticking his tongue on it. We had a winner. But Miniskirt Stacy wanted one more chance. She flashed her thong. It didn't sway Morganti. The Paint and Feathers Guy had a thong, too, Morganti noted, and the Licking Guy had put his tongue on the wheels of a shopping cart.

"I'd like to know what you'd like me to lick," Stacy said.

"This is a supermarket," Angelo said. "Do I have to remind you?"

"This is the Eagles, hon," Stacy said.

Morganti awarded two tickets to the Licking Guy. The Paint and Feathers Guy would also get two tickets if he agreed to lick the wheels of the shopping cart.

"The Paint Guy entourage, and a larger collection of losers would be hard to find, said that what the Lick Guy did was nothing," Angelo said.

"Oh, it was something," Morganti said.

Was Paint and Feathers Guy prepared to lick the shopping cart?

"I'll lick the wheels and the floor," Paint Guy said.

He did, licking the same wheels that the other guy had just licked.

"What did he just do?" Angelo asked.

"Well," Rhea Hughes said, "if we were in another state, they'd be married."

An old friend of WIP called before the end of the morning show. A familiar contestant named Damaging Doug wanted back in Wing Bowl. The entries had already been filled, Angelo said.

"Where were you?" he asked.

He was away, Damaging Doug said. Away, as in behind bars.

"Do they just have your own suite there?" Hughes asked.

"I have stock," Damaging Doug replied.

An old warrant from a domestic dispute kept being reissued, he explained. Baseless charges and all that nonsense, he said. But it was cutting into his ability to eat massive amounts of chicken wings for fun and prizes.

"Basically, this arrest warrant has been stalking you?" Hughes asked.

"This warrant is outside in the bushes waiting for me right now," Doug said.

That was his fear, Cataldi chimed in. That Damaging Doug would qualify for Wing Bowl, and be under house arrest, necessitating use of the first Wing Bowl satellite setup.

"No, we'd have to make a stipulation with the judge that I'd be out by Wing Bowl," Doug said.

Even though the lineup was set, Angelo agreed to do Damaging Doug a favor. He could enter a wing-off among several potential contestants. Or he could get into Wing Bowl with an eating stunt: Fifty chicken McNuggets and five Big Macs.

Damaging Doug agreed. "It's a done deal," he said.

"Contact your cardiologist," Angelo said. "And please bathe before arriving here."

• • •

At practice, Donovan McNabb held his weekly news conference. The best was yet to come for this season, he assured. He loved pressure. He loved to step out on the field with all the fans on their feet, mouths wide open, wondering what he was going to do next.

"Buckle your seatbelts and enjoy the ride," McNabb said.

This is what people had been waiting to hear. His words soothed like a comfort blanket. For a moment, anyway, a nervous city seemed to exhale.

Thursday, January 13

This being Philadelphia, McNabb's remarks could sustain community enthusiasm only for so long. Thursday afternoon, a caller name Dan phoned Howard Eskin's drive-time show on WIP. "Donovan's due to get hurt," Dan said. "If the only thing we have in the backfield is [Brian] Westbrook, we're doomed. I'm scared to death, man. I'm scared to death."

I was surprised Eskin didn't pass the guy to the suicide hotline. Then Eskin gave the good news. He had seen Terrell Owens at the Eagles' training complex, wearing flip-flops, walking without any kind of brace on his ankle. T.O. looked fine. No cast, no crutches, nothing.

10

Friday, January 14

Up the street from my house, I stopped by Butch's Deli to get a paper. Butch DeLuca had gotten over his initial despair at Owens's injury. Now he had Eagles streamers hung in the window of his store, along with his neon Eagles helmet. And he had a table for Eagles gear set up near the front, triangulated between the newspaper rack, the dairy case and a life-size cardboard cutout of Donovan McNabb. Eagles hats and scarves were selling as fast as he could stock them.

"I need a dozen pink scarves as quick as I can get them," Butch said over the phone to his supplier.

A crazy restlessness suffused the city. People seemed less nervous about Minnesota than about having to wait two more days for the game. At the airport, workers discovered the Vince Lombardi Super Bowl trophy in transit, removed it from its protective case and waved it over their heads. At schools all over the region, students and teachers wore their Eagles jerseys to class.

"Believe," said the front-page headline in the *Daily News*, an odd encouragement given that the Eagles were eight-point favorites, but a knowing sign that many still needed convincing.

Fans performed more desperate acts for tickets. On radio station Q102, a woman offered to spray-paint her car green. Some guy ate five cockroaches with a side order of maggots and mealworms. Another woman had part of her head and an eyebrow shaved. A guy coughed up ice cream for his girlfriend to drink.

The winner was a man who spun a tattoo roulette wheel and

agreed to have a six-inch likeness inked on his calf of William Hung, the *American Idol* contestant who became celebrated for his warbling incompetence.

"He put it on the line and took a chance," said Shaun Young, one of the contest judges. "It could have been a picture of Clay Aiken."

On WIP, Angelo Cataldi said he had never experienced such a fever pitch of emotion in his sixteen years on the air. He wondered whether thousands of Eagles fans would moon Randy Moss on Sunday. "Tomorrow, I'm getting my ass waxed, just in case," he said.

Sister T, who called herself an Eagles nun from Reading, Pennsylvania, phoned from a convent in north Jersey. "I'm up here in Giants territory," she said. She had her yearly playoff predictions. She liked the Eagles over the Vikings, twenty-seven to seventeen. Not only would they win, but they would cover the spread.

The *Pioneer Press* of St. Paul, Minnesota, has warned Vikings fans traveling to Philadelphia that verbal and physical abuse awaited them, as if they were headed to Altamont instead of a football game.

"Don't look like a Vikings fan if you want to enjoy the game and value your safety and possessions," Steve Erban, who operated Creative Charters of Stillwater, Minnesota, told the newspaper. "The stadium is beyond civilization."

At a 2004 playoff game in Philadelphia, Erban wore the green and gold of the Green Bay Packers and said he was showered with beer and pennies.

"This is not normal," Erban said. "It's like the movie *Wolfen*."

Other cities had their idiots, too, Shaun Young told me, unruly places like Oakland and Cleveland. It's just that Philadelphia was the rowdy flavor of the month every month, he said. There were lines he would not cross as an Eagles fan, even one wearing a painted face, shoulder pads, jersey and football pants. He would not fight and risk a permanent loss of his season ticket. He would not taunt women beyond accepted jibing. And he would not throw things. But there was a certain pride, and advantage, to be had in a reputation for raucous behavior.

"I don't agree with the violence, beating people up, but I don't want to see anyone wearing Cowboys or 49ers or Giants or Packers stuff," Young said. " I want to see every seat filled with Philly supporters. We thrive on the fact that everyone can't stand us, that we're a bunch of filthy, dirty, nasty, drinking bums. In a sense we take pride in that. We don't want you here. We want you to be afraid to come. We want you to know we're the landlords, and it's time to pay the rent."

The quietest, most relaxed place in town seemed to be the Eagles' locker-room. In early afternoon, defensive end Hugh Douglas sat at his locker with an amused look as he talked about the restless fans and their reaction to Terrell Owens's injury.

"It's crazy," Douglas said. "You have to understand, man. We've been in this situation before. Things happen in football, and you have to adjust, let it run its course. But you can't tell the fans that. They don't want to hear it. They get out there, 'Aw, T.O. is hurt, oh my God, what are we gonna do?' They're ready to commit suicide."

His teammates had ambivalent feelings about their own fans. "When you're winning, there's nobody better," fullback Josh Parry said. "When you're losing, there's nobody worse."

Darwin Walker, the defensive tackle, called it tough love.

"You accept it and you deal with it," Walker said. "It's Philly, a grimy, gutty city. That's the way we do it."

Still, Douglas admitted, he missed this jittery passion a season earlier when he left Philadelphia for Jacksonville as a free agent, and was happy to return. Kids knocked on the door at his house and yelled, "Hugh Douglas, you in there? Come out and sign my jersey."

"Where are your parents?" he would ask, and they would say, "Down the street, but don't worry about that, sign my jersey."

In a begrudging way, he respected the kids for their audacity. That's how it went in Philly. People were always in your face, telling you what they thought. One thing about an emotional place like Philadelphia. You always knew where you stood. Douglas went out at night in the city and people approached him and said, "We're winning Sunday, right?" They looked him dead in the eye, and felt they were owed a championship, that they deserved it, that a debt had to be paid, but they also needed hand-holding reassurance.

"They just want you to say, 'Yeah,' and they want you to mean it," Douglas said. "If you say anything else, they're upset."

He had played in New York for the Jets, but the urban big top of New York City possessed a manic energy that had nothing to do with sports. In Philadelphia, the Eagles occupied center ring.

Howard Eskin told Douglas of the infamous Monday night game on November 3, 1975, a forty-two-to-three defeat to the Los Angeles Rams, when fans took Coach Mike McCormack at his word that there were a couple of "dogs" on the team. At Veterans Stadium, a huge dog bone was paraded around, bearing this admonishment: "Hey, Beagles, here's your dinner."

"They threw cans of Alpo at the players when they went off the field," Eskin said.

That was in some dispute. Others said that fans chanted "Alpo" and threw dog biscuits. Still, the story illustrated the bottomless frustration of fans whose team had not had a winning season in nine years. Ron Jaworski was a member of the Rams that night. As he stood on the sideline, hearing the boos, watching objects being thrown toward the field, he thought, *It must be awful to play in a place like this.* Two years later, he would be the Eagles' quarterback.

Bob Grotz of the *Delaware County Daily Times* told Douglas that fans had tossed pork chops at Buddy Ryan after he choked on a piece of meat. Eskin recalled how fans ate cockroaches in a bent devotion to the Eagles, and I recounted the story of the guy who won tickets by licking the wheels of a shopping cart.

"He's nasty," Douglas said, sitting back in his locker and rubbing his eyes in astonishment. "Hopefully, he doesn't have a wife or kids. I wouldn't want to be a woman having to kiss that guy. That's ridiculous. But that's what being passionate about football is."

He had not wanted to come to Philadelphia from New York in 1998. Then he felt the energy of the stadium and the undomesticated hope of the fans, who cheered deafeningly in celebration and threw snowballs and batteries in anger, and he knew this was where he wanted to be.

Sometimes this consuming interest grew tedious. Fans had to be taken with a grain of salt, Douglas said. But he was given to over-the-top behavior, too, chatting so much before games that Coach Andy Reid refused to ride on the same bus to the stadium. Douglas loved them, these gritty, hard-working fans for whom the Eagles were an heirloom, handed down from grandfather to father to son.

"It's passion, man," Douglas said. "Diehard craziness. You never know how much you miss it until you're gone."

In the *Daily News*, columnist Sam Donnellon tackled the psychology of heartbreak. Studies showed that testosterone levels rose for male fans in victory and fell in defeat, the way they did for animals that fought over a desired mate. Passion stemmed from feelings of love and of "us against the world," a psychologist named Belisa Vranich told Donnellon. "Romeo and Juliet—their passion also fueled their sadness. And ultimately, their tragedy."

The close association of fans to teams in older cities fueled an intensity linked to "how much the group identifies with failure," Vranich said. "It comes from saving your own ego. When someone threatens your ego—'You're not as good as I am'—you are going to get more passionate."

The problem was, Jon Gordon, author of a book called *Energy Addict*, told Donnellon, the mentality of despair could seep from fans to players like tea from a tea bag.

"If the group believes something is destined to occur, it has a greater chance of occurring," Gordon said.

Nobody believed failure was destined to occur the way Eagles fans did. That's okay, Freddie Mitchell said, pulling on his shirt and jeans at his locker for a meeting of wide receivers. The Eagles had been successful because they "don't focus on the outside environment."

"See who the best 'away' team is in the NFL," Mitchell told me. "That's us, because this team is full of characters who really zone out the outside noise."

Well, most of the noise. Mitchell, Todd Pinkston and the other Eagles receivers heard the bullhorn shout of doubt in the absence of Owens. Mitchell was upset with Angelo Cataldi on WIP, saying he didn't know a cover-two zone from a school zone. He would shut up all the doubters by doing what he was paid to do—catch the ball, Mitchell said. Fans had to understand that he did not call the plays. He ran the routes, and he needed a coach to call a play for him and a quarterback to spot him when he was open.

"That's been the hard thing, trying to get them to understand the different stages," Mitchell said of the fans.

He attributed their edginess to Philadelphia's proximity to New York. "They've always been second to New York," Mitchell said. "Everybody's sick of New York being the big city and being number one. I think the fans say, 'We can be better than New York and we can be ruder than New York.'"

During the 2003 season, when the Eagles lost their first two games and fans were booing Donovan McNabb and screaming for his backup, A. J. Feeley, Mitchell grew infuriated. He said fans had a responsibility, just as players did. Most of the fans were great. The rest, he said, had to decide whether they were groupies, with ephemeral allegiances for whatever was hot and glamorous at the moment, or true fans, who stuck by a team through thick and thin.

"You'll find out Sunday who's the groupies and who are the fans," Mitchell said. "Then it'll be, 'I knew you could do it without T.O.' Because now everybody is going, 'Hell, no way.'"

The Eagles had reached the NFC championship game for three consecutive seasons without Owens, Mitchell said. And they had won five of six games while McNabb recovered from a broken ankle at the end of the 2002 regular season.

"They gotta understand, we won without T.O. and we won without Donovan," Mitchell said. "We're lucky to have Donovan now."

•   •   •

As R&B music played soothingly in the locker-room, while a city nearly burst with emotion outside, McNabb combed his hair and dressed unhurriedly. Asked about the fans who booed him at the draft, he said he didn't think about it anymore. That was more than five years ago, he said. But clearly, he did think about it. How could he not?

"It's a difference between being accepted and understood," McNabb said. "It took a while for people to accept the fact I was drafted high, the first African American quarterback drafted that high to play for the Eagles. I don't think people understood about the mindset of the pick. I think people understand it now. But the fans are Philadelphia fans. They won't change. For me to say I forgive them, I don't forgive. I forget, but I don't forgive."

In another wing of the training complex, which included a theater and a vestibule of photographs of the great Eagles teams of the past, Garry Cobb held a microphone and did the opening and closing for a television report. A television and radio personality, he had played linebacker for the Eagles and the hated Cowboys and had graduated from Southern Cal with a degree in sociology.

Like many others, he detected an inferiority complex in Philadelphia, given its location between the muscling skyscrapers and Broadway lights of New York and the brawny political power of Washington. Although Philadelphia had its important place in the founding of the nation, Cobb said, "It seems like the city, the people, are looking for an identity. A lot of it has been placed on sports."

Earlier in the season, he traveled to Chicago for an Eagles game. Even after the Bears lost, Cobb noticed how the fans were still buoyant and friendly, even offering him food.

"Here, you lose and people are nasty," Cobb said. "They take it personally, because they feel like defeat is the same as saying, 'We're not anything.'"

Years ago, he had nicknamed the city Negadelphia.

"There's been such a long time that people have been disappointed," Cobb said. "They almost anticipate it. People are ready to devour the team. We do eat our own. You see the devouring of Todd Pinkston. You let us down, we turn on you. We want to boo, shred 'em up, cut 'em up. Years ago, if a criminal did something bad, people enjoyed that they strung him up. Here, they string people up verbally, emotionally. They strung Todd Pinkston up the last three weeks. Women are calling the radio station, 'He's not a man.' They would like Andy Reid to be nastier. He doesn't blast his players. They are like, 'Throw us a body. Throw Pinkston out here so we can string him up. He's a coward.' That's worse than anything."

A wall of separation between fans and the team did not exist in Philadelphia as in other places, Cobb said. Fans of the Eagles felt not like mere supporters, but actual owners of the franchise, and their allegiance was not to the players, but to the team and its history.

"I've heard people say," Cobb said, "'These players come in here and put on our jerseys, but that's our team. We're going to be here twenty years from now. They can leave and they'll retire and get traded, but that's our team and we deserve it.'"

There was one theory, held by some, that Philadelphia fans actually enjoyed losing. That defeat confirmed Philadelphia's second-rate status. That failure gave them a chance to enjoy their second-favorite sport: complaining.

"I think they really want to win, but when the team was winning all this year, you heard fans say, 'This is boring,'" Cobb said. As he saw it, defeat did not confirm Philadelphia as a second-tier city, but validated the fans' belief that they were first-rate supporters. Psychologists called the phenomenon Cutting Off Reflected Failure. The "we" of victory became "they" in defeat.

"It allows them to say, 'We tried everything we can,'" Cobb said. "It kind of confirms that 'These guys let us down.' Somebody says they're animals, and they can say, 'We're not animals, we're the best fans in the league.' I think a lot of the hurting is part of the enjoyment. 'We're tougher than everybody. We are the best fans, but we got shortchanged with these teams. We are true, regardless of whether the team is up or down.' There's a lot of that here."

Some called Eagles games a validation of public drunkenness. The cops had even discovered tailgaters inhaling nitrous oxide—laughing gas—from balloons. With all the attention paid to football, some fans developed maladies in their personal lives and deluded themselves into believing the team was the cause of their problems, Cobb said. Satisfaction became difficult or impossible. If the team won it all once, "They've gotta win again," Cobb said.

If the Eagles did finally win a championship, Cobb said, he could imagine fans visiting the graves of their relatives, wearing their Eagles gear and saying, "We're champions." By that, he believed, they would mean the city of Philadelphia was champion of professional football, and each of them individually was a champion.

"It's not just a football team," Cobb said. "It's part of people's lives."

Linebacker Ike Reese called WIP after practice and said that fans had done an unwitting favor for the Eagles. Players were always looking for the tiniest sliver of motivation, and fans had provided it with their hesitation and uncertainty. The Eagles had circled the ego wagons, a classic gambit. If nobody else believed in them, at least they believed in themselves.

"There's a little edge because of all the doubters," Reese said. "There's a little uneasiness in the city. No one has seen what the offense is going to look like over the past three weeks. That's a little understandable. That's no dislike for the fans, but there's a little edge there, the edge we need going into this game because Minnesota is going to catch it."

11

Saturday, January 15

John Kleinstuber got into work by eight thirty. It didn't take him long to start pacing. The other chefs at the Gulph Mills Golf Club, where he was assistant manager, kept telling him to stop. He couldn't. The Eagles game was only twenty-four hours away. He had a tiny office just off the stainless-steel kitchen. The radio was tuned to WIP. The Eagles website was a mouse click away. "Do Not Feed the Alligators," said a sign above the office door. Kleinstuber was starving for football.

A couple of nights earlier, I ran into John on my jogging route in Havertown. He had been to the corner pizza joint and was walking home with a hoagie. Even then he was anxious.

"My hand is shaking," he said, standing on the front steps, spreading his fingers.

He was the jock in his family, and at forty-two, he still had a tight end's muscular build. His receivers' coach at Haverford High in suburban Philadelphia had been Ted Dean, who scored the winning touchdown for the Eagles in the 1960 NFL championship game over Green Bay. Everybody remembered Chuck Bednarik's final tackle of Jim Taylor, but it was Dean who had provided the decisive points in the waning minutes. He had returned a kickoff for fifty-eight yards, then swept around left end from five yards for the seventeen-to-thirteen victory. Two decades later, Dean showed film of the game once or twice to the players at Haverford High, and Kleinstuber watched transfixed.

In 1981, John's senior year of high school, the Eagles reached the Super Bowl for the first and only time so far. He could relate to quarterback Ron Jaworski and his tall receiver, Harold Carmichael, and to the toughness with which everyone seemed to play, a toughness he saw in himself. In those days, the Eagles seemed like regular guys. Jaworski and linebacker Bill Bergey were Everymen. You saw them in the grocery store or the dry cleaner's, and you went up to them: *Nice tackle. Great game. How the hell could you have thrown that pick?* John watched games with his father and he became fiercely devoted to the team. "It was religion to watch the Eagles," he said.

Five years ago, John purchased season tickets for himself and his wife, Helen. She had been a student at Villanova when the Wildcats won the NCAA basketball championship in 1985, the last title for any prominent team in Philadelphia. John and Helen now lived on Darby Road, a main thoroughfare in Havertown, and the night Villanova won, John said, "People were climbing light poles, and half of them didn't even know where Villanova was."

That's how euphorically championships were embraced here, and, how achingly they had been missed. *If the Eagles ever won the Super Bowl, they'd better get the National Guard,* John thought. *It could get ugly.* In the front yard of his row home, John had installed green terrace lights. Last year, he even placed green cellophane in the windows. When the lights were on, he and Helen seemed to be living in an Eagles aquarium.

Others adorned their yards with plastic Santas or inflatable snowmen for the holidays. John had other decorating ideas. He made an eagle head out of plywood and also fashioned a wooden likeness of safety Brian Dawkins in his uniform. A warrior-like visor covered Dawkins's eyes. His gloved hands were clinched in the celebration or anticipation of violent contact.

John had planned to make wooden torsos of the entire Eagles defense. He would stick them on the lawn the way people placed wooden cows and pigs in the yard for fiftieth birthdays and thirtieth anniversaries. But the project took longer than expected. So he stuck with Dawkins. He was the epitome of a football player, a guy who put his head down and hit hard. John liked tough guys. Guys like Bergey, guys who chewed nails. Dawkins would run through a wall to make a tackle.

"Philadelphia people don't like pansies," John said.

It broke his heart when Coach Dick Vermeil resigned after the 1982 season. By then, Vermeil had squeezed all the juice out of his team, out of himself. The workaholic stories once had been amusing. Like the time he visited the team psychiatrist and reported back, "It would take me a week to straighten that guy out." Or the time, on July 4, 1976, when Vermeil became incensed that booming fireworks interrupted his film study at training camp.

"It's the birthday celebration," Carl Peterson, then the Eagles' personnel director, told him.

"Who's having a birthday?" Vermeil wanted to know.

"The country," Peterson responded. "America is two hundred years old. It's the Bicentennial."

"I don't care whose birthday it is," Vermeil said. "Tell 'em to shut off that noise."

By 1982, Vermeil was burned out and the stories weren't funny anymore. He slept and ate in his office and drove to practice and sat there, unable to let go of the steering wheel. There had been a players' strike that fall, and on one of his free Sunday afternoons, Vermeil remarked to his wife, Carol, about how red and yellow the leaves were. "They get red and yellow every year," Carol replied. Funny, Dick hadn't noticed before.

This decline saddened John Kleinstuber, but one thing always bothered him. Why did Vermeil have to cry all the time, especially at his farewell press conference? Coaches weren't supposed to cry. "Thought it was kinda wimpy," Kleinstuber said. "The macho thing, I guess."

He suffered through Marion Campbell, Vermeil's successor, an austere time when John could buy a ticket to a game and end up on the fifty-yard line as the Vet emptied of people and hope. Then came the reviving impudence of Buddy Ryan, who spoke dismissively of the globe-trotting team owner Norman Braman, calling him "the guy in France." Ryan distrusted authority in a city where everyone seemed to distrust authority. He put together a concussive defense and spoke in the vernacular of bounties and body bags. John showed Buddy the ultimate respect. He named his cat after him.

At first, John didn't like Jeffrey Lurie, the current owner of the Eagles. Lurie seemed like some Boston rich kid playing an expensive game of fantasy football. And his buddy, Joe Banner, the team president? Was there a nerdier looking guy in football? But both Lurie and Banner had grown on John. They had built the team into one of the best in the league, done a terrific job constructing the Eagles for this year and future years. Same with Andy Reid.

"It all turned around for me," John said.

He listened to WIP four or five hours a day. He loved Angelo Cataldi for the same reason he loved Buddy Ryan. He was a wise guy. At the Vet, John and Helen found a place to smoke a cigarette before each game, an alcove, and they'd see Angelo heading for the elevator. They'd met him a couple times. "A knucklehead," John said. "That's the best thing I can say about him. Doesn't care what he says or sounds like or if he looks stupid."

He watched Governor Rendell, too, on the Eagles post-game show. At first, he was shocked that an elected official spent so much time on football. "I wonder how he gets away with it," John said. "People in Pittsburgh must be mad as hell." Today, Rendell was in Pittsburgh, watching the Steelers play the Jets. Rendell was all right, as far things went, though John didn't think the governor was all that knowledgeable about football. The guy John really liked was Ray Didinger, the Hall of Fame sportswriter and NFL Films producer and radio host. Didinger was a homeboy but not a homer. John viewed him as a guy who said what his eyes saw, not what his heart felt. He always waited for Didinger on WIP on Saturdays.

Just before one o'clock today, Didinger had heard enough of the moaning and groaning. He began to lecture his listeners. This was rare for him. He was a mild-mannered guy who avoided the scream-fest model of talk radio. But this week, Didinger had enough with the fear in callers' voices. Come on, people, Didinger said. Philadelphia was supposed to be a tough town, a town of Rocky Balboa and Smokin' Joe Frazier and Concrete Charlie Bednarik and the Broad Street Bullies. Had the city suddenly lost its backbone?

"When did we all of a sudden become a city that is afraid of its own shadow?" Didinger said.

Having admonished the faithful, he began to console them. The Vikings had lost seven of their last ten games for a reason. They were ranked twenty-eighth in the league in defense for a reason. The Eagles lost to tough, prepared teams, but they didn't lose to dumb teams. Andy Reid knew his players better than the fans did. If Reid thought the Eagles could prepare for the playoffs by resting starters at the end of the regular season, then he deserved the benefit of the doubt.

Didinger's prediction: Eagles twenty-seven, Minnesota fourteen.

John also felt pretty confident. He just hoped Didinger was right about resting the starters. "No one knows what to expect," John said. "No one has played. No one knows what we're looking at."

He appreciated Donovan McNabb's remarks, his assurance that everything would be all right without Terrell Owens. That everyone should just buckle their seat belts and enjoy the ride. For once, McNabb had not seemed to John like a clone of Andy Reid. Instead, McNabb seemed to be insulted. *Everybody's crying about T.O., but I'm still here and I can win games.*

Without Owens, though, it was "time for Big Mouth Freddie and them to step it up," John said of the other receivers. The defense should be monsters. Everybody was healthy this year.

"The D line spent the last two weeks in a hot tub," John said. "They might be ready to tear somebody's head off."

He was, too.

He was tired of all the hype, tired of reading the papers and watching television and seeing the TV reporters and anchors wearing Eagles jerseys, more cheerleaders than journalists. He had grown impatient hearing players asked the same questions over and over. *Just play the damn game, will ya?*

At home, everything was in its place, ready to go. He had his clothes laid out, his long johns and gloves and hat and jacket. His tickets sat on the dining room table, along with his binoculars and quarters for the subway. Breakfast food and Bloody Mary mix were also ready. John was still trying to decide between two coats.

He had a bomber jacket that would keep him warm in any weather. But Helen had worn it to the last two NFC championship games and the Eagles had lost both times. Superstition would not allow it out of the closet this year.

If the Eagles lost to Minnesota, well, he didn't want to think of what might happen. "I'm a sore loser," John said. "I'm the first to tell you." Last year, when the Eagles lost to Carolina in the NFC championship game, he walked silently from the stadium to the subway, didn't say a word on the ride to the Sixty-Ninth Street Terminal in West Philadelphia and completely ignored other friends in the car on the ride home. "If someone touched me, I'd have been in jail," he said. Back in Havertown, he walked into the house and went right to bed. Helen unfastened the plywood eagle head from a railing on the porch and let it drop out of sight, until she could hide it the next morning. She thought John would throw it in the street or set it on fire.

"I'm not sure what I was mad at, myself, the Birds, I'm not sure," John said. "Or it could have been the twenty-five beers, which always helps."

Two days later, he went into work at the golf club, and everybody knew to steer clear of him. They walked on eggshells, until John said, "Okay, I'm over it, I'm not going to kill you guys."

"We spoke a few days later," Helen said. "Things improved."

Still, for a week, John did not bring a paper in the house or listen to WIP or watch the local cable sports channel. *Real mature stuff for a forty-year-old man.* If the Eagles beat Minnesota and reached the conference championship game for the fourth consecutive year, he joked ruefully, Helen would probably want to sell their tickets.

"I'm not sure she wants to be with me again," John said.

He would get home tonight in time for both playoff games. He would watch Pittsburgh–New York on the couch, which was decorated with Eagles blankets and pillows. He had Donovan McNabb bobble-head dolls on the television and the refrigerator, and two footballs, one that played the Eagles fight song, the other that had announcer Merrill Reese calling a touchdown play. Helen's jewelry box was stuffed with Eagles ticket stubs. As usual, John would have his homemade penalty flag ready to throw anytime he spotted holding or pass interference.

The second game, he'd probably watch in bed. That would take him to midnight. Then he'd only have to sleep until seven or eight, and it would be time to go to the Eagles game.

"Alarm clocks will be set," John said.

The Jets could not manage a touchdown on offense against the Steelers, but the struggle became gripping. I watched at home with my wife, Debby, and I couldn't turn away from the television. A Pittsburgh victory would keep alive the possibility of a Pennsylvania Super Bowl. But the Jets were coached by Herm Edwards, a former Eagles cornerback who made one of the most famous plays in the team's history, scooping up a fumble against the Giants in 1978 and returning it twenty-six yards for a touchdown in what became known as the Miracle of the Meadowlands. For the first time in eighteen years, the Eagles made the playoffs that season. More impressive was Herm's personality. A nicer, more effusive guy you'd never meet. He was still with the team when I began covering the Eagles in 1982. An undrafted free agent, Herm would make the roster each year and say, "Fooled 'em again," laughing that the only thing a free agent got when he was cut was a jelly sandwich and a road map.

Improbably, his Jets kept coming back against Pittsburgh, on a punt return for a touchdown by Santana Moss and an interception taken to the end zone by Reggie Tongue. Twice in the final two minutes of regulation, New York had a chance to win on field goal attempts, but one hit the crossbar and the other drifted wide left. For the third week in a row, the Jets were headed to overtime. Now I was pacing back and forth in the living room from my chair to the fireplace. But the Jets were spent, and they lost on a field goal, twenty to seventeen.

"At least now it won't be the Eagles against Herm," Debby said. "That would be hard."

John Kleinstuber was not happy with the outcome.

"I can't stand Pittsburgh," he told me earlier, saying he was put off by the demonstrative Steelers coach, Bill Cowher. "He starts with the spitting and grunting and screaming. I can't stand looking at him."

But John's interest would really be focused on the second game—St. Louis at Atlanta. The winner would play the victor of the Eagles-Vikings game for the NFC championship. Almost as soon as it started, it was over. The Falcons rushed for 327 yards. Michael Vick ran for more than a hundred of those yards at quarterback. Early in the fourth quarter, Atlanta sacked St. Louis quarterback Marc Bulger in the end zone for a safety, putting the Falcons ahead, forty to seventeen.

"If this were a fight, they'd stop it," Dick Stockton, the Fox announcer, said.

The final score was forty-seven to seventeen.

"I don't know if it's going to be Philadelphia or Minnesota playing them, but they better watch out," said Jimmy Johnson, the Fox analyst and former Dallas coach.

This outcome would be unsettling to Eagles fans. Undoubtedly, many of them were already worried about next week's game even before this week's had been played.

12

Sunday, January 16

Finally, the wait was over. The Eagles would play their first relevant game in four weeks. I got up at seven and went for a run through Havertown. Windows of the tiny business district on Darby Road were decorated like the storefronts in small towns when the high school team reached the playoffs. "Go Eagles," said a placard in the barbershop. The trading-card shop had a pennant and an Eagles license plate in the window. The hair salon was strung with streamers and a football mobile. At an apartment down the street, green-and-white icicle lights framed the front door. A candelabrum in the window had been stripped of its electric Christmas lights and fitted with Eagles green.

On the jog home, I ducked into Butch's Deli at eight thirty. Butch's son, Brian DeLuca, and his daughter and son-in-law, Melissa and Tim Kelly, had left for the stadium two hours earlier. Butch would soon be on his way, too. I noticed another Eagles trinket in his window, a green inflatable hand with the index finger signaling "We're number one." His anguish over Terrell Owens had been replaced by a brash confidence.

"I like 'em, I think they'll win by two touchdowns," Butch said. "If they lose, everybody's gonna say they had too much rest, they were too rusty. Aah, they're gonna win. They're all right."

Michael Vick looked good for Atlanta last night, he said, but the Eagles would take the Falcons next week. "Money in the bank," Butch said. "Money in the bank."

Too bad about Herm Edwards, though. "If that game was in

New York, they woulda hung that kid," Butch said of the Jets' errant kicker, Doug Brien.

As I jogged down the hill to my house, I noticed a guy walking his dog. He was wearing an Eagles hat and bulky green jacket. He seemed to be staring at me. Then I realized I was wearing a purple-and-gold LSU watch cap and purple-and-gold gloves. These were also Vikings colors. Had he mistaken me for a Minnesota fan? Could his dog sniff out opposition from the NFC North?

At nine o'clock, I met up with John and Helen Kleinstuber. We would take their car to the Sixty-Ninth Street Terminal in West Philadelphia and ride the elevated train and the subway to Lincoln Financial Field.

Greeting me at the front door, John said, "I'm still feeling good."

To a point.

"The game last night was a little tough to watch," he said of Atlanta's throttling of St. Louis.

"Are you nervous about next week already?" I asked him.

"I don't know. Maybe," he said. "But let's deal with today first, one day at a time."

One day at a time. The twelve-step mantra of Eagles fans and recovering addicts.

John was layered up and had an Eagles flag dangling from his back pocket. *We're not going to a fashion show, we're going to a football game.* Helen wore Eagles Mardi Gras beads. John had been up since six thirty, reading the paper, pacing. He had already spoken with his mother, Pamela, who was worried about his moodiness in defeat.

"Will you promise me, if they lose, you'll behave yourself?" she asked

"Mom, I'm forty-two years old."

It was only a short drive to Sixty-Ninth Street, where Helen saw the first good omen of the day. We parked behind a Mercedes, and the first three letters of its license plate read EGL.

"Going to the game?" a woman outside of a restaurant asked.

"Yeah."

"Are they going to win?" the woman asked timidly.

"Absolutely," John said.

"You sure?"

"Yeah, we're sure," Helen said. "We believe."

John wanted to sit in the first car on the elevated train. That would put us nearer the Broad Street subway line when we reached City Hall. Football, after all, was a game of inches.

"I'm a tad impatient," he said.

On the ride in, we compared the Linc and the Vet. John missed the Vet, the noise and bawdy character and outrageousness, the ease of moving around and talking to people. Still, the place was a toilet, and everyone who had ever been there had a bathroom story. "Anything with a hole in it was able to be peed in," John said.

The higher the level in the concrete bowl of the Vet, the fewer the women, Helen noticed. By the time one reached the infamous Seven Hundred Level, which had a reputation for hostile taunting, fighting, public urination and general strangeness, there were no lines at all in the women's bathroom.

The Vet was a dank arena where a mouse-chasing cat once fell through the ceiling onto the desk of an assistant coach, where visiting players looked through a peephole into the dressing room of the Eagles cheerleaders, where now-Governor Rendell once paid a fan to throw snowballs or threw them himself, where the Washington Redskins' mascot was hospitalized after a knee-capping.

My favorite Vet story involved my wife, Debby, and her friend Jeanette Miller. In the early 1980s, they sat in the Seven Hundred Level at one game, when Jeanette removed her shoes. Next thing she knew, the guy in front of her was sucking on her left big toe. They got his phone number as a goof, and Debby kept it for years on her Rolodex as Tom the Toe Sucker.

John and Helen liked the Linc, even though, with the giant viewing screens, sometimes they felt trapped inside a video game. They had good seats, on the Eagles' side of the field, four rows up from the goal line at the northwest end of the stadium. Before each game, Helen walked to the rail and tried to high-five linebacker Ike Reese.

"I'll be reminding myself to relax my shoulders and breathe, that there's nothing I can do to affect the outcome," Helen said.

The two-year-old Linc, with its pretense at sophistication and winged upper decks, seemed unfinished and reminded me of a fishing tackle box opened to the spinner bait. While fussy attention was paid to copying European architectural styles, Eagles owner Jeffrey Lurie neglected water fountains and sufficient parking for the handicapped. And, in an overreaction to September 11, he disallowed food to be brought in from the outside until the *Daily News* sparked a backlash with its famously ridiculing headline, "Hoagies of Mass Destruction."

Many suspected the Eagles were more interested in profit than security. The contretemps reached all the way to City Hall and the governor's office. Angelo Cataldi was suspended for two days from WIP for comparing the Eagles' officiousness to Nazi Germany. Michael McGeehan, a state representative from Philadelphia, threatened an "endangered hoagies bill" in protest of food bans at publicly financed stadiums, saying the biggest threat caused by the sandwiches was gastric, not nuclear. Finally, the Eagles relented, although Lurie showed yet again that his rich palate for luxury was matched only by his tin ear for public relations.

"He has no clue what it's like around here," the title character of the play *The Philly Fan* complained about Lurie. *"This guy wasn't born with a hundred million bucks, he'd have trouble gettin' a job at the car wash. When they give ya a Super Bowl ring for comin' under the salary cap, we'll finally have a champ."*

At City Hall, we changed to the Broad Street subway line. Helen bought a black scarf from a vendor for ten bucks. John took a swig of iced tea spiked with vodka.

"Antifreeze is a must," he said.

We hopped a train to the sports complex in South Philly, and John rode up the escalator carrying a bag full of gloves and hoodies and hand and foot warmers. It was not yet ten o'clock. The game was three hours away.

"Bring it on," John called out.

"We're here way too early," Helen said.

We walked out of the subway and crossed Broad Street to meet some friends of John's who were tailgating in FDR Park. The temperature was thirty degrees and the sun was only a smear in the gray sky. That was fine with John.

"I hate football when it's warm," he said, wearing three shirts and three pairs of socks over his long johns.

He loved the cold, and preferred a muddy track. The thing he liked most about the Linc was natural grass. He wanted to see someone get dirty. Helen worried about the running of Daunte Culpepper, the Minnesota quarterback who came packaged in a linebacker's body. She worried about the freelancing of Michael Vick next week, too.

"I'm scared of either of these teams," Helen said.

"Neither play any defense," John said.

"The Falcons scare me," Helen said again. "The playoffs start, the game gets even faster. Vick is explosive. Culpepper outside the pocket is even scarier. I'm a little nervous."

"Take Culpepper and Vick, especially Vick, stack his ass up, hit him until his teeth bleed," John said. "He won't do anything. That's my type of football. That's Philly football."

John turned toward the stadium complex and said, as he had a day earlier, that if the Eagles won the Super Bowl, they'd better get the National Guard down here. Then he grew pensive for a moment. He wondered how he would feel if they ever actually won.

"Am I going to lose my gumption, my longing?" he said. "Is it going to be disappointment? I don't know. If we win, I'll be deflated, as well as in the hospital with a heart attack or a stroke."

Someone in the tailgating party needed his help. A set of portable barbecue pits stood aligned like a double tight end formation. Except for one thing. Somebody forgot the grills. John was a chef, maybe he could figure something out. He had an idea. Someone had wire hangers from the dry cleaner's in the car, and John fit them over the pits to accommodate hot dogs and ribs.

"Focus," he said. "You gotta stay focused."

•   •   •

Before noon, I left John and Helen and walked back across Broad Street to the WIP pre-game show in a Linc parking lot. Angelo Cataldi and Howard Eskin sat on a stage wearing mink coats. Cataldi even had his furrier in tow. This might have seemed odd at other times, in other places, but not in the parking lot at an Eagles game. Arlen Specter, the head of the Senate Judiciary Committee, showed up as a guest, wearing a rolled-up bush hat and a trench coat. He looked like a cartoon version of an Australian spy, Crocodile Dundee joins the CIA. Shaun Young had arrived, too, face painted, dressed as usual in his Eagles jersey, shoulder pads, football pants and a hand warmer around his waist.

Shaun bounced back and forth in his turf shoes as if getting ready to field the opening kickoff. He had been up since four thirty, jogging a few miles along a highway in the western suburbs while wearing a jacket that said, "I bleed green." He wanted to run all the way to the stadium.

"I've never been so ready," Shaun said.

Cataldi sensed a little terror in the audience. Eagles fans were always nervous. Not Shaun. Shaun had no doubts.

"Minnesota is not a good team," he said. "We're the elite team in the NFC. They have no shot. It's a lock. I don't know why we're playing the game."

A guy named Helmet Man appeared on the stage. He wore a green helmet with a visor, a cape and knee-high black boots. Tomorrow he would phone WIP and say that his head swelled during the excitement of the game and he couldn't get his helmet off for hours. Today, Helmet Man had two babes with him, the Helmettes, Nicole and Kelly, who wore tight Eagles tank tops and tighter jeans. As suave and sophisticated as he was, Helmet Man had outkicked his coverage with these two women, Cataldi said.

"Helmet Man wears his Eagles helmet no less than twelve hours a day," Cataldi said on the air. "As you can imagine, when you wear an Eagles helmet all the time, groupies begin to form. It's inevitable."

Being the welcoming sort that they were, the fans gave the

Helmettes a typically warm Philadelphia embrace, chanting, "Show us your tits."

Another guy, Mike Borish, arrived without a shirt. His chest had been shaved into a kind of jersey. E-A-G-L-E-S was spelled out in hair across his pecs, while Donovan McNabb's hirsute number five curled around his navel.

Borish began to pound on Shaun Young's shoulder pads, and Shaun began to pound on his shoulders, their faces leaning toward each other, both of them shouting, "Super Bowl! Super Bowl!"

All over the parking lot, fans carried placards that said "Jacksonville or Bust."

Did this mean Borish had to watch the whole game without a shirt? Cataldi asked. If that's what it took to get the Eagles to Jacksonville, he'd do it, Borish said. He was a hurtin' Philly fan. He had to see a winner.

But surely he had some kind of insulation against the cold? I asked him.

"Beers," he said.

A brave or stupid man named Ragnar, the Vikings' mascot, appeared on the WIP stage, dressed in purple and gold. He might as well have had a bull's-eye painted on his back.

"You going in like that?" Cataldi asked. "Do you understand the danger you face inside that ballpark?"

"I come in fun," Ragnar said.

"You're screwed," Rhea Hughes, the WIP cohost, said.

The crowd chanted, "Asshole," and booed Ragnar.

"Listen to that," Cataldi said. "It's like a T-bone at a zoo."

As Ragnar left the stage, Shaun Young stared him down, mascot a mascot. During a commercial break, Cataldi told me, "These people are drunk and fucked up. They're damaged psychologically. There could be violence."

His posse of imbeciles, the Dirty Thirty, began to gather. Like Brazilian soccer players, they needed only one name. Rocco took the microphone and said, "I'm sick and tired of looking at Cowboys fans saying, 'We got the ring,' and Giants fans and Redskins fans. This is our year, and now we can say, 'Take those rings and shove 'em up your ass.'"

Clark, the official chef of the Dirty Thirty, was formally inducted into the group, which also had an official cookie girl. Clark raised his right hand and took the oath of allegiance, saying, "I plan to uphold the honor of the Dirty Thirty by being a moron at all times."

Kenny, another charter member, took his turn at the mike and delivered a blistering riposte of the Vikings, elegantly declaiming the incompetence of their football abilities and the girth of their female fans. He summoned the oratorical flourishes of the Lincoln-Douglas debates and the urbane put-downs of the Mailer-Vidal literary dust-up. Then he removed his Randy Moss wig and wiped his butt with it.

"I believe, in four quarters, the fans of this city will verbally and, in other ways, abuse the Vikings the way they have never witnessed in the annals of professional sports," Cataldi said.

His prediction: Eagles thirty-five, Vikings seven.

Finally, it was Shaun Young's turn at the microphone. He limbered up his vocal cords by calling Ragnar a "punk-ass, cheap, maggot-infested, yellow-bellied Vikings fan," then growled his way through a rant in which the words rammed into each other like a linebacker into a ball carrier.

"Minnesota, you have got yourself into some shark-infested waters," Shaun screeched. "You have no clue what you're getting yourself into. Randy Moss, you moon the Philadelphia fans, you will be destroyed. You have no reason to be here to play us. We as Philadelphia fans are the greatest fans in the world."

Later, he could not remember a word he had said.

"His eyes are bugging out now, ladies and gentlemen," Cataldi said, describing Shaun to the radio audience. "He's going into that catatonic state."

These next eight days, through the NFC championship game, Cataldi assured, would be the biggest eight days Eagles fans had ever had.

•   •   •

After he entered the stadium, John Kleinstuber made a pit stop. Outside the bathroom, he was greeted by another Eagles fan who said, "You'll enjoy yourself in there."

At a urinal stood a Vikings fan, serenaded by ten Eagles fans, who rhythmically chanted, "Asshole, asshole." The guy kept turning from side to side until he gave up and walked out, relieving the tension but apparently not his bladder.

John and Helen took their seats, and the man sitting to John's right seemed oddly subdued. He appeared to be a Vikings fan, but would not admit it. The man sat with his son and would say only that his brother-in-law gave him a blue-and-yellow University of Delaware jacket to wear. It appeared to be a wary disguise.

The Vikings themselves did not appear any more assured.

The Eagles needed only a little grease to lubricate the rust of a month's inconsequence. On Philadelphia's second possession, Freddie Mitchell caught a two-yard touchdown pass from McNabb as he fell out of the end zone. In celebration, Mitchell lampooned the half-moon that Moss had performed a week earlier in Green Bay. Instead of pretending to pull his pants down, Mitchell pretended to pull his up, to the roaring delight of sixty-seven thousand fans at the Linc.

"Something to make somebody smile," Mitchell said later. "I'm just glad I got the opportunity to actually make plays."

On Philadelphia's next possession, McNabb threw a fifty-two yard pass to Greg Lewis. Then he spotted Brian Westbrook over the middle from seven yards for a second touchdown pass, and the Eagles jumped ahead fourteen to zero.

The guy sitting behind John Kleinstuber began tackling him and pounding him on the back. John would go home with bruises and he didn't play a down.

"You're not as fired up as you used to be," the guy said.

"You're wearing me out," John replied.

With ten minutes, eight seconds remaining in the second quarter, and Philadelphia ahead fourteen to seven but not yet in control, McNabb threw to tight end L. J. Smith inside the Minnesota ten-yard line.

Smith was flipped onto his head at the four, and the ball squirted forward into the air. Mitchell, a former center fielder as well as a receiver at UCLA, shagged the pop fly in the end zone. The Eagles held an insurmountable lead of twenty-one to seven.

Moss, on the other hand, seemed injured and disinterested, his ankle twisted, his enthusiasm sprained. He caught three passes for fifty-one negligible yards. Late in the first half, with a chance for Minnesota to close the deficit to twenty-one to fourteen, Moss was supposed to feign walking off the field. Then he would catch a touchdown pass on a fake field goal attempt. But everything went wrong.

A Vikings lineman, Cory Winthrow, misinterpreted the play, leaving Minnesota with too many men on the field. So Moss was forced to the sideline to avoid a penalty. This unplanned exit left the Vikings without their target receiver. Futilely, Coach Mike Tice tried to call a time-out. On fourth and goal from the Eagles' three-yard line, the stunned holder Gus Frerotte, a backup quarterback, took the snap, looked for Moss, couldn't find him, scrambled and threw a pass to nowhere. Trying to outwit the Eagles, the Vikings had outsmarted themselves.

The Eagles were not perfect, either. Mitchell fumbled at the goal line on a second-half reception. Still, after weeks of ceaseless worry, fears about corrosion of the offense had proved unfounded. Terrell Owens had hardly been missed. For the fourth straight year, Philadelphia had reached the NFC championship game.

On *Post Game Live*, Governor Rendell praised Andy Reid and his decision to rest his starters in previous weeks.

"When people asked us in the last two games—was Andy Reid doing the right thing?—each and every one of us had our doubts," Rendell said. "But we said, 'Trust Andy,' and Andy got it right on the nose."

So did Ray Didinger. He had predicted the exact score: twenty-seven to fourteen.

Freddie Mitchell appeared at a post-game news conference wearing a bowtie and an Indiana Jones hat. He looked like some studious fossil hunter. What he had discovered was his petrified career.

Mitchell was my favorite Eagle. He had been a first-round draft pick out of UCLA in 2001, and he had a daffy self-absorption and a worldview beyond the wide world of sports. He had traveled from the Vatican to Rio, where he discovered that "Brazil is a melting pot, America is a crock pot." He thought about land ventures in Cuba ("I still want to kick it with Fidel") and he practiced yoga and he saved the Eagles in the divisional playoffs in 2004 with a fourth-and-twenty-six reception against the Green Bay Packers.

He called himself the People's Champ, and after each reception, he pretended to buckle a championship belt. He was also known as FredEx because he always delivered. But this season, with Terrell Owens as the main target, Mitchell seemed to catch one pass a game, which became a kind of running joke around town and a great irritation to himself. He began to complain with hurt audacity and people began to tune him out.

In today's post-game news conference, Mitchell mentioned sarcastically that he wanted to say hi "to all my new friends out there." By this, he meant fans who had questioned him but would say now they had faith in him all along.

"I'm a special player," Mitchell said. "I just want to thank my hands for being so great."

The stadium was long empty by the time I left and walked to the subway for the ride home. Waiting for the train to pull out, I heard a woman in the next car say, "I didn't know you could have so much fun at an Eagles game without drinking."

On the elevated train to Havertown, I sat behind Crystal Morris, a health inspector, who was dressed in an Eagles watch cap and jacket. She was approaching the upcoming Atlanta game with cautious optimism.

"Am I worried? Just a little," Morris said. "We didn't have any fear about the Vikings. This one is kind of questionable. They do it to you every time. They make it to the final four and choke. I have my fingers and toes crossed. I have everything crossed."

Emotionally worn out by the day, John Kleinstuber went to bed by eight o'clock. *They finally played like they were supposed to all year. Not many turnovers. They played like a team. Defense stepped it up. Minnesota didn't have a chance.*

On the television news, a father and his sons had shaved their heads in anticipation of the Atlanta game next Sunday. Bald Eagles beat Falcons any day, the father said.

13

Ron Jaworski called in to WIP.

"Can everyone relax now?" he said.

Philadelphia didn't do relaxed.

Not after three consecutive defeats in the NFC championship game. Plus, there was talk of snow for next Sunday. Snow might favor a running team, and Atlanta had the best rushing attack in the NFL. The Eagles could be in trouble if this football game turned into the Iditarod.

"I think it's a tremendous psychological hurdle," a worried caller, Arlen from Washington, otherwise known as Senator Arlen Specter, said of the championship game defeats. "I have a lot of confidence in the players. I think they can do it, but there's no denying the hurdle."

Superior Court Judge Seamus McCaffery also phoned the station. As a municipal judge, he had adjudicated Eagles Court at Veterans Stadium. The court had been established in the basement of the Vet in 1997, after a game against San Francisco in which approximately sixty fights occurred, a season-ticket holder broke his ankle trying to rescue a friend and a flare gun was fired into empty seats.

McCaffery attributed violent behavior at Eagles games to alcohol and anonymity. He did have a sense of humor about the football miscreants, though. He once told me he had proposed to television executives that *Sport Court* would make for great viewing as a kind of *People's Court* for misbehaving fans.

"Can you imagine the wack jobs?" the judge said. "It would be the funniest sitcom going."

At the penultimate game played at the Vet, a Saturday night playoff against Atlanta on January 11, 2003, McCaffery had a classic exchange with a Temple University student, majoring in criminal justice, who was nabbed trying to sneak into the stadium under a fence.

The judge recounted the exchange in *The Great Philadelphia Fan Book:*

"How do you plead?" McCaffery asked.

"Judge," the student said, "I plead stupid."

"I can't do that," McCaffery said. "Is it aggravated stupid or simple stupid?"

Whichever was the lesser offense, the student said.

He appeared contrite.

"Tonight," he told the judge, "I was majoring in dumbass."

News reports said that Eagles Court had been closed down when the team moved to Lincoln Financial Field in 2003. It was bad publicity, and, anyway, the crowds were better behaved at the new stadium.

Until Sunday, anyway.

Apparently, an inglorious christening of the Linc had occurred during the Minnesota game. And contrary to news reports, when bitter rivals like the Giants and Redskins and Cowboys came to town, and when the playoffs began, Eagles Court was still held, McCaffery told Angelo Cataldi.

On Sunday, McCaffery said, the court was in session with another judge presiding. A "whole van full of clients" was brought in, removed of their tickets and shorn of a few hundred bucks in fines.

Rhea Hughes told of looking down from a press box window and seeing fans pushing to get through an entrance where several Mercedes-Benzes were on display.

"Some people thought it was a good idea to rock them back and forth," Hughes said. "I'm thinking, 'They're going to trash this one.' People were climbing on the roof of the car. It was wild."

Apparently, the Vikings' team bus got a similar Philadelphia welcome.

"I was told they mooned and egged the Vikings' bus," Hughes said.

Once inside, a few fans apparently suffered flashbacks to the Vet and could not resist a fistic encounter.

"Security said they had never seen as many fights, including two men rolling around in an elevator," Hughes reported.

A guy named Jesse called the station to confirm Hughes's account. He had driven six hours from Buffalo to display his artwork, a ten-foot sign that said, "Moss Sucks."

When the Vikings' bus came down a ramp at the stadium, a dozen or so Eagles fans had mooned Moss, Jesse said. Not a fake moon, as the Vikings' receiver had pantomimed in Green Bay.

"It was a real moon," Jesse said. "I think Eagles fans were trying to show Moss how to do it."

Players on the bus could be seen nudging each other and pointing.

"There might have been a couple of eggs thrown," Jesse said. He seemed sad about missed opportunities. "It wasn't a group effort like the mooning was."

Showing admirable restraint, Jesse said he had not dropped his pants in front of the bus, "but I did moon some Vikings fans walking into the stadium."

Cataldi wanted to know if mooning was unlawful. It could be a free-speech issue, McCaffery said.

Or, Cataldi retorted, "If you're not well equipped, it could be insufficient evidence."

According to the *Minneapolis Star Tribune*, Vikings fans had been treated as roughly as Vikings players. Marie Hoppe, the mother of lineman Chris Liwienski, made the mistake of wearing a replica of her son's jersey to the game. She felt like an arcade-game gopher, popping out of the ground only to get bopped on the head with a mallet. She told the paper she was pushed repeatedly by Eagles fans. Her daughter-in-law was conked on the head by a plastic beer bottle.

"We were warned that Philadelphia fans would be rough, the worst in the league, and my son begged me not to wear this jersey," Hoppe told the paper. "Fans are supposed to come to games, not thugs. But these people had their hands on me constantly. What are these people doing at sporting events like this?"

Another of her sons, Joe Liwienski, said he had attended the basketbrawl earlier in Auburn Hills, Michigan, where players from the Indiana Pacers scuffled in the stands with fans of the Detroit Pistons.

"This was ten times worse," Joe Liwienski told the *Star Tribune*.

At his noontime press conference, Andy Reid discounted a Fox television report that Terrell Owens had suffered a setback with overly aggressive rehabilitation.

"He's really doing fine," Reid said.

Owens had been running and cutting in a pool. This week, he would begin running on hard ground.

"When he really has to get out there and push off, we'll see how he does," Reid said.

At Chickie's and Pete's, the South Philly restaurant where Cataldi did his Monday night cable television show, I met up with Shaun Young. He wore a Jeremiah Trotter jersey over his shoulder pads in honor of the Eagles' middle linebacker, who was scheduled to appear with teammate Brian Westbrook.

"I don't think you could have played any better," Shaun told Trotter in a VIP room at the back of the restaurant. It was a kind of beer library, with cans shelved like books on one wall.

On Sunday, as he awaited the introduction of his teammates, Trotter watched the fans waving towels in howling anticipation and began crying. He had spent two seasons in Washington after leaving the Eagles bitterly as a free agent. Now he was back, and his presence had given the defense a swaggering brawniness.

"I feed off the crowd, and you got crazy Eagles fans, and that doesn't do nothing but raise the energy level and allow us to go out and play crazy," Trotter said.

Shaun cheered with the vigor that he played, Trotter said. "That cat is awesome," Trotter said. "If you cut him, he'd literally bleed green."

Some Eagles fans offered less sanguine endorsements. Chris Clark, a longtime season-ticket holder, said he could never forgive Shaun for booing Donovan McNabb at the draft.

"I have a bad spot in my heart," Clark said. "Idiots like that make the rest of us look bad."

Joe Weachter, Cataldi's producer on WIP, said, "That guy's got his own issues. He's nuts. I'm an Eagles fan, too, but my appendix burst, I'm in the hospital."

Shaun occupied a singular position among the Eagles faithful, something less than a player but more than a fan. Tonight, he was a kind of hyper Ed McMahon, getting the crowd pumped up for the beginning of Cataldi's show. Climbing on a railing, Shaun played one side of the restaurant against the other as they went through the letters of the Eagles cheer. When it ended, he was hyperventilating.

"You all right?" I asked him.

"I can keep it up all night long," Shaun said. "Gotta let the guys know we got their backs."

Sean Murphy, the reporter on Cataldi's show, dead-panned, "He usually ruptures a blood vessel, but not until the sixth or seventh segment."

Shaun signed autographs and posed for photographs, and, in the VIP room, he spoke with three Eagles fans standing at the bar.

"He's the face of the Eagles," Anthony Palma said.

In a sense, he was. If the players in the real uniforms seemed remote and unapproachable, Shaun was always there to bump fists, to have his shoulder pads pounded, to high-five, to be asked about next week's game.

"You put WIP on, every Yuppie is jumping off a bridge," Russell Lamplugh said. "They don't count. You gotta live it and breathe it and go for it. Shaun counts. He goes for it. Guys make a hundred thousand dollars and get tickets for free, they don't count. You go to an Eagles game and can't name the five offensive linemen, you shouldn't be there."

Palma and Lamplugh and their friend, Bill Peruso, began talking about just what it meant to be an Eagles fan. Their answers spooled out like a garden hose, looping and coiling, tied in hoarse knots of beery logic.

"I don't like losing, but I like having something to bitch about," Lamplugh, a twenty-five year-old restaurant manager, said. "If you can't bitch, what's the point?"

"I want them to lose," Peruso, forty-one, a painter, said. "I gave up on them. They broke my heart. My wife is so high with them. Yesterday, I voted for the Vikings and she threw me out the house."

"You really want them to lose?"

"They hurt me too much."

"You expect us to win," said Palma, twenty-one, who worked with Lamplugh. "At the same time, you prepare for the worst."

Peruso: "I'm against them. They're going to win to freakin' spite me."

No, that's not what he meant.

"I want them to win," Peruso said. "I don't want to say I want them to win."

So it was a matter of psychology? I asked him. By saying you didn't want them to win, you secretly hoped they might actually do it?

It was this seeming inconsistency and contradiction, I realized, that was the essence of being an Eagles fan. It required adherence to a string theory of sport, a belief in multiple dimensions and parallel universes, where emotions collided in a vibrating, oscillating permanence along the space-time-beer continuum.

"Philadelphia is the place where one day you love 'em, the next you hate 'em," Lamplugh said. "You contradict yourself in every statement. By three o'clock on Sunday, you want them to win. By three thirty, you want them to lose. In three minutes you can go from dream to nightmare to dream to throwing up. You can't do that until you live in Philadelphia."

After Trotter's appearance on Cataldi's show, Brian Westbrook took his turn. There must have been seven hundred people in Chickie's and Pete's, with a line out the door. The players appreciated the love, Westbrook said. But apparently they didn't appreciate it enough on this night to hang around and sign autographs.

This was a blurred line in the fan-player relationship, where rules were fuzzy and the bond was tense. Cataldi made it clear that Westbrook and Trotter were not there to mingle with the crowd, but the audience had other ideas. To them, public appearances came with public responsibilities.

A line of parents and kids, most wearing Eagles jerseys, formed outside the door to the VIP room. Trotter had signed a few autographs before he left. Westbrook sat at a back table with friends, and the parents and kids became impatient.

Someone who worked at the restaurant asked Shaun Young to explain the situation to the fans.

"You putting that on me?" he asked incredulously.

"They're not heroes, they're scumbags," Peruso said. "They wouldn't be anything without us. We don't ask for a championship, we ask for a signature. What about these kids? They're out here with their parents. It's a school night. It means everything to them. It's like Christmas."

But Trotter was a nice guy, Peruso said in the next breath, holding an autographed T-shirt. Again, the contradiction, the knotty, convoluted, cat's-cradle devotion.

"I won't remember being here tonight drinking, I'll remember meeting Jeremiah Trotter," Lamplugh said. "We want his autograph. We kissed his ass when he came in, but he's still a scumbag. We still did it because we're fans. We don't have nothin' else. I'm not saying we don't have nothin' else, but that's what you live for as a fan."

Peruso nodded in agreement.

"He's a scumbag, but we still like him."

Shaun Young, though, was not happy with this end run by Westbrook.

"That's bad, that sucks, a third-year player shunning us already," he said. "I don't know, that's not good. People were waiting for hours, kids. But it is what it is."

He walked out of the restaurant in the windy cold, the temperature having dropped to twenty-two degrees, wearing his football pants and a sleeveless T-shirt, carrying his shoulder pads and jersey in his hand.

14

Tuesday, January 18

Governor Rendell had a political tightrope to walk. The AFC championship game would be played in Pittsburgh, immediately following the NFC championship game in Philadelphia. The governor couldn't be in both places at once. His heart, his stomach and his post-game television duties belonged to the Eagles.

"We understand that," Sean Logan, a state senator from Allegheny County, whose seat was Pittsburgh, told the *Inquirer*.

At least the Democrats understood.

"Perhaps voters will remember this in two years," Senator John Pippy, a Republican from Allegheny County, told the paper.

At a news conference, Rendell said he would send a warning to the mayor of Jacksonville, Florida, if both Pennsylvania teams reached the Super Bowl. Perhaps he ought to lend a few state troopers on horseback.

"If people from Pittsburgh and Philadelphia come down there for a whole week before the game, all I can say is, the citizens of Jacksonville should beware," he joked.

On WIP, Angelo Cataldi compared Philadelphia and Atlanta as sports towns. Atlanta was notoriously indifferent about its professional teams. As a participatory sport, the Falcons ranked a distant third behind college football and Jack Daniel's.

"For us, to lose would be to amputate a leg," Cataldi said. "For them it would be a pimple."

Just how devastating another defeat would be for Philadelphia could be heard in the flammable words of Arson Arnie, a longtime caller.

"I want no more excuses," Arnie said, his voice quivering. "I want a return on my investment of twenty-five years. I have given this team thousands. I could have bought another house, okay? I want to be able to brag to everyone. I want to call my relatives in Texas. I want to rub it in their fans' faces. Specifically Dallas. I'm tired of hearing, 'Oh we won in 1931.' I'm sick of it. I want none of those excuses. I want to quit lookin' at next year. I want a reward for my damn pain. I want to hear Freddie Mercury sing 'We Are the Champions' and know he's singin' about us. I want to take my son to a parade. I want to make him see this is the greatest sports town in the Western Hemisphere. I want it all and I want it now. I want nothing less than everything."

This was far and away the most emotion Cataldi had felt in his sixteen years on the air. The interest, concern, worry, excitement. A guy named Joe phoned and said he needed the Eagles to win for one reason: "If they don't, my brother-in-law may take his own life."

The few remaining tickets for Sunday's game went on sale at ten o'clock. They sold out in two minutes. A guy named Ed Krushenski said on television that he had consulted a friend with an atomic clock. Exactly at ten, he called for tickets. Even with an atomic clock, he wasn't quick enough. "You have dreams," Ed said. He wanted to surprise his wife, ask her if she had any plans for Sunday. "She would have exploded her head."

Tim Peterson of Wilmington, Delaware, made a trip to the Shop Rite store in northeast Philadelphia. They were giving away tickets to the person whose loaded shopping cart matched the weight of Eagles tackle Jon Runyan. Runyan was listed at 330 pounds. Only three different items from the store could be placed in the cart.

Peterson's cart tipped the scales at 313. He won. His strategy had been simple but effective.

"Kitty litter," he said. "Lots of kitty litter."

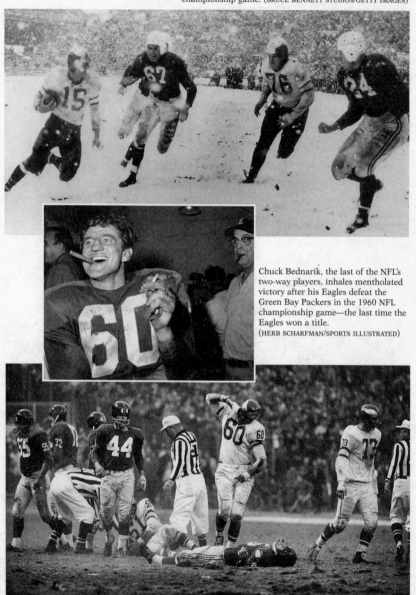

Steve Van Buren, the battering ram of a punishing Eagles team that dominated the league in the late 1940s, runs through a blizzard in the 1948 NFL championship game. (BRUCE BENNETT STUDIOS/GETTY IMAGES)

Chuck Bednarik, the last of the NFL's two-way players, inhales mentholated victory after his Eagles defeat the Green Bay Packers in the 1960 NFL championship game—the last time the Eagles won a title.
(HERB SCHARFMAN/SPORTS ILLUSTRATED)

Bednarik knocks out New York running back Frank Gifford.
(JOHN G. ZIMMERMAN/SPORTS ILLUSTRATED)

Shaun Young, the "unofficial official" mascot of the Eagles, turned his apartment into a shrine to his favorite team, to whom he is so devoted that he attended one game with a burst appendix. (PHOTO BY TIM SHAFFER)

Pennsylvania governor Edward G. Rendell, who analyzes each Eagles game on television as if it were an appropriations bill, conducts a pep rally at the state capitol. (AP PHOTO/PATRIOT NEWS, JOE HERMITT)

Birdman and beaked friend cheer from the Eagles' nest, where many an eccentric fan has been known to flap his wings and his jaws. (PHOTO BY TIM SHAFFER)

John and Helen Kleinstuber are such big fans of smashmouth football that they named their cat after former Eagles coach Buddy Ryan, who put together a concussive defense and spoke in the vernacular of bounties and body bags. (PHOTO COURTESY OF THE KLEINSTUBERS)

Melissa and Tim Kelly pose for wedding photos on the playing surface at Lincoln Financial Field, a bridal quarterback and her tuxedoed center. (PHOTO COURTESY OF THE KELLYS)

Butch and Sue DeLuca, whose Havertown deli is decorated like an Eagles Christmas tree. (PHOTO BY MELISSA KELLY)

Governor Rendell;
Ray Didinger, the
authoritative voice of
the Eagles; and for-
mer Eagles running
back Vaughn Hebron
discussing the Eagles
on *Post Game Live*, a
kind of *McLaughlin
Group* for sports.
(AP PHOTO/H RUMPH JR.)

Terrell Owens
winces in pain after
tearing ligaments in
his right ankle and a
city's championship
swagger is reduced
to a limp.
(AL TIELEMANS/SPORTS
ILLUSTRATED)

Terry Funk, Jen Clark, Sue Harrigan, Ernie Clark, and Chris Clark—the family, who has followed the Eagles for four generations, celebrates as the team reaches the Super Bowl for the first time in twenty-four years.
(JESSICA GRIFFIN/PHILADELPHIA DAILY NEWS)

Donovan McNabb holds up the NFC championship trophy and lifts a heavy Super Bowl burden from the city's shoulders.
(AL TIELEMANS/SPORTS ILLUSTRATED)

Unconventional receiver Freddie Mitchell, the "People's Champ," wears his 'Frohawk hairdo after the Eagles KO'd Atlanta in the NFC championship game. (BRIAN BAHR/GETTY IMAGES)

While other people put Santas and reindeer on their lawns for the Christmas season, John and Helen Kleinstuber festoon their yard with a plywood Eagles head and a wooden likeness of safety Brian Dawkins.
(PHOTO BY HELEN KLEINSTUBER)

Bill Simmons, aka "El Wingador," goes for his fifth Wing Bowl title, having strengthened his jaws for munching on chicken wings by eating frozen Tootsie Rolls. (JEFF FUSCO, PHILADELPHIA WEEKLY)

Sonya Thomas, aka the "Black Widow," attempts to win her second Wing Bowl title, having previously stuffed her ninety-nine-pound frame with 167 wings in thirty minutes. (JEFF FUSCO, PHILADELPHIA WEEKLY)

WIP radio personality Angelo Cataldi checks out the action at the boozefest known as Wing Bowl, knowing that someone will win, hoping that no one will die. (JEFF FUSCO, PHILADELPHIA WEEKLY)

Donovan McNabb is sacked by the Patriots' Tedy Bruschi during the Eagles' first drive of the Super Bowl.
(JOHN IACONO/SPORTS ILLUSTRATED)

The Philadelphia faithful suffer through yet another disappointing Eagle performance in the Super Bowl.
(WILLIAM THOMAS CAIN/GETTY IMAGES)

(JERRY LODRIGUSS, PHILADELPHIA DAILY NEWS)

•   •   •

Later, I stopped by John and Helen Kleinstuber's home. The afternoon was frigid, with thin clouds on the horizon. Their row house
was already in shadow. John was waiting for the weather on television. His feet had frozen on Sunday. They got so cold they hurt.
Helen was out looking for boots. John had asked the
groundskeeper at his golf club what he wore. Snowmobile boots
might do the trick.

John had mentioned the bomber jacket again to Helen. The
jinxed one she wore to the last two NFC championship games. If
she didn't want to wear it Sunday, he would. "No you won't," she
said.

He knew Helen was already worried about his reaction if the
Eagles lost again. Last year, John barely talked for days. Helen had
to hide the wooden eagle head in the yard so he wouldn't toss it
like a Frisbee. But John was going with a different attitude this
time. He felt the Eagles were going to win.

Atlanta was a dome team coming to play outside in the cold.
All the Falcons had was a running game. And not even a power
game at that. Plus, Atlanta had absolutely no passing game. Zilch.
John was tired of all the anxiety over Michael Vick on WIP. "Who
died and made him King of the National Football League?"

Of course, McNabb would be under a great deal of pressure.
"This hasn't been a star game for him," John said. "How he deals
with the pressure, I don't know. But I can't believe it's not in the
back of his mind."

Still, John had a good feeling about this one. Terrell Owens
had brought a welcome boastfulness to the team. None of this
"one game at a time" coach-speak. They were talking smashmouth, baby. They were going to hit somebody. Atlanta'd better
look out.

"This is a man's game," John said. "You want to come here, we
play a man's game."

His favorite player, besides Dawkins, was Runyan, the six-foot-
seven-inch tackle. "Just a big ol' country boy that likes to knock
the crap out of people."

We sat and watched *Daily News Live* on Comcast SportsNet. Leo Carlin, the Eagles' ticket manager, made an appearance with sportswriters from the *Daily News*. Everybody wanted tickets, Carlin said. And he meant everybody. Even his sister called, asking for a pair. He turned her down cold.

"Everyone thinks there's just two left in the drawer," Carlin said.

A meteorologist from AccuWeather said there was a 70 percent chance of snow for Sunday and a fifty-fifty chance of ten inches or more.

"God help us," John said. "Those snowballs are going to be going somewhere."

He didn't have any extra work at the club this week. No dinners or parties or anything to distract him from football. By the end of the week, he'd be climbing the walls.

"The wife'll have to calm me down," John said, "or I'll get out of my mind."

About eight thirty, I dropped by Butch's Deli to get a paper. He was home sick in bed, said Dot DeLuca, his sister-in-law. He was going to the doctor tomorrow.

Was he going to miss the game?

"Nah, he's a diehard," Dot said.

15

Wednesday, January 19

Amy Shaw and her husband, Bill, arrived at WIP to get their heads shaved for Eagles tickets. Amy wore a pink shirt that said, "Bald Is Beautiful." This was not the first time she'd become a chrome-dome. Last March, upset with what she considered a pathetic corps of receivers, she promised to shave her head if the Eagles signed Terrell Owens. The team obliged and Amy, a bartender, let her drunken bar guests shear her locks on St. Patrick's Day. Today, she would be using a professional stylist, Raymond Orsuto, whom Cataldi referred to as the "Mickey Rooney of haircutters."

Orsuto, it seemed, had more wives than scissors. He said he'd been married three times.

"All his wives have the same first name—plaintiff," Al Morganti chirped.

Bill Shaw was not exactly thrilled with the cue ball look as a fashion statement. Or as an aphrodisiac. The last time Amy did this, he said, their love life flew at half-mast.

"It's like looking at Uncle Fester next to me in bed," Bill told me.

But for Eagles tickets, what the hell.

"For Super Bowl tickets, I'll shave anything you want," Amy told Cataldi during a commercial break.

Back on the air, Bill went first. Orsuto, the stylist, offered him one hundred, two hundred, five hundred bucks to walk away. No way, Bill said. He loved the Eagles, and he was willing to sacrifice what little hair he had left for the team.

Orsuto sheared Bill as if he had just joined the Army, and hair fell in ribbons to the floor of the studio. A few minutes later, it was Amy's turn. Cataldi offered her seven hundred fifty dollars, then a thousand, to keep her thick, dark hair on her head.

"No way. I'm an Eagles fan," Amy said. "Get the hair off. I'm ready."

The offer went to fifteen hundred dollars, then two thousand. Again Amy declined.

"When we return, Amy loses her hair," Cataldi said. "She's already lost her mind."

Orsuto shaved a furrow down the middle of Amy's head, then pretended that his shears broke. When he finished up, Amy looked like Squeaky Fromme.

"Amy, do me a favor," Cataldi said. "Do not go near a mirror today. It will shatter. She's a nice-looking woman. Not currently, but she's nice-looking."

Amy's sister, Shana Goldberg, phoned to say that she was watching Bill and Amy's kids while their mother and father were being groomed to resemble a pair of testicles.

"Tell her kids their mom is a moron," Cataldi said.

"Why didn't you take the money?" Rickie Straff, Amy's neighbor, asked on the air. "What kind of Jewish girl are you?"

"Rickie, I'm telling you right now," Cataldi said. "Every village needs an idiot and yours is in our studio right now."

Morganti referred to these eccentric Eagles fans as "Tarantino Nation."

"It's a participatory sport," Morganti said. "They actually believe if they bang their heads against the wall, it's an extra inch at the line of scrimmage. They're convinced of it."

For the first time, two African American quarterbacks would start a conference championship game. And one of them, Donovan McNabb or Michael Vick, would become only the third black quarterback to start in thirty-nine Super Bowls.

"It shows how far we've come, how far the league has come," Vick told a gaggle of reporters on a telephone conference call.

Earlier, in the *Washington Post*, Doug Williams, who quarterbacked the Redskins to a Super Bowl title in 1988, said, "It helps the league move further away from the old stereotypes that a lot of us had to deal with coming up: not smart enough, can't lead, that kind of garbage."

At his weekly news conference, McNabb reiterated Williams's point, and said, "This is the new generation of quarterbacks that are able to do a little bit more than just sit back in the pocket and pass the ball."

And yet, defensive end Hugh Douglas said, this resourcefulness was sometimes used by commentators and the news media to reinforce lingering stereotypes about black quarterbacks.

"Every time you talk about Michael Vick, you always talk about how athletic he is," Douglas said. "If you talk about Peyton Manning, they always say how smart he is picking up blitzes."

This was a particularly sensitive subject with McNabb. He restricted his own running to force people to appreciate that he could play a classic style. Some fans thought he avoided running to the point that it undermined the completeness of his skills.

"He has to run for us to be maximum on offense," Governor Rendell said earlier in the season.

Asked today how a forecast snowstorm on Sunday might bother a "running quarterback," McNabb gave a sly smile to a roomful of reporters and said, "I wouldn't know."

Said Douglas: "Donovan, early on, I think he subconsciously tried to fight this. Everybody talked about how athletic he was, how he would take the ball down and run. I guess he took it upon himself to become a [pocket-style] quarterback. You still never hear about how he changed his game. You hear about how athletic he is."

McNabb and Randall Cunningham had enjoyed great success and popularity as black quarterbacks with the Eagles. McNabb's replica jersey was among the most popular among fans around the NFL. But his career was always tugged by a racial undertow.

Success, of course, could be colorblind. When the Eagles won, the color of the jersey mattered, not the color of the skin. It was failure that black quarterbacks were not afforded on the same terms as whites. Too often, defeat did not come on its own merits, an off-day, a bad pass, an alert defense. Defeat became a complexion, a shade of deficiency, a pigment of imperfection that suggested larger, bell-curve flaws of intelligence and aptitude. McNabb understood this acutely. With black quarterbacks, there was a difference between acceptance and understanding, he said. The issue of color was always there, just below the surface. A year earlier, Rush Limbaugh accused the news media of inflating McNabb's value because they wanted to see a black quarterback succeed. Limbaugh's remarks were widely discredited, but even McNabb's most sensitive and vociferous white supporters, who were legion, could become self-conscious in their judgment of him. Was it biased or prejudiced to want him to run more, to refer to him as "an athlete," to criticize his readiness for big games?

"You feel like you have to defend him against people who attack him," said Ernie Clark, a season-ticket holder since 1961. "Often, there is an underlying race issue. You feel like you have to defend against this all the time. When you are in a defensive mode, you find yourself overlooking his shortcomings."

Jim Mora Jr., the Falcons' coach, couldn't wait to return to Philadelphia for Sunday's game. He lived here in the 1980s when his father coached the champion Philadelphia Stars of the now-defunct United States Football League.

"It's going to be awesome," Mora told reporters on a telephone conference call. "They might be throwing batteries at us. They might be dumping dog shit on us. They might throw snowballs at us, [be] spitting on us, throwing beers at us."

He wanted his players to feel good about any success in Philly, because they would be playing against, not only the Eagles, but the seventy thousand fans who would be rooting for Philadelphia.

He did offer some advice, though, to his players and their wives, girlfriends and parents. Any Atlanta fans should wear green, not red and black, because "they'll get the shit beat out of them."

His father, Jim Mora Sr., wanted to sit in the stands, but the son would hear nothing of it. Dad would sit in the press box, where he might lose a finger in a stampede at the buffet table, but would otherwise suffer no harm.

"No, no, I'm sitting in the stands," Jim Sr. had protested.

"No way," Jim Jr. said. "They know who you are and they'll kill you."

"No, no, they love me in Philadelphia."

"They might love you," Jim Jr. said, "but they don't love me and the Falcons."

The son did have some additional advice, though, just in case Atlanta won. "They'd better dispatch one hundred thousand grief counselors" to Philly, he said, "because I don't think people will be able to take another loss."

Governor Rendell held a news conference to talk about football. If the Eagles and Steelers both lost on Sunday, he said, "I can hardly think of anything worse that could happen to the entire state."

If either team won the Super Bowl on February 6, and a parade was scheduled for the eighth, he would consider changing the date of his state budget address.

"Sick as it is," he said, "we've thought of it."

A mere inch of snow fell today, and paralyzed Philadelphia. A half-hour trip home from the Eagles' training complex took two hours. At practice, Mike Quick, the radio commentator and retired all-pro receiver, said he had begun to wonder whether climate would again play havoc with an Eagles game. Quick was in the lineup on December 31, 1988, when the Eagles played in the infamous Fog Bowl in Chicago, losing a playoff game by twenty to twelve to the Bears.

"It was almost like playing in a dream," Quick remembered. "I'd run downfield fifteen yards and I couldn't see Randall [Cunningham]. I could see the linemen and their feet, but I couldn't see the upper part of their bodies. And when the game was over, it was perfectly clear. A bad dream."

•   •   •

At practice, Terrell Owens walked through the locker-room wearing a white sweat suit with powder blue trim, not showing any
signs of a limp. He declined to speak with reporters, but if his
mouth kept quiet, his gait spoke wonders. Later, on his drive-time
show on WIP, Howard Eskin said, "I'm going to guarantee you
that right now. Terrell Owens will play in the Super Bowl, if the
Eagles are there." Eskin had a pipeline to Coach Andy Reid. Not
only would Owens be in uniform, Eskin said, he would "play a sig-
nificant number of plays." His recovery, Eskin said, was beyond
what "anybody in their wildest dreams could have imagined."

Two more signs that Philadelphia was the world's biggest small
town: The Business Owners and Management Association asked
that the city's tall buildings be switched to lights that shined
Eagles green. And the *Daily News* spent a full page on a mascot
version of rock-paper-scissors, just to prove that actual eagles
ruled the skies over actual falcons.

  While a falcon wingspan might extend to three feet, the harpy
eagle of South America could spread its wings to ten feet, the
paper reported.

  "They eat monkeys out of trees!" Nate Rice, an ornithologist
with the Academy of Natural Sciences said. "It's a bad-ass bird."

  Tonight, I talked with Butch DeLuca. He got sick after Sunday's game and still hadn't been back to work at his deli. It was a
little stomach virus, he said. He'd be all right. Then he said he had
been to the doctor for an electrocardiogram. This sounded more
serious. Chest pains. The doctor wanted him to see a cardiologist.
Still, he said, he'd make it to the Eagles game.

  "Hell or high water, I'm going," Butch said. "How could you
miss something like this?"

  He had been a little down, he said, a little depressed. It happened when you got sick. But he was trying to remain positive.
The Eagles would be fine, he thought. Hell, they'd better be.

  "I'd hate to see 'em lose," Butch said. "I'm fifty-nine years old.
How many more of these things can you go through?"

16

Thursday, January 20

It was Inauguration Day for President George W. Bush, but few here seemed to notice. Philadelphia was looking for a coronation, not an inauguration. By six thirty, Butch DeLuca was back at his deli, shoveling a coating of snow, making coffee, scraping his spatula across the grill. He met the bread man at the door. Things were looking up. He felt better, thought he'd make the game on Sunday. Butch was a one-man neighborhood watch. Everybody stopped by, cops, politicians, heating-oil guys, contractors, landscapers, painters, mothers who dropped their kids at the dance studio next door. The store was a nerve center for gossip and Butch seemed to know about everything, from kids sneaking beer in the park to one neighbor borrowing a box of macaroni and cheese from another.

He was short and stocky and wore frameless glasses and a mustache and combed his hair straight back. He had the plump hands of a man who was a natural greeter and did his business in cash. He had become a big Eagles fan four or five years earlier. Dave Spadaro, who ran the Eagles' website, lived down the street and was in the store all the time. Spadaro hooked Butch up with season tickets, and when the Linc was built two years ago, the Eagles' ticket manager took him around in a hard hat to help him pick out his seats in the end zone.

Brian Mitchell, the running back and kick returner, came to Philadelphia in 2000 and did a radio show from a restaurant in Havertown. Butch and his wife, Sue, went each week and sat at a front table. They became friends. Mitchell bought them dinner and tooled Butch around a time or two in his Ferrari and sometimes mentioned their names and the deli on the air. A few times, Mitchell called and invited him and Sue to his Center City apartment. Duce Staley, the running back, came over to play dominoes. Domino Duce, they called him. Once, Mitchell got Butch and Sue tickets to an Eagles game in Washington, and when he came out of the tunnel he waved to them.

"It gets you more involved when you know somebody," Butch said.

Mitchell had since left to play for the New York Giants, then retired, but Butch kept his autographed Eagles jersey on the wall of the deli. He also kept renewing his four season tickets, going to the Linc each week with Sue and their kids, Melissa and Brian. Butch loved to hear the *Rocky* theme played at the stadium. He went nuts. They had a good group of tailgaters, a guy with a forty-foot mobile home and Shaun Young's brother, Mike, who bought an ambulance and painted it Eagles green. But this season had been difficult for the DeLucas. Brian's girlfriend, Lauren Joceville, had died of cancer in October, a young woman just out of college, a magna cum laude graduate of Arcadia University. Brian and Lauren had met in school and had talked of marrying. Now he felt displaced, unsure of what he wanted to do. He had worked for the Eagles as an intern last season. Through this season's playoff run, the team became a kind of solace for him. "There's a good group of people to go to the games with," Brian said. His tailgating party grew to forty, fifty people during the playoffs and had its own website. "It eases things," Brian said. "It makes you not forget about things, but it makes things a little easier."

Sue's interest in the Eagles ebbed after Lauren died, and Butch, too, had missed a few games. He wanted Brian to go with his friends, wanted him to have a reason to get out of the house. Brian and Lauren had been inseparable. He was hurting and Butch wanted to do what was best for his son. "You can see it when he comes home," Butch said. "The distant look on his face. He's just empty. I'd like to get him out to do something. It's gonna take time."

Brian usually rode to the games with his sister, Melissa, and her husband, Tim Kelly. Tim came into the store this morning, his work bag slung over his shoulder, on the way to catch the train into Center City. He worked for a benefits outsourcing company, and, at twenty-eight, he got wound up over the Eagles.

"They lose, he won't even talk to his parents," Butch said.

Tim had played lightweight football, for players under 165 pounds, at Penn. He went to Eagles games with Melissa and Brian, but sat with his brother and two friends. That was his time alone, to hang out with the guys. Win or lose, he'd be taking next Monday off, to celebrate or suffer after the NFC championship game. Last year, after the Carolina loss, he and his brother and his friends remained in their seats until the ushers made them leave. They walked to the parking lot and sat in the car for what seemed like an hour, devastated. *I can't believe they did this to us again.* Then the waiting began, an entire year just to get back to the same point. This whole season, prior to the Minnesota game, was just preamble, an interminable, impatient buildup. Only this week really mattered. A fourth consecutive NFC championship game.

"It's the worst thing," Tim said. "It's not like you expect them to lose. They get your hopes up that they're gonna win, then they lose in the worst possible fashion. Why do I keep coming back? Because I'm an idiot. I'm a glutton for punishment. I was a glutton for my first twenty-eight years, and I'll be a glutton for the next twenty-eight. Every year you are like, 'No, I'm not going to get into it,' then you get back into it. It's just in you. You're used to the losing, but they're your team. There's always something inside that says this is going to be the year."

He was trying not to get too worked up. It was only Thursday and he had to focus on work for two more days. It would be hard. Football was the ultimate team sport, Tim thought, offense and defense and special teams working together like links in a chain. He knew the Eagles were stronger than Atlanta. He just hoped none of the links broke.

"Of course I'm nervous," he said as we talked in the front of the store. "Anybody that says they aren't is lying. As good as they are, they've broken your heart so many times before. There's always that unexpected thing that could happen. That turnover, the snow."

His earliest memory had been of his father watching the Eagles lose to Oakland in the 1981 Super Bowl, sitting in disbelief, *What are they doing? I can't believe this*. But at least his father had seen the team play for a championship. Now Tim wanted the same opportunity. Sure, he'd want the Eagles to win if they got to Jacksonville, but if they didn't win, at least they had finally reached the ultimate game.

"We absolutely have to get over this hump," he said.

Butch's regulars began filing in for newspapers, coffee, donuts, eggs, gossip. They grabbed chairs at tables in the back. It was a casual place. Some made their own omelets. Frank Frayne said he was glad to see Butch back. Everyone called him Butchie. "If you're going Sunday," Frayne said, "you better bring some good booze."

At age seventy, Bill Pergolini was a spitting image of Buddy Ryan with his gray hair and oversized glasses and garrulous cursing. He still worked as a contractor, and had a "Jacksonville or Bust" placard on the front of his pickup.

Pergolini began to tease Tim Kelly about showing up at the deli just as Butch, his father-in-law, began having chest pains.

"You know the old story, where there's a will, there's relations," Pergolini said.

He had been at Shibe Park in 1948, as a thirteen-year-old, when the Eagles won their first NFL championship. It had snowed that day, too. He remembered his uncle leaving a dollar under the visor of the car. A guy would come around and take the dollar and watch the car.

"We hadda walk because my uncle hadda drive," Pergolini said. "No little shits getting in the car, just the big shots. All them crazy dagos. They're all dead now."

He went to a lot of games in those days, Pergolini said, but he couldn't remember any of them.

"Maybe you had something to drink," said Walt Clinger, another regular.

"I was a kid. I was only thirteen."

"He took a vow of abstinence when he was in grammar school," said another of the morning crowd, Al Santoleri.

Pergolini was skipping the Atlanta game in person. He'd watch on TV.

"Too cold," he said. "I wouldn't give a shit if they were playing in my backyard. I'm not going down to see 'em."

He had grandkids in Atlanta who thought the Falcons would win easily. They were big fans of Michael Vick. "They got his name tattooed on their ass," Pergolini said.

How were the Eagles gonna stop Vick, his grandsons wanted to know? "We're gonna tear them up," Pergolini said. "They get that raisin head, they'll throw him in the stands."

The Eagles would get to the Super Bowl, Pergolini said, but they wouldn't win.

"You know why? That jerk-off white kid Brady. Buckwheat can't do the job."

Brady was New England quarterback Tom Brady. Buckwheat was Donovan McNabb. Pergolini liked McNabb, thought he was a terrific quarterback, but blamed him and receiver Todd Pinkston for the loss to Carolina in last year's NFC championship game.

"Pinkston dropped everything in sight," Pergolini said. "Whadda they call him, Freddie Ex? FredEx? That horse's ass. In the wrong spot all the time."

"You gotta say one thing," Gene Kelly, another regular, said. "They stepped it up last week."

"One little game against the Vikings," Pergolini said.

"Two touchdowns, fellas," Butch spoke up, predicting the victory margin over Atlanta.

"He said to put on two seat belts this week and enjoy the ride," Kelly said of McNabb.

"He's the best," Pergolini said.

"I was hoping they'd lose so we wouldn't see all that hype," Clinger said. "I get sick of all that hype. Every channel has it on.

They kill it. It's too much. But I'd like to be on the winning side once."

Dave McCullough, another customer, walked in and said that snow would cause the Eagles to lose to the Falcons. Snow was the great equalizer, he said. The better team always got hurt in bad weather.

"New England really gets hurt in that bad weather up there," Pergolini said in rebuttal. "They only won seventeen games in a row. They don't know shit."

"You comparing the Eagles to New England?" McCullough said. "Get the freak outta here. Get outta town. The Eagles are good, but they're not like New England. Please. Nobody's like New England."

At forty-two, McCullough was a Cowboys fan. The Eagles stunk when he was young, so he followed Dallas.

"If I was an Eagles fan like Butch, I'd probably have had a heart attack three years ago," McCullough said.

"That's why I got these pains right now," Butch said, standing behind the counter, a hand on his chest. "That's why I'm all stressed out. It's the Eagles."

The Eagles were going to win, Butch said. A no-brainer. They were the better team.

"They were better than Carolina last year, too, and they didn't win," McCullough said.

No problem, Butch said. The Eagles would stop the Falcons' running game and clamp Vick in a defensive vise.

"Watch out, McNabb'll fumble," McCullough said, goading him.

"The only way the Eagles lose is they beat themselves," Butch said.

"I'll agree with that," McCullough said. "But how many times do they beat themselves?"

McCullough smiled.

"All's I can say is, I'm the only happy one around here when they lose," he said. "Everybody else can't go to work because they're sick."

Brad Lane, the Tastykake deliveryman, came in to check the

shelves. Butch tried to enlist him in a double team against the Dallas interloper.

"I might not be as sure as you are, but they should win," Lane said.

"Easy win," Butch said.

"They should win, Butch," Lane said, "but I been watchin' them since 1962, so I'm a little leery, you know. A little leery."

This afternoon, I drove out to Warminster in Bucks County, to see Ernie and Anne Clark. Ernie was one of the few fans who had been in attendance when the Eagles won the 1948 NFL championship at Shibe Park, the 1960 NFL championship at Franklin Field and the 1981 NFC championship at Veterans Stadium.

After a couple of wrong turns, I arrived at the Clarks' home. Ernie met me outside. He would be seventy in a few days and was a retired bank vice president. He had a ruddy, plump face and wide-frame glasses and also bore a resemblance to Buddy Ryan. We sat in Ernie's favorite room, which was decorated with lithographs of Shibe Park and the local sports teams. "Go Eagles," read a placard in the front window. The ornamental curtains above the window were done in Eagles green and silver.

"I've been called a degenerate sports fan," Ernie said with a laugh.

He had gone to high school across the street from Shibe Park. On December 19, 1948, he and his father took the trolley there to see the Eagles play the Chicago Cardinals in the NFL title game. He was thirteen, and it might have been the first pro football game he had ever attended with his father.

"It might have been the first pro game I went to," Ernie said.

What he remembered about that day was what everyone remembered: the snow. Some still referred to the game as the Blizzard Bowl. The players appeared almost ghostlike on film. Steve Van Buren scored the only touchdown and the Eagles won seven to nothing. According to Van Buren's legend, he awakened that morning, thought the game would be canceled, went back to sleep and nearly missed the championship altogether.

As he recounted to Ray Didinger in the *Daily News*, Van Buren got a call from his coach, Greasy Neale, who said, "Hey, you'd better get here."

"Greasy, have you looked out the window?" Van Buren replied. "There is no way we will play today."

"Go to the park for God's sake," Neale said. "It's the championship game."

From Upper Darby in the western suburbs, Van Buren took a bus to the Sixty-Ninth Street Terminal, rode the Market Street elevated train to Broad Street and took the subway north to Lehigh Avenue, walking the final seven blocks to Shibe Park at Twenty-First and Lehigh.

Al Wistert, an all-pro tackle on that team, told me that Neale was hesitant to play the 1948 game in the snow. A year earlier, the Eagles had lost the NFL championship to Chicago at Comiskey Park, twenty-eight to twenty-one, on a frozen field. The Eagles had filed down their cleats trying to get traction, and Van Buren later said he fell twice just coming out of the huddle.

A vote was taken and both teams wanted to play in 1948. Players helped to shovel snow and remove the tarp from the field. "We had trouble," Wistert told me. "It was like rolling a big snowball."

Ropes tied to stakes were used to mark the sidelines. Flags were planted at the goal line. Because snow kept falling and covering the yard markers, referee Ron Gibbs was made the sole arbiter of first downs. Finally, Philadelphia got a break late in the third quarter, recovering a fumble at Chicago's seventeen-yard line. Van Buren punched the ball over the goal line from the five, running to his right, behind Wistert, guard Bucko Kilroy and end Pete Pihos.

"Hell, he was big," Wistert said of Van Buren, who now lived in assisted-living quarters in Lancaster, Pennsylvania. "He was about 205, that was as big as some linemen. I played at 215. He was fast as hell, too, a track man. When someone came up to tackle him, they paid a serious price."

The Eagles won another NFL championship in Los Angeles in 1949, as Van Buren sloshed through the rain for a then-championship game record of 196 yards. Clark Gable, one of Hollywood's most visible stars, approached Van Buren and told him he was the greatest athlete he had ever seen, according to Didinger. "This fella seemed like a nice guy," Van Buren told a teammate. "What's his name again?" To which the teammate, George Savitsky, replied, "Steve you really ought to get out more."

On December 26, 1960, at Franklin Field, Philadelphia won its third NFL title by defeating Green Bay seventeen to thirteen, as Chuck Bednarik stopped Jim Taylor to end the game. Ernie and Anne Clark were dating at the time. He was working in a paper products factory with his father, and she was attending college and teaching at a Catholic school. It had snowed the day before, Anne said, and they tromped through the snow to their seats, she in stockings and heels, he on crutches with a broken toe, both of them dressed for a wedding after the game.

This was Anne's first pro game, and both she and Ernie still vividly recalled the flamboyant Eagles' receiver Tommy McDonald catching a touchdown pass and skidding into a snowbank. Tom Brookshier, a teammate, sometimes joked that McDonald often ended up in the lap of a blonde. Years later, when Ernie was president of a Little League chapter, he invited McDonald to be guest speaker at a banquet.

"He talked about his divorce," Ernie said. "These were ten-, eleven-, twelve-year-old kids. It was almost like, 'Don't get married kids, it won't work out.' Everyone sat there with their mouths agape. Unbelievable. He is a goofy guy."

The next year, 1961, Ernie bought ten season tickets at eighteen bucks apiece. They went for seven hundred nowadays. He couldn't have known at the time, but the Eagles were entering a barren period that would provide two winning seasons in seventeen years. Sometimes he got mad—Anne used to call him Archie Bunker—but other times he almost had to laugh at how pitiful the team was. The worst for him was 1962, when the Packers returned to Franklin Field and beat the Eagles forty-nine to nothing.

"They must have run Taylor on that tackle sweep forty times and we couldn't stop it," Ernie said.

Football evolved for him, and as his four children grew, the

game became less about championships and more about family
and friends. Their former neighbors from Feasterville, Pennsylvania, had sat with the Clarks for thirty years at Eagles games. When
the kids were young, one family drove and the other paid for parking. Now that the Clarks' four children were grown, the Eagles
meant renewal and congregation and the maintenance of strong
familial bonds.

The kids still lived nearby, but three of them were married and
had kids of their own. Each Sunday, Ernie went to see the Eagles
with his son Chris and his three daughters—Terry Funk, Sue Harrigan and Jennifer Clark. Anne stopped going regularly because of
the coarse behavior of many fans. She grew worried that her husband's chivalry in protecting her from cursing and other rude con-
duct might get him injured. But she also thought it was heartening
that a father could go to a game with his four kids.

"We see the kids a lot, but because we have nine grandchil-
dren, it's certainly a different environment when we see them,"
Ernie said. "It's kind of neat for me to go to the game with them.
It's something we all love. It's like it was. We have a good time,
we're together, they're my kids."

Ernie once had season tickets to the Flyers, too, but after they
won consecutive Stanley Cups in 1974 and 1975, he sold them.

"I figured I'd seen everything there was to see in hockey," Ernie
said. "What's left after two Stanley Cups?"

The Eagles tickets he kept. The beauty of football was its
reliance on collective performance. Baseball, to him, seemed like
an individual game with a team score. Basketball was a star's
game more than a team game. Football was like a puzzle. All the
pieces had to fit precisely to build something complete.

While the Eagles were floundering, Ernie and Anne did get to
see how the other half lived. On March 8, 1971, Ernie attended the
first Ali-Frazier fight at Madison Square Garden with a business
associate named Bob Egan. Bob's wife, Loretta, was the sister of
Joe Namath's roommate, Ray Abruzzi. After the fight, the Clarks
and the Egans met up with Namath, who gave them a tour of his
famous bachelor pad apartment, decorated in expected out-

landishness, all red and white and black, with a mirrored ceiling in the bedroom. Anne Clark looked at her friend Loretta and they began laughing hysterically at the decorated absurdity of it all.

"It was Joe, it was what you thought it would be," Ernie said. "I don't think Norm Van Brocklin had an apartment like that. But I bet Terrell Owens's is pretty nice."

A decade later, in 1981, the Eagles had been sufficiently revived under Dick Vermeil to play for a chance to reach the Super Bowl. The NFC championship was played in the frigid cold, this time at Veterans Stadium against the hated Dallas Cowboys. Wilbert Montgomery's early touchdown of forty-two yards made victory inevitable for Philadelphia. The game meant so much—an exorcism of mediocrity as much as a victory over an archenemy— that the run seemed to grow longer over the years, at least fifty yards, more like fifty-five.

"I probably had tears running down my eyes," Ernie said. "We had beaten Dallas and were king of the mountain. Beating Tom Landry was special. I thought he was arrogant, standing on the sideline in his hat. It was like watching Ed Sullivan on tape, seeing everyone in suits and ties. Like the forties. They thought they were better than everyone else. We finally put them down. It was great, probably too great."

By all accounts, the Eagles were emotionally spent and uptight for the Super Bowl match-up against Oakland two weeks later. Ernie did not attend the game in New Orleans. *I'll go the next time. They'll be back soon enough*. He watched on television, and during the introduction of the players, the eyes of the Eagles seemed "as wide as saucers." The game had not yet begun and he felt the Eagles had already lost, which they did, twenty-seven to ten.

And they had never gotten back to the Super Bowl. But this might finally be the year. Earlier this week, Chris Clark had surprised his father. He had a couple of tickets to Jacksonville. If the Eagles went, father and son were going, too.

First, Philadelphia had to get past Atlanta. Again, snow and cold figured to play a major role. Ernie had never seen the Eagles lose a championship game in the snow. Still, he was concerned.

He had followed the team too long not to be. Donovan McNabb had thrown one touchdown pass and five interceptions in the previous three NFC championship games.

"I think a lot of snow and wind, which might be the bigger issue, is not a plus for the Eagles," Ernie said. "If you're the better team, you want to play in optimum conditions. But I think a lot of us forget how well-rounded this team is. The pressure is on Donovan to get it done."

17

Friday, January 21

A nor'easter was on its way, and up to fifteen inches of snow were expected Saturday into Sunday. Game-time temperature would be in the twenties, with winds up to twenty-five miles an hour. Today was sunny but fourteen degrees.

The *Atlanta Journal-Constitution*, in an effort to plumb the hostility of Eagles fans, had sent a reporter to Philadelphia dressed in a red Michael Vick jersey. He had promptly encountered a reporter from the *Allentown Morning Call*, who was also wearing a Vick jersey and pulling the same stunt, according to the *Daily News*.

I spent the day with Ray Didinger and a crew from NFL Films, taking the pulse of the city before the NFC championship game. Still boyish in appearance at age fifty-eight, Ray grew up in southwest Philadelphia and worked for many years as a sportswriter at the *Evening Bulletin* and the *Daily News*. No one in Philadelphia had a more encyclopedic knowledge of the Eagles than he did. His parents would come home from Shibe Park, renamed Connie Mack Stadium in 1953, with Eagles game programs that contained names and photographs of the players. Ray learned his numbers from the numerals on their jerseys and the alphabet from the spelling of their names.

"I was the only four-year-old in America who could spell Alex Wojciechowicz," Ray said with a laugh.

His grandfather owned a bar on Woodland Avenue, the main commercial drag through southwest Philly at the time. Ray and his parents lived two and a half blocks down the street, atop a shoe store. He often said that the language his family spoke at the dinner table was not English but football. His father, also named Ray, had been a superb end on a semi-pro team, and had flown in B-24 bombers during World War II, as had Eagles' star Chuck Bednarik.

With an unlimited supply of Cokes and games of shuffleboard, the younger Ray spent much of his free time in his grandfather's bar. It was a sports bar before anyone knew to call it a sports bar. Ray listened for hours as his grandfather and his friends argued endlessly over baseball and football, and it began to dawn on Ray that these were grown men and they really cared about these games and it was a big part of who they were.

His grandfather—the patriarchal Ray—was one of the first Eagles fans who bought season tickets in a bloc. At one point, he had upwards of seventy tickets. He'd buy them and his patrons would pay him back. Behind the counter, he kept a tab of who owed what on the tickets that, in the late 1950s, cost fifteen bucks apiece.

Ray was sure there never was a year when his grandfather got all his money back. There must have been five or six guys carried from one season to the next. But they were customers, it made good business sense, and Ray was certain his grandfather made up any losses in the beer they drank and the sandwiches they ate.

On Sundays, after Mass, patrons would gather at the bar in their church clothes and ride a chartered city bus, first to Connie Mack Stadium, then to Franklin Field, where the Eagles moved in 1958. Maury, a patron who smoked cigars dipped in wine, handled the dollar betting pool. Another guy made hoagies that he carried in a box and sold on the bus for a buck.

"That was my Sunday—Mass and the Eagles—and I couldn't tell you where religion left off and football began," Ray said. "It all ran together. I went from one congregation to another. The only difference was, the second one smoked."

His grandfather, whom Ray called Boo, had attended the 1948 championship game, driving his old DeSoto toward North Philly until it got stuck in a snow bank. He opened the trunk, grabbed burlap sacks, wrapped them around his feet and walked the final miles to Shibe Park. Did he exaggerate? The miles, perhaps, but not his passion for the Eagles.

"Why would you do something like that?" Ray asked him once.

"What, you kidding?" Boo said. "It was the first championship game they were ever in. Think I'm not going to go?"

Ray's first Eagles game had been the home opener against Washington on October 6, 1956, a rainy Saturday night at Connie Mack Stadium. He was a boy of ten. When he walked through the concourse to the seating area and the night opened up for him and he saw the lights and the wide expanse of green and the band playing, his heart began to pound. He had never felt anything like this before, this physical sensation, his body changing and beginning to tingle. He had heard games on the radio, sitting at the kitchen table with his father, and he had seen the black-and-white photographs in the newspaper, but here he was, at the stadium, getting a boy's first look, and it took his breath away.

The season ended with three victories, eight defeats and a tie, and as Ray walked out of the stadium for a final time with his father, he began to cry. He couldn't remember exactly why, whether it was the day's loss or a realization that the season was over and, to a ten-year-old, it seemed the next one might never arrive.

Ray felt as deflated then as he had been excited on opening day. His father saw the tears, and Ray wondered whether his dad would admonish him, "Come on, be a man, buck up, it's only a game." Instead, his father put his arms around his shoulders and said, "I know how you feel."

His father was reserved in his emotions, as were many veterans of the war. Ray could never remember him cheering. But he cherished the Eagles as much as anyone and he let his son know it was okay to feel hurt. They were many seasons, before and after, when feeling wounded was all there was to feel.

"It was so revealing," Ray said. "He didn't belittle the emotion I was feeling. He understood how much I loved the game."

In a quiet, dark studio at NFL Films, Ray interviewed Vai Sikahema, a former Eagles punt returner and now a sports anchor at

WCAU-TV, the local NBC affiliate. He sensed a manufactured boldness among Eagles fans, Sikahema said. Whistling past the graveyard, he called it.

If there was one thing that players loved and loathed about Eagles fans, Sikahema said, it was that people approached them in stores and clubs and stopped them on the street and told them exactly what they thought.

If they thought you were great, they said you were great. If they thought you stunk, they said you stunk. They jawed at you and wanted you to jaw back, Sikahema said. He told a story about Jim McMahon, the former Eagles quarterback, who left Veterans Stadium one day in the early 1990s to a chorus of boos and obscenities.

"McMahon, you suck, you stink, you're terrible," two guys yelled as the quarterback walked up the tunnel toward the locker-room.

His teammates ignored the cursing fans, but McMahon flipped them the finger. As he did, the two guys stopped, looked at each other and began yelling, "You're the man. You . . . are . . . the . . . man!"

"That to me is the essence of a Philadelphia fan," Sikahema said, sitting forward on the balls of his feet, all kinetic energy even in retirement. "They want to abuse you, but they love you if you respond. They just want to banter with you. We like pointing our fingers in someone's chest. If they back off, recoil, we think they're lesser for that. But if they pump their chest out and stick their finger right back in your chest, all of a sudden we walk away and think, 'That's a man's man, he's worth his salt.'"

We hopped into Ray's car and headed to Moorestown, New Jersey. Paul Campise had a court reporter's business that reflected his obsession with his favorite team from a boyhood in South Philly. An Eagles flag flew on a pole, and the shutters and the porch furniture were painted Eagles green.

"We going to Jacksonville, Ray?" Campise asked Didinger.

He was seventy-four and he didn't know how many more chances he would get to see his team in the Super Bowl. Before he started having heart problems, he ran through Veterans Stadium carrying banners, and he made another one out of a horse blanket that hung from the owner's box. Time had slowed him, but in his basement he had spent six months and three thousand dollars building an Eagles train platform, complete with an Eagles diner, restaurant, gas station, souvenir shop and movie theater. An Eagles jet flew over the village, whose centerpiece was a stadium built to scale and with knowing detail. Cops wrote a ticket in the parking lot to misbehaving fans. Campise wasn't sure what they were doing, drinking maybe, but whatever it was the cops didn't like it and they needed a van and a police dog to clean it up.

The scoreboard said Eagles fifty-four, Cowboys zero.

"I hate the Cowboys," Campise said.

It drove him crazy that his mailman, his barber and his accountant were all Cowboys fans. Even his ex-son-in-law was a Dallas fan. "We got him out of the family," Campise said.

In a little room off the basement, he had Eagles cookies on a plate, and a twenty-three-year-old soft pretzel from a forgotten game at the Vet. He had found the pretzel in a bag, along with a packet of mustard.

"I should sell it on eBay," Campise said. "They sold a piece of cheese."

He would be on vacation in Florida during the Super Bowl, and if the Eagles were in it, he had to be there. His miniature stadium was built on hinges, and Campise flipped it up and stood in the middle of his Eagles village. He said he felt it in his bones that this would be the year. Last year, he had open-heart surgery and doctors replaced his aortic valve with a cow's valve. Before the surgery, he told his doctor to keep him alive for three reasons. He wanted to celebrate his fiftieth wedding anniversary, he wanted to shoot a hole in one and he wanted to see his Eagles win the Super Bowl.

His fiftieth anniversary had come in June.

"All we need is the Super Bowl and a hole in one," Campise said. "I think the toughest is the hole in one. I'm a twenty-six handicap."

Back in the car, we headed over the Ben Franklin Bridge toward Philadelphia for an Eagles pep rally. WIP had wanted ten thousand fans in Love Park, but the temperature was fourteen degrees, and only two thousand hardy souls braved the frigid conditions. The cheering was muted, as if everybody's lungs were in need of ice scrapers.

On the way in to Center City, Ray talked about the other time in his sporting life that he felt his heart pound and his knees go weak. Tommy McDonald, the Eagles' flanker, had been his boyhood idol. McDonald played with a boy's enthusiasm, not wearing a face mask or long sleeves and popping right up when he was tackled. If he could play, he would play like Tommy McDonald, Ray always told himself. Then he became a sportswriter and began to champion McDonald for the Hall of Fame. In 1998, McDonald was voted in, and he called Ray before he called his own mother. "It's you and me in Canton, baby," McDonald yelled into the phone, and that summer Ray was in Ohio, riding in a parade with his onetime idol and giving the speech that inducted him into the Hall of Fame. Bart Starr, Gale Sayers, and Otto Graham sat and listened, and so did Don Shula. Ray was so excited and overwhelmed that he could feel his legs shaking, and it seemed as if the trembling moved all the way up his body, into his ears, and he thought he could hear his voice begin to quiver.

But, for Philadelphia fans, celebratory moments like these were brief and scattered. Sweetness always turned bitter. For a certain generation, this sense of dread lingered from the 1964 Phillies. A six-and-a-half-game lead with twelve to play. And they blew it. Flat-out fuckin' blew it. Once something like that hits you in the stomach, you never really catch your breath again.

Ray had enrolled as a freshman at Temple that fall. He had followed the Phillies all summer. In his lifetime they had never been this good. Never. Everything seemed to be going their way. Jim Bunning threw a perfect game. Johnny Callison hit a ninth-inning homer to win the all-star game. All summer, Ray had watched, never being sure, and then September came and they were still ahead and he began to tell himself, *God, it's going to happen*. This was going to be their year. Then school started and everything began to fall apart, the team, his grades, everything.

He couldn't not watch. That was impossible. Every night there was a game on, and he couldn't study during the game, and after the game he was too devastated to hit the books. He watched a lot of games with his grandfather, or spoke with him on the phone, and when Ray began to agonize, his grandfather would say, "Don't worry, Champ, they'll be fine, they'll win tomorrow."

His grandfather was everything a fan should have been, passionate without being judgmental, supportive without being hostile. He calmed Ray with the same soothing words every day until a Saturday game when the Phillies held a big lead over the Braves, then blew it as Rico Carty hit a shot off the scoreboard. This time his grandfather had no words to comfort him. He got out of his chair, turned off the television and walked into the kitchen. Ray knew at that moment it was over.

"When they blew the pennant, I was catatonic for weeks," Ray said. "By the time I finally snapped out of it, I was so far behind in my work, I damn near flunked out my first semester, and I would have blamed it all on Gene Mauch. I don't know that my parents would have accepted that as a legitimate excuse, but that was my story and I was sticking to it."

We parked downtown and walked a couple of blocks to Love Park, near City Hall. Ray stood in the park and closed his eyes and inhaled and said he could still smell Eagles games at Franklin Field, the pretzels and roasted chestnuts and hot chocolate. He and his parents and grandparents sat in section EE, in the base of the horseshoe in the end zone. He remembered how civil it was back then, how men wore coats and ties and women wore dresses and how his father could fold his topcoat and leave it on the bench with his binoculars and go to the concession stand or the restroom and be sure that his belongings would be there when he returned.

People kept coming up to Ray in the park, asking, "Whaddya think? What's going to happen?"

All week, Didinger had noticed the peculiar Philadelphia blend of confidence and uncertainty in the words of people he met around town.

We're going to win. Right?

Over and over he heard the ambivalence in their voices.

They can't lose again. Can they?

A few days earlier, he had interviewed Governor Rendell on the difference between Philadelphia and Pittsburgh fans. Last week, as the Jets attempted a field goal at the end of regulation, Steelers fans were waving their Terrible Towels, stomping their feet, saying, "Miss, miss, miss," certain their team would prevail in overtime.

If the same thing had happened in Philadelphia, Rendell said, the stadium would have gone dead silent. "All the fans would have been standing with their hands over their eyes, saying, 'He's gonna make it. I can't believe we're going to lose this way.'"

But Ray had been saying all along this was the Eagles' year. He wasn't going to change now.

On stage at the rally, Angelo Cataldi said he had never seen more on the line for one game. "It's either going to be dancing in the streets or a funeral procession," he told me.

Shaun Young was on stage, too, dressed in his bandanna and his Eagles uniform, screaming, "Atlanta's got no shot, no clue what they're getting themselves into."

"Ours" guaranteed today's front-page headline in the *Daily News*, which ran a forty-eight-page special section on the Eagles.

At a news conference, Donovan McNabb said, "I have visualized winning the game and holding up the trophy and getting hit by confetti and having all of our fans getting excited and it being chilly out there and the snow on the ground."

But some fans needed more persuasion. As we left the rally at

Love Park, I spotted a guy named Steve Swenk. He was wearing his Eagles underwear on the outside of his pants.

"It's our good luck, to get us to the Super Bowl," he said. "You gotta do something."

We ducked out of the cold into the Friends Center on Cherry Street. Tom Hoopes, the center's director of education, told us the widely held belief that Philadelphia sports teams were cursed or jinxed was a misunderstanding of the city's Quaker heritage.

Many thought a curse was placed on the city's teams by William Penn, the Quaker statesman and founder of the "holy experiment" of Pennsylvania. For those who believed in such things, Penn was supposed to be upset at the lapse, in the mid-1980s, of a gentleman's agreement to construct no building taller than his statue atop City Hall.

The sense of being cursed, of spiritual hopelessness, was a mark of Puritan theology, Hoopes said. While the notion of a jinx or curse applied to the Red Sox in Calvinist New England, it did not have resonance with the Eagles. What Philadelphia suffered from, in its collective shame and negativity and low-self esteem, was a string of broken promises, Hoopes said.

Original plans for the statue of Penn called for him to face south from City Hall so he could survey his city, Hoopes said. Instead he faced northeast. That was one broken promise.

In facing northeast, Penn was forced to look in eternal shame toward Treaty Park, which commemorated the treachery of his sons, who cheated the Indians out of land in what was known as the Walking Purchase of 1737. A second broken promise.

Penn was also left in urban shadow after the gentleman's agreement expired. At least half a dozen skyscrapers now topped his statue above City Hall. Broken promise number three.

No major professional team in the city had won a championship since.

Philadelphia had to reconcile these broken promises, Hoopes said. A symbolic act might help. He recommended placing an Eagles jersey on Penn's statue, but putting it on backward.

Metaphorically, this would allow him to face southward, as sculptor Alexander Calder had intended. South also happened to be the direction of the city's stadium complex.

"Not only will that allow him metaphorically to watch the game," Hoopes said, "but it will address the original sin of betraying the Native Americans and correct the misdeed of rotating the statue of Billy to face Penn Treaty Park."

Last on the day's itinerary was Pat's Steaks, the cheesesteak institution in South Philly. As we navigated the narrow, crowded streets, Ray began telling his favorite stories about Leonard Tose, the high-rolling team owner who brought the Eagles to the Super Bowl in 1981 and basically fumbled the franchise away a few years later because of his forty-carat hedonism.

By his own estimate, Tose lost $25 million to $50 million in drunken, destructive gambling. While his fortune held out, he served the media filet mignon and lobster Newburg when the Eagles played on Monday nights, and he often arrived at practice in a helicopter. Sometimes, he landed right in the middle of practice. Once, Ray said, the dust cleared to find Steve Zabel, a former first-round draft pick, writhing on the ground with a knee injury.

Finally, Tose's profligate ways caught up to him, and he threatened to move the team to Phoenix in 1984 unless the city built luxury suites at the Vet. The city caved in, but in 1985, his pockets were as empty as his drinks were full, and Tose sold the Eagles to an automobile dealer named Norman Braman. Then he got a small measure of revenge.

The 1986 Super Bowl was held in New Orleans, and although he was now out of the NFL and reduced to tattered extravagance, Tose still loved a party and knew how to make a florid gesture. According to Ray, he made his customary appearance at Brennan's restaurant, where lavish tipping made him a popular guest. Tose noticed Braman waiting in line outside, and called over the headwaiter. He peeled off a couple of fifties and said, "Make him wait."

When the waiters could not stall Braman any longer, Tose

peeled off more bills, and said, "Okay, but make sure he gets really bad service."

Even though Tose rationalized that he was the man who kept the Eagles in Philadelphia, Ray wrote harshly about him and thought his near-move of the team was reprehensible. Once, he said, Tose called and threatened to have him killed, saying, "I know people who can take care of guys like you."

Ray reported the threat to his sports editor at the *Daily News*, but didn't take it seriously. "At that point, Leonard didn't have enough money to hire a decent hit man," Ray said. "If he was going to get anybody killed, he was going to have to do it himself."

The two didn't speak for about ten years, then finally patched up their differences. Destitute, Tose was assisted by a small group of people, including former Eagles coach Dick Vermeil and former general manager Jim Murray. He lived alone in a downtown hotel suite until he died in 2003.

These days, Ray preferred to think of the generous side of Tose, who had started an Eagles leukemia charity and who famously had a soft spot for people in need. One day, Tose approached Ray at practice, with a story ripped out of the *Bulletin* about a young music prodigy. She was struggling because her parents couldn't afford transportation for her training. Tose called over his driver, John Fitch, and said, "Get this little girl a piano so she can practice at home."

That afternoon, she had a piano.

"For the most part, I liked the guy," Ray said of Tose. "I do think there was a lot more good to him than bad. He had a good heart, but also terrible weaknesses that became his downfall."

After a short stop at Pat's, we headed back to NFL Films, and as we walked back to the lobby, the sun a frozen ball near the horizon, Ray said he hoped the Eagles would win on Sunday. Not for himself. Journalism had long ago dulled his rooting interest. No, he wanted them to win for the fans, for people like his mother and father, who followed the team for decades and always gave more than they got in return.

Each summer, while others went to the Jersey Shore or the Poconos, Ray and his family traveled to Hershey, Pennsylvania, to watch the Eagles at training camp. In the 1950s and 1960s, players were more approachable. Many of them lived in the same apartment house in West Philadelphia and hung out at a bar called Donoghue's. At training camp, they stood in the sun on Camera Day, posing with fans for photographs. A kid could feel that a guy who shook his hand and signed an autograph and reached down and rubbed his hair really knew him. There was a loose charm to it all, not like today, when the crowds were bigger and autographs were signed in assembly line fashion and the players sometimes seemed as if they'd rather be at the dentist.

At night, back in the hotel room, Ray would watch television and his mother would read a book while his father sat at the desk with a mimeographed roster, drawing a line through names, making his player cuts, saying, "This guy's not going to make it, that guy won't be around," whittling the team to the league limit. By the time vacation was over, he had done in two weeks what it took coaches a whole summer to do.

"I root for my mother and father," Ray said. "Before they die, they want to see the Eagles win a Super Bowl. There is a thread of family that really runs through the city and the team. We all have relatives that make us mad, that disappoint us and let us down, that borrow money and don't give it back. You get mad at them for a while, and you have a fight, but ultimately, they're still your family. You always keep the faith. There's always one relative who's a screw-up. But you know what, he'll be fine. Just give him time. He'll work through it. He'll be okay. That's the way the Eagles are. You go through periods when you're mad because they're doing everything wrong, but you never turn your back on them because they're family. You think, 'One of these days, they're going to make me proud.'"

18

Saturday, January 22

By five, John Kleinstuber was already awake in squirmy anticipation, the championship game and the snow on his mind. By eight, dressed in a hooded sweatshirt, work boots and khakis, he drove his pickup to the Gulph Mills Golf Club to prepare for a paddle tennis tournament and a skeet-shooting competition. They were trying to get both in before the nor'easter hit.

In his cramped office, John had pictures of McNabb and the Eagles' running backs on his computer. He wasn't worried about the game, he said, he was worried about the weather. Fifteen inches of snow and a wind chill below zero would test any fan's resolve.

"I have to go to the game," John said. "If they win, I'd kill myself if I'm not there. I hope there's not a letdown. I've had urges for ten years to win this game. If we win, I'm not sure if I'll be excited or go, 'Now what?'"

Last night, John and his wife, Helen, had coats and snow pants and hats strewn about the living room. The place looked like a department store. Helen had picked out a faux fur hat. John mentioned the bomber jacket again, but Helen said no, it was bad luck.

She wasn't worried about the cold, Helen said, she was worried about John's reaction to the score. If the Eagles lost for a fourth consecutive time, she wondered if John would go silent again, walking twenty paces in front of her, sullen, inconsolable.

"I'll have to bring my own money and subway tokens," she said with a nervous laugh.

No, things were different this year, John said to me this morning at the club. He had a new, lighter attitude. And he was sure the Eagles were going to win. They'd better, said the club's other chefs as they took a cigarette break. They teased John about how he wore an Eagles shirt every day of the season. And they recounted how he moped about for a week after the loss to Carolina in 2004, sitting in his office with the door closed, probably not even eating.

"They lose again, I come in here Tuesday, these people will be afraid to talk to me," John said, leaning against a counter, jingling change in his pocket.

"I'm calling out sick," laughed Donna Wright, one of the chefs. "I'm definitely calling out."

A few minutes later, we ran into Mike Estock, one of club's bartenders. He wore a pinstriped Eagles baseball shirt. John joked that his coworkers always wondered whether his vehement devotion would land him on page one of the paper or in jail.

"He'll be the first one arrested," Estock said.

"I haven't done that yet," John said, "but they know I have it in me."

It hurt everybody last year, Estock said. They were all Eagles fans. Everyone felt let down, somber.

"They're gonna win this time," Estock said. "No problem."

We got into John's pickup and hauled two tanks of propane to a cabin where the skeet-shooting tournament would be held. It was ten o'clock. The snow had begun to fall, tiny, insistent flakes. Ray Didinger and Glen Macnow were on WIP.

"Are we going to Jacksonville?" Macnow asked Didinger.

"I believe we're going to Jacksonville," Didinger said.

John nodded several times.

"It gives me more confidence," John said. "Ray'll give it to you straight. But it's not going to keep me from being nervous."

The snow might do him some good, John said, force him to shovel and use the snow blower on Sunday morning, take his mind off the game. The more snow, the better.

"It'll give me something to do for two or three hours," John said. "The wife'll say no beer or Bloody Marys 'til noon. If I start at ten, I'll be a mess by three. Late games aren't good for me. I like early games."

It was fourteen degrees, and the snow began sticking to the roads and lawns and sidewalks. It was so cold that Didinger and Macnow asked listeners to bring a couple of portable heaters to the hoagie restaurant where they were broadcasting. Within a few minutes, things were getting toasty.

"Another hour, and I'll be working in a thong," Didinger said.

It was the kind of weekend of bitter cold and snow that decorated the Eagles' history and inflamed the villainy of their fans. The NFL championships in 1948 and 1960, the NFC title game against Dallas in 1981, the throwing of snowballs at Dallas Coach Jimmy Johnson in 1989, the pelting of Santa Claus in 1968. Weekends like this, Didinger said, people remembered with a cozy distance and forgot about the frostbite and said, "I lost a big toe, but it was worth it."

There was desperate hope to be found in geometry, according to the *Daily News*. David Zitarelli, a math professor at Temple, noted that the Eagles had been in the playoffs for five years, four times in the NFC championship game, with three past defeats.

"In a right triangle, the length of the legs are three and four while the hypotenuse is five," Zitarelli told the paper. "It all comes back to the Pythagorean theorem. The whole triangle is completed and now is the time to move on."

By two o'clock in the afternoon, snow was falling so heavily that I couldn't see Butch's Deli up the block. Kids were sledding and snowboarding down my street. I took a train into Center City to pick up my press pass for the game, and the place was quiet, deserted. I was supposed to take the train to Washington with Governor Rendell, but he canceled. Indoor lacrosse and soccer games were postponed, and so were classes and dance recitals and church services. On the radio, they said the airport had shut down for the first time in nine years. The Falcons made it in, though, and Coach Jim Mora Jr. wore only a suit, no coat, when the team arrived at its hotel. It was another in a series of psychological games Mora had been playing all week. Atlanta would revel in the snow and the howling of both the wind and the Eagles fans, he kept saying. All the pressure was on the Eagles.

I walked in the snow up to Butch's Deli, and Butch seemed a little solemn. He might have to skip the game, he told me. His employees were hesitant to get out in this weather. "No one wants to work," he said. Plus, it would be cold as hell and he had gotten sick last week and he didn't want to suffer a relapse. Maybe he'd be there. He'd have to see. If he couldn't go, maybe his son, Brian, would take some friends. Brian was still having a hard time after the death of his girlfriend.

"I'd feel better if he went," Butch said.

There was some good news, though, on the Super Bowl front. Butch had a line on tickets.

"If I had tickets, I'd go in a minute," he said.

Now all the Eagles had to do was get there.

"If they lose, I won't even talk to him," Butch's wife, Sue, said at the cash register. "I'll leave the house."

Know what he'd have to put up with on Monday if the Eagles lost? Butch asked. He was a diehard. They'd be bustin' his balls all morning. God forbid.

"They say McNabb in the big games, he can't do it," Butch said. "I don't want to see 'em lose. If they lose, it's gonna be McNabb this, McNabb that. I can hear it now, 'black quarterback, blah, blah, blah.' I know what they're gonna say. If they win, boy, it's gonna be something."

Know what he hated? He hated when guys came in, negative guys, guys who thought the Eagles won only because the other team screwed up. Guys, all they had were excuses. He couldn't stand that. Lucky, whaddya mean lucky?

He went on for a bit, then his confidence began to droop like branches in the snow.

"What about turnovers?" Butch said. "Think we gonna have turnovers?"

The snow kept falling, and the plow-truck guy came in and made a call, and the street up the hill to Butch's house still wasn't plowed. He'd spend the night at the store if he had to.

"I got a bed in back, there's a TV back there, there's heat back there, I got everything I need," Butch said. "There's booze back there."

He laughed.

"Oh gosh."

At least ten inches had fallen into Saturday night. I went out to shovel the sidewalk and the driveway. I loved snow. I even enjoyed shoveling it. The perfect year for me would be snow beginning on Labor Day and ending on Memorial Day. Growing up in Louisiana, I spent too many Christmases with the air conditioner on. When a rare snow came, no one had a sled, so we pulled each other around on coffee-serving trays.

Hundreds of workers shoveled through the night at Lincoln Financial Field, clearing the field and the stands. One of them, James Phillips, didn't have a job, and needed the eight-fifty an hour, so he worked for thirty hours straight, he later told the *Inquirer*. In exchange for his services, he would get to stay and see the game for free while others paid thirteen hundred dollars for tickets on eBay. Eventually, Phillips would pay, too. He didn't wear gloves and his hands became severely frostbitten and finally they were useful only for one hand catching blood that dripped from the other.

"I'm kind of an Eagles aficionado, so I overlooked it," Phillips would tell the *Inquirer*, explaining that he hadn't understood about frostbite. "We live and die Eagles in this city."

A month later, eight of his fingers would be amputated.

"Fanaticism is something that takes on a whole different form," he would say.

19

Sunday, January 23

At eight thirty, it was sixteen degrees. Six and a half hours before game time, snow was still falling. Butch DeLuca's daughter, Melissa Kelly, her husband, Tim Kelly, and her brother, Brian DeLuca, followed a convoy of snowplows to Lincoln Financial Field. A strong wind slapped at tents and signs in the parking lot, just as hopes of Eagles fans flapped between optimism and doubt.

January always seemed to batter faith with a desolate hopelessness. This irredeemable grief felt, Ray Didinger said, like "the cold rough edge of a razor dragged across the skin, nothing good about it, pain followed by loss of blood."

Tim Kelly and his friends often played a drinking game called Beer Pong, which involved tossing Ping-Pong balls into cups of brew. But the wind was too strong today, and the beer developed a slushy crust.

"One of the few days when the beers got colder as you drank them," Tim said.

Snow had reached the chest on the wooden likeness of safety Brian Dawkins standing in John Kleinstuber's front yard in Havertown. John woke up to find it forty degrees in his living room. His oil heater had broken. He had a service contract, so he called the company, which sent a repairman. To speed up the work, the guy ran a new fuel line and told John, "Don't tell anybody about this, they'll charge you. It's on me. Go Eagles."

Shaun Young had taken a hotel room near the stadium so he wouldn't get caught in the snow. He awakened, did pushups by the side of the bed, painted his face and put on his jersey and shoulder pads. Later in the morning, the snow stopped and the sun broke through, and a dishwater sky gave way to a pale blue gusty cold.

Shortly after noon, the Clark family began gathering at the General Davis pub in Southampton, Bucks County. A limousine would take Ernie Clark and his four children to the game. His son, Chris, and one of his three daughters, Terry Funk, did not want the limousine. Sometimes all you could control were your superstitions. They had taken a limousine to the previous two NFC championship games, and the Eagles had lost both times. But another sister, Jennifer Clark, prevailed. Let's stick to our routine, she convinced her siblings. What better way to toast a victory, or drown sorrows in defeat, than a limo?

Sue Harrigan, the third sister, walked into the General Davis wearing a pink Eagles hat and a green boa. A nurse, she had been in Atlanta all week at a conference. "I walked through the whole airport with my Eagles sweatshirt and my hat," she said. "Not one heckler. Not one anything. Nobody cared. I couldn't believe it."

Chris Clark, forty-one and a partner in a printing firm, wore an Eagles sweatshirt and sipped on a Miller Lite. As a fifteen-year-old, he had played quarterback for the Little Quakers, a youth team that won tournaments in Arizona and Florida. Apart from his marriage and the birth of his three children, he told people those victories were the highlight of his life. Later, he played as a backup catcher at the University of Dayton and still kept a pinch of smokeless tobacco between his cheek and gum.

He had the assured jaw of an ex-athlete, but a year ago, after the Eagles lost a third straight time in the NFC championship game, he wanted out. Chris had gone to games with his father since he was eight or nine. He had been a senior in high school in 1981 when Wilbert Montgomery took that early handoff to the end zone against Dallas and put the Eagles in the Super Bowl. Chris came out of his seat as Montgomery got the ball, seeing the hole open, a whole stadium seeing it together, that one glorious moment becoming a validation of a family's and a city's loyalty through all those years of aching defeat.

But three consecutive losses in the NFC championship game
had been too much for Chris. During last year's loss to Carolina,
he had begun grumbling. *I can't deal with this anymore. Why do we
keep doing this to ourselves?* Finally, his father had heard enough
and snapped at him, "Aah, shut up, Chris, would ya?"

After that game, Chris said he was finished, but his sister Terry
confronted him first, then Jen, as their father walked a couple of
steps ahead, saying, "You know what? You're gonna do it. You're
gonna do it 'til he's gone, and you're gonna do it with your son and
he's gonna do it with his son. 'Cause this is what we do."

Chris was out and his sisters dragged him back in and here he
was, a year later, going to another NFC championship game. He
had stepped back a little this season, going to five home games
and missing three to spend time with his wife and three young
children. He knew he couldn't live and die with the Eagles anymore. Tomorrow morning, his kids would be jumping on the bed
at six thirty, asking for their father, and they wouldn't care if the
Eagles won or lost.

Sometimes he felt guilty leaving his family on Sunday to make
a whole day out of an Eagles' game, but there was another side to
it. He got to spend six or seven hours with his father, sitting next to
him, and that made it justifiable. And if the Eagles won this week,
he'd be taking his father to the Super Bowl. If it sounded silly or
sentimental, that's just the way it was.

"It's what we do," he said.

Ernie Clark grabbed his coat and a seat cushion and put them in
the trunk of the limousine, a white Lincoln with an Eagles flag on
the rear window. Sue Harrigan carried a trash bag full of clothes
to the trunk, and her cousin, Nora Harkins, said, "You movin' in?"

Anne Clark wanted a picture of her husband and her kids, so
they posed in front of the limo, then climbed in. In the bar, Anne
had described her reaction to news that Terrell Owens would need
surgery, making a fist and punching her stomach. But that was
weeks ago, and optimism seemed to be rising today along with
the sun.

"Good luck," Harkins told her cousins. "It's only football."

"It's not only football," Jen Clark said.

Terry Funk sat just behind the driver. She was four and a half months pregnant with twins.

"If the Eagles win, I'm naming them Donovan and Freddie," she said.

A civil engineer, Terry also refereed college basketball games. Yesterday, she had a game in Connecticut and drove home in the snow to make sure she wouldn't miss the Eagles. Six and a half hours, without so much as a restroom stop.

"I'm a camel," she said.

Beer and vodka began to flow, but because she was pregnant, Terry waved off the alcohol.

"Maybe that's the key," she said about the Eagles' playoff hex. "Maybe I need to be sober through this whole run."

She had been offered six hundred and fifty bucks to referee a game at LaSalle University today, but turned it down. The Eagles came first on Sundays. Terry had three kids, all born in autumn, and she had planned all of their christenings around the Eagles, making sure the baptisms were performed when the team was off or away. Her parents had made their first trip to Hawaii this fall, and they scheduled it during the Eagles' bye week.

"First thing you do is look at the schedule," Terry said.

Some people just didn't get it. The worst thing was sitting at a baby shower during an Eagles game, Terry said. "You're like, 'Oh my God.'" Sue missed the Minnesota game last week because her son's high school held its football banquet the same weekend as the NFL playoffs.

"That's moronic," Terry said.

The windows on the limo fogged up in the cold, but the roads were remarkably clear for Philadelphia in the snow. The limo eased down Interstate 95 without the usual clutter of traffic.

It had been the longest week of work that Chris Clark could remember. He tried to stay busy and get to the next day, but it seemed like Tuesday would never become Wednesday. When Owens needed surgery, Chris and his sister Jen, who worked together at the time, had looked at each other and said, "It's over." Then they gave it another thought and said, wait, maybe Freddie Mitchell would bring them through. It kept going back and forth, hope and despair sloshing around like beer in a bottle.

In a way, Chris said, he thought it would be better if the Eagles got to the Super Bowl without Owens.

"He's kind of a hired gun," Chris said. "Don't get me wrong. I'd much rather have him here. But for guys that have been through it the last three or four years, Donovan, Andy Reid, I think it's great they can do it without T.O. He's an interesting guy to Eagles fans, a guy that traditionally in Philadelphia wouldn't play very well. He's a 'me-guy.' He delivered, so people accept it, but the underlying current is, he's a 'me-guy.' That's a tough sell."

Jen kept worrying that another season would just fizzle out, go flat like a tire with a slow leak. She had been nervous for the Minnesota game. This week was better, much easier than last year when she had a horrible, anxious feeling leading up to the Carolina defeat.

"We should be fine," she said. "We'll see."

If the Eagles won the toss, they should kick and play defense, Chris thought. The first quarter was the key. This would be like a hockey game, the team that scored first getting a big emotional lift. If Atlanta scored, the Philadelphia fans might be taken right out of the game.

"Because of where the Eagles have been," Ernie Clark said. "The monkey on their back."

Still, a family that followed the Eagles for more than half a century had to have a huge reservoir of optimism and faith. Otherwise, rooting would be impossible. Chris remembered his father coming home after some god-awful rainy game in the 1970s, and taking his hat off and throwing it against the wall in disgust and, later that night, lightening up and saying, "If we can just win next week, that'll be a step in the right direction."

Chris looked at him, stunned. *Dad, what are you talking about?* But now he was a father, too, and he understood this was what the Eagles demanded, a devotion as wiggly and resilient as Jell-O.

When he was younger, Chris and his father would huddle around a black-and-white television in the kitchen to watch road games, or crane past the mashed potatoes and roast beef during Sunday dinner to see the television in the living room.

When Ernie and Chris returned from home games, Sue said, holding her hands together as if in prayer, it always seemed to be twenty minutes after five and the mood of Sunday dinner depended on whether the Eagles won or lost.

"It had nothing to do with the meatloaf," Jen said.

For Sue's thirteenth birthday, Terry said, they had gone to celebrate at their grandmother's apartment in northeast Philadelphia. The Eagles were on and her father was hooting and hollering at the television and Sue sensed her grandmother's irritation and went outside and sat on the porch, knowing a fight was coming on.

"Now my dad and my grandmother are going at it and we're piling in the car and going home," Terry said, laughing.

The others began picking up the story, finishing each other's sentences in the retelling.

"Where are we going, Dad?"

"Home, so we can watch the game."

"I think my mother asked us to leave," Ernie said.

"We didn't talk for a month," Sue said.

Chris remembered another game, this one a Monday night grudge match against Dallas on September 23, 1974. He was only eleven and it was a school night, so his parents made him stay home with his sisters and their maternal grandmother. Everybody went to bed, but Chris snuck into the living room and turned on the television with no sound and sat with his face near the screen.

In the third quarter, Philadelphia trailed seven to nothing, but Dallas fumbled and Joe Lavender scooped up the ball for the Eagles and ran ninety-six yards for the tying touchdown. The Eagles won on a late field goal and Chris couldn't hold it inside. He began screaming and yelling and he woke up the whole house.

"My grandmother comes running and grabs a broom and starts chasing me, 'If I get my hands on you I'll kill you,'" Chris laughed. "It's funny what you remember. I can't remember the

name of my first-grade teacher, but I'll never forget my grandmother chasing me around the living room with a broom."

With surprisingly light traffic, we reached the stadium before
one thirty, an hour and a half before kickoff. It was too windy and
cold to go inside this early, so we sat for a while next to Citizens
Bank Park, across from the Linc.

Jen Clark stepped outside for a cigarette.

"I'm going with you," Chris said.

He didn't smoke, but he was getting nervous.

"I just hadn't considered the possibility of them losing again,"
Chris said. "Now I'm starting to think about that a little bit."

At the WIP tent, the soldier known to listeners over the months as
Chris from Falluja made an appearance. He had arrived home
from Iraq yesterday. He stood on the stage and dropped and began
doing military-style pushups.

"The first time he called us, he said, 'We faced heavy fire last
night, we lost a couple of guys,'" Angelo Cataldi told me later. "He
was calling from Iraq and he timed it because we were on the air.
I'm like, 'You mean to tell me you're lucky to be alive today,' and
he's like, 'Yeah, but let's get back to the Eagles.' I'm going, 'How's
this possible? This guy's following the Eagles and dodging real
bombs.' It puts things in perspective. I realized I want as little of
the real world as possible. Give me a lot more of this fake stuff that
we do. It's a lot safer."

The Eagles' locker-room was so loose and confident that Jeffrey
Lurie, the owner, joined an impromptu dance party that defensive
end Hugh Douglas held in the training room.

Lurie busted a move, and the players busted out laughing. "He
needs to come to my dance school," receiver Greg Lewis said.

At the moment, Lurie's ungainliness didn't seem to matter. It
was just another sign of certitude in a locker-room full of self-
possession. Later, players would say that they looked in the eyes of
their teammates and saw conviction and knew they had the game
won before it was played.

On Comcast SportsNet's pre-game show, Governor Rendell spoke assuredly on the air, but during off-camera asides, Ray Didinger sensed that he was less certain of victory. Finally, Rendell said he felt anxious, like Gary Cooper waiting for the clock to strike twelve in *High Noon*.

After the Clark family stood for the national anthem, bundled in scarves and hats and bulky coats, layered against another inconsolable loss, Terry Funk noticed her brother Chris leaning down the aisle toward her.

"I'm so nervous I can't stand it," he said.

At kickoff, the temperature was seventeen degrees, with winds from the northwest at twenty-six miles an hour, gusting to thirty-five miles an hour. The wind chill was zero to minus five. The field and the stands were remarkably clear of snow. There would be no fusillade of snowballs hurled at the Atlanta bench. When the wind kicked up, though, squalls of white blew from the upper deck like smoke from a barbecue fire.

Atlanta won the toss and elected to receive. Helen Kleinstuber turned to her husband John and, knowing how grief-ridden he would be in defeat, said, "Regardless of the outcome, will you please walk with me?"

He nodded and said, "I will."

On the game's first play, quarterback Michael Vick lined up in the shotgun for the Falcons and ran to his right. Linebacker Keith Adams smothered him after a gain of two yards. Running back Warrick Dunn tried to punch through at left tackle, but Adams tackled him after a yard. Vick tried right end on third down but defensive tackle Corey Simon quickly dragged him down. The NFL's leading rushing team had tried three plays and managed but five yards. Already, the Falcons were in trouble.

Philadelphia had made a clever tactical decision, flip-flopping its defensive ends. The fleet Jevon Kearse moved to right end to slow Vick, a left-handed quarterback who preferred moving to his left. Derrick Burgess switched to left end, the side he preferred. The effect was to cast a wide net around Vick, forcing him toward the middle, where linebacker Jeremiah Trotter poached and defensive tackles waited with their paunchy agility. Kearse and Burgess would collect three of Philadelphia's four sacks. Unable to run, Vick would be left to throw wildly into the wind. A team that had rushed for more than three hundred yards against St. Louis would gain only ninety-nine against Philadelphia. Vick's meager total would be twenty-six yards. Atlanta was too predictable, too reliant on one player, to defeat a team as resourceful as the Eagles.

"You want to be a one-man show, play golf," Eagles cornerback Sheldon Brown would say.

Atlanta kept Philadelphia's second possession alive with a penalty for illegal use of hands. In that moment, the game began to turn the Eagles' way. Brian Westbrook burst up the middle for thirty-six yards, then Donovan McNabb passed to tight end L. J. Smith for twenty-one yards to the Falcons' four-yard line. Running back Dorsey Levens bulled into the middle, and the play seemed to stop in a pile of bodies, then Levens regained his forward motion, pushed ahead by teammates until they spilled across the goal line. Eagles seven, Atlanta zero.

The crowd erupted and began whirling their white towels, ecstatic but also guarded in their celebration, knowing it was too early to be certain of victory. Two years earlier, Brian Mitchell had returned the opening kickoff of the NFC championship game seventy yards and Duce Staley had muscled to the end zone from twenty yards and Chris Clark had turned to his father and said, "We're going to win." But, of course, the Eagles hadn't won. That early lead against Tampa Bay melted into somber, incredulous defeat and some people had burned their McNabb jerseys in barrel fires as they left Veterans Stadium for the final time. So, while this first touchdown by Levens against Atlanta was a good start, it was only a start—encouraging but insufficient.

I don't think seven-nothing is going to get it done, Ernie Clark thought to himself.

Four minutes into the second quarter, Atlanta had a chance to level the score. On third and three from the Eagles' three-yard line, Vick settled in the shotgun, looked to pass then sprinted up the middle. A lane seemed to open, but it closed quickly as defensive tackle Hollis Thomas rushed forward, lowered his shoulder and slammed Vick with a pummeling tackle back at the five. The Falcons settled for a field goal and trailed seven to three.

Relieved and inspired by Thomas's rattling tackle, the Eagles moved seventy-two yards in nine plays, passing into the starchy wind. McNabb threw forty-five yards to Greg Lewis, who made a brilliant adjustment as the ball hung in the wind and an Atlanta cornerback spun with indecision. From the three-yard line, McNabb passed to tight end Chad Lewis, who caught the ball and tightroped the end zone before rolling out of bounds. The referee signaled touchdown, but Atlanta challenged the call.

Ernie Clark and his son and daughters stood at the opposite end of the stadium, with a distant view, so they dialed their cell phones to the rest of the family, who watched on television.

Did he get both feet down?

I think it's going to stand up.

We think he's out.

There was no consensus, so Terry Funk called her son, Matthew. He was only nine, but his mother joked that he was the little old man of the family. He was adept at these things, at knowing which way the referees would rule, and he had become the family arbiter.

"How's it look?" Terry asked her son.

"Left foot down, right foot close," Matt reported. "I think it's going to stand."

Chris Clark wasn't so sure. In this moment of uncertainty, he remembered other moments, so many of them, when calls had gone against the Eagles and hopefulness had fluttered away into ominous reversal.

"Oh, no," Chris said, turning to his dad, thinking, *What bad is going to happen?*

For once, nothing bad happened. Replays confirmed that Matt Funk was right. Lewis did drag both feet in bounds, and the referee raised his hands and the crowd roared and Terry Funk shouted, "Never a doubt."

Fourteen to three seemed a solid lead, but it proved a rickety advantage. Atlanta counterpunched immediately, driving seventy yards in five plays, assisted by an Eagles penalty for roughing the passer. From the ten, Dunn skittered off right tackle to the end zone, the defense undisciplined and ragged for one costly instant. Philadelphia fourteen, Atlanta ten.

Ernie Clark wasn't worried, but he was disappointed the margin wasn't greater. He didn't want a close game in the fourth quarter with Atlanta holding the ball and him holding his breath. *My heart can only take so much after all these years.*

At halftime, Brian Dawkins gathered his teammates and reminded them that penalties had gifted both of the Falcons' scoring drives. Earlier in the week, he had cautioned against playing uptight, saying, "When we're loose, we're lethal." Now he had one final exhortation.

"We gave them everything," Dawkins said. "They not gettin' nothing else."

On that Atlanta touchdown drive, Vick had thrown for thirty-one yards over the middle to tight end Alge Crumpler. Dawkins roamed from his safety position and pile-drived his body into the Atlanta tight end, punishing him to the ground in awkward collapse, hitting him so viciously that it seemed a miracle of concentration for Crumpler to hold onto the ball.

The hit sent a message. *It's not going to be flag football when you come across the middle.* Crumpler got to his feet, but he would not catch another pass until the game's final, inconsequential minutes, and the Falcons would grow just as wobbly as their tight end.

John Kleinstuber had been hit like this once, as a tight end in high school. When he came back to the huddle, a teammate asked if he was okay, and he said, sure, then he noticed that everything was green. All the other colors had been drained out of the spectrum. That's how Alge Crumpler must have felt, John thought. Everything going green.

How you doin? John said to himself in his best Rocky Balboa greeting.

The second half started and Tim Kelly had a conflicted thought. He couldn't feel the toes on his right foot. *I'm going to lose a toe today,* he thought to himself. *It'd be bad, but it'd be kinda cool to say I lost it at an Eagles game.* Then he came to his senses. He got up and went to the bathroom, bending his toes, walking around until the feeling returned in his extremities.

Meanwhile, Philadelphia's lead began to expand. David Akers kicked a field of thirty-one yards. Dawkins intercepted a pass intended for Crumpler and Akers kicked another field goal, this one from thirty-four yards. Soon the third quarter became the fourth. Philadelphia twenty, Atlanta ten.

People began turning to each other and saying this year felt different. Victory seemed inevitable. But ten minutes remained. Chris Clark wanted more affirmation. Weird things could happen. He turned and looked at his father and sisters and said, "Donovan, one drive. All we need is one drive and this thing is over."

McNabb ran around right end, then passed for twelve yards and twenty more. He sprinted up the middle, dinked a short pass, then found Chad Lewis again in the end zone from the two-yard line. Eagles twenty-seven, Atlanta ten. Less than three and a half minutes remained. As Lewis fell in the end zone, a whole stadium stood on its feet, strangers hugging and jumping, their faces full of disbelief and acquittal and liberation at victory gained and failure avoided and history defeated.

Lewis ran off the field as Dorsey Levens screamed, "We're going, we're going," but something was wrong. Lewis looked at Freddie Mitchell and said, "I broke my foot."

"You didn't," Mitchell said in a moment caught by NFL Films.

"I broke it," Lewis said.

He had suffered ligament damage that would keep him out of the Super Bowl, but no one else knew it at the time, certainly not the fans who were screaming and jumping and hugging in their bundled, insulated exhilaration. Jen Clark kept saying, "Unbelievable." Terry Funk felt a jumble of emotions. She felt almost sorry for Vick, so much talent as yet unformed, and she felt a pang of sympathy for Jim Kelly, the Buffalo quarterback who had played in four Super Bowls without winning. *How did he keep playing. Did he think in his mind he could win that fourth time?* The moment seemed almost surreal, dislocated, just as it had seemed when the doctor told her she was having twins. She felt nothing for a moment, then she felt more than she ever thought she would feel. She always thought this moment would come, but wondered if it ever truly would.

"Is it better having been on the other end three times?" she asked her father.

A longtime neighbor spoke to her from a row behind, saying, "I can't believe we win and you have to go through it without drinking," and Terry thought, no, this was better. At the Tampa Bay game two years earlier, there had been miserable anger and words, a guy screaming at her father and her screaming back. She didn't want any of that again.

"I think the key is being sober and enjoying it," Terry told the neighbor.

She nudged her sister, Jen, and they looked at their father and he was crying. And they began to cry. Some days, Terry thought it would be easier just to stay home and watch the Eagles from the couch, but who knew how long the whole family would be together? It was moments like this, the look on her father's face, that made coming to the games worthwhile. Her brother, Chris, had a look of delirium, his tension uncoiled, worry having evaporated like sweat. He had tears in his eyes, too. After all these years of ups and downs, he felt a satisfied equilibrium. *Finally, we're winners. So many people out there are going to be calling Philadelphia fans and the Eagles winners.*

Counting down the final seconds, six, five, four, three, two, one, Merrill Reese, the Eagles' radio announcer, said in his baritone, his body all voice and jubilation, "The Eagles, after twenty-four years, are going to the Super Bowl!"

In two days, Ernie Clark would turn seventy.

"Not a bad birthday present," Sue Harrigan told her father.

"A great present," he said.

In the north end zone, Shaun Young began crying, too. He had looked at the clock with five minutes, thirty-five seconds left, and the tears began to come, and now the players came over to high-five the fans and to see their families and Shaun stood at the railing to meet them. Tight end Mike Bartrum pounded on his chest and pointed at Shaun and Shaun pounded on his own chest and said, "Thank you, thank you, thank you." Fullback Josh Parry hugged his brother Neil, who lost part of his leg after a horrific college football injury and came back to play with a prosthetic leg. "You're the only reason I'm on the field," Josh told Neil. The brothers hugged for what seemed like two minutes, and Shaun stood next to them and started bawling. *I'm all Niagara Falls here.* People banged on Shaun's shoulder pads and hugged him and he looked up at all the cheering and the towel waving and the release from losing and thought, *It's like a wet, sloppy piece of clay was put into a kiln and out came a piece of pottery, nice and glossy and everything. Artwork, pure artwork.*

Jevon Kearse ran to the Eagles' bench and took a bow before the crowd. Freddie Mitchell carried his boxing-style "People's Champ" belt aloft, his hair braided and bushed into a 'Frohawk. McNabb slipped on a victory T-shirt and hat and Owens kept jumping and whooping and chest-bumping his teammates, his repaired ankle apparently sedated by victory. Brian Dawkins climbed a makeshift stage on the field and shouted, "Hallelujah" and the crowd howled in deliverance under a nearly full moon.

Andy Reid, wet from a Gatorade soaking, said yes, he thought Owens would play in the Super Bowl. Confetti cannons boomed a glittery shower and fireworks exploded in feathery arcs from the rim of stadium and Terry Funk turned to her father and said, "You think they had all those fireworks stored up there last year and didn't use it?"

Ernie Clark was elated, but tired, too, standing all those hours, his ankles beginning to talk to him, and his daughter Jen helped him toward the limousine. He needed a kidney transplant two years earlier, and Jen had donated one of her kidneys. She was the youngest child, and she looked after her father at Eagles games as Ernie had once looked after his kids. They reached the limo and champagne began to flow.

"It doesn't mean everything," Ernie said to me as I reached him on his cell phone, with the perspective of age and two more grandkids on the way. "Somebody asked if it was worth the wait, and I guess that's true in some respects. When you win, you say it was worth the wait. I feel great."

Linebacker Ike Reese, wearing a championship T-shirt in the cold and a breath strip across his nose, walked off the field and said into a camera, "This is the greatest feeling in the world. You know who I feel happiest for? The fans in this city, who have been called losers, who have been called whiners, who have been called all the names in the book. It's the happiest I've ever been in my life. All the pain from the last three years doesn't add up to the joy I feel right now. We persevered. We did it. We gave this city another opportunity to get to the Super Bowl, and we're going to cash it in for them when we get to Jacksonville."

In the parking lot, a fan jumped on Shaun Young's back and Shaun carried him for what seemed like a hundred yards. People were high-fiving the cops. Shaun got into his truck and drove up and down Broad Street, honking his horn, pumping his fist, getting out to hug a few people. They came out in the street by the hundreds and rocked his truck and, at that moment, he realized it was time to get out of there before they started dribbling his vehicle like a basketball. In northeast Philadelphia, two thousand fans rushed into the intersection of Cottman and Frankford Avenues. In South Philly, Danny Grimes, a sixteen-year-old, ran up Broad Street with no shirt on, explaining to the *Daily News* that the capital E carved into his chest hair was backward because he had shaved in a mirror.

As John and Helen Kleinstuber left the stadium, Helen thanked her husband for walking with her this year, not ten or twenty glum paces ahead as he had a year earlier after the Carolina defeat. On the way out, they saw two couples wearing Atlanta gear from head to toe, and then they noticed something even more remarkable.

No one said a word to them. At any other time, these visiting fans would have been serenaded with chants of "Asshole, asshole," but now they walked along in their red-and-black outfits and Eagles fans ignored them in their bliss.

In the Eagles' locker-room, the team huddled around Jeffrey Lurie, the owner, and he said, "It's not just about the Super Bowl; it's about winning it." Doors were opened to the news media and Jeremiah Trotter screamed, "We're going to Jacksonville. Could you have imagined it? We're going to the Super Bowl." At his locker, Freddie Mitchell sat limp, exhausted by victory. Later, Donovan McNabb, who had been nearly flawless during the game, dressed impeccably in a dark pinstripe suit and sunglasses and told reporters, "There's no relief for me. I have relief after the Super Bowl. I set a goal to win the Super Bowl, and that's where I'm going with it."

At his news conference, Andy Reid said he wanted to credit a few people, first of all the fans.

"They were incredible," he said. "And they were so loud and obnoxious when they needed to be."

One of the last to leave the locker-room was Reese, who gave a final shout-out to the fans for a fealty that was rude but durable.

"This city has endured a lot of heartbreaks, a lot of disappointments and a lot of letdowns for their sports teams," Reese said. "To still be able to stick in there with us, I just felt like they deserved the game, even more so than some of the players. You have some players that have been here from the start of this thing, but as players, we come and go. This city is going to be here. That's who this team belongs to, the city, and they're the ones who deserve it today. We still have one more gift to give them because this is just part of what we wanted to do."

Governor Rendell brought out two bottles of champagne on *Post Game Live* and sang "Fly Eagles Fly" with host Michael Barkann and panelist Vaughn Hebron. Ray Didinger demurred, the journalist in him forbidding him from popping the cork on any celebration.

Wearing a gray sweater, Rendell held up what appeared to be a measuring cup for his toast and said, "To the Birds."

"There's nothing like sports, and in this town nothing like football, that brings people together," Rendell said. "Black, white, Hispanic, Asian, it doesn't matter. Rich, poor. The biggest executive in town, talking to the shoeshine guy, it doesn't matter. They're equal. They're both Eagles fans. Nothing lifts a community like this. This is going to be an awesome next two weeks. This community is going to be floating on air."

Later, New England would defeat Pittsburgh, forty-one to twenty-seven, in the AFC championship game, setting up a match against the Eagles in the Super Bowl. With the Steelers eliminated, the governor was off the hook politically.

When Chris Clark finally got home, he could not stop saying, "We won." Over and over, he kept saying it, as if to convince himself it had really happened. After what seemed like the sixtieth time, his wife, Deb, told him, "Enough already, I get it. I'm happy for you. Now let's go to bed."

Chris was going to the Super Bowl with his dad. Ernie Clark had been reluctant, wanting to watch the game with his entire family, but this had been a dream for Chris, to take his dad to a Super Bowl with the Eagles in it. He had told his father, "Look, Dad, they'll understand. You gotta go."

Now they were going.

On my way home, I caught a cab at Thirtieth Street Station and it was mostly empty, except for stragglers headed for New York and Washington. A dozen or so people came through, in a kind of conga line, singing the Eagles fight song, walking in one door and out the other.

Shaun Young drove home and blew his horn in the parking lot of his apartment complex and began shouting "E-A-G-L-E-S, Eagles!" A few people came out on their balconies and opened their doors and joined him in the cheering. He got something to eat and watched the end of the Pittsburgh–New England game. His cell phone kept ringing, and he answered the first couple of calls, then he let his voice mail pick up. The ring on his phone was the Eagles fight song and he let the calls go so he could hear the song play all the way through.

20

"Finally!" screamed the front-page headline in the *Inquirer*.

"Heaven Freezes Over," announced the *Daily News*.

Melissa Kelly woke up at six thirty at her home in Havertown. First thing she did was turn on the television. *I had to make sure it really happened.* Her husband, Tim, had the day off. He dreamed all night about the Eagles and when he awakened at ten, he thought to himself, *We did win, right?* He called his brother, Ed, who also kept having to remind himself that the Eagles prevailed. For three straight years, everything had gone wrong in the NFC championship game. They weren't sure how to react now that everything had gone right.

Tim's father-in-law, Butch DeLuca, arrived at his deli at six thirty, a king awaiting his court. The Eagles were in the Super Bowl. All day, customers would be coming in to congratulate him as if he scored the touchdowns and called the plays. They knew how much this meant. How could they not? The license plate on the front of his van said "Number One Eagles Fan." And the walls of his deli were covered with Eagles jerseys and miniature helmets and photographs. They knew all right. They knew.

"I think they win the Super Bowl," Butch said, standing behind the counter, scrambling eggs. "I still don't think they played their perfect game."

It killed him to miss the game, Butch said. Killed him. But he had to stay at the store. Nobody wanted to work in that weather. Anyway, his son and daughter went. That made his day.

"Here's South Philly Louie," Butch said in a singsong voice as the bread man, Louie Fareri, walked into the deli.

"Step on up, baby, it's about time," Fareri said. "They been waitin' for this the longest time, twenty-four years. It's the best thing that ever happened to Philly. Best thing that ever happened to the fans. We been losers for the past twenty-four years."

"Not anymore," Butch said.

"Not anymore, man," Fareri said. "They can't say nothin' negative about us anymore."

Butch thought the Eagles could win the Super Bowl, even without Terrell Owens.

"No, they can't win without T.O.," Bill Pergolini, one of the morning regulars, said.

"They can win without him," Butch said. "They got this far."

Another customer, Sam Nangle, came in to get a paper and said it was nice the way the fans reacted, no snowballs, no riots.

"People acted civil," Nangle said.

"Civil as they ever been," said Louie the Bread Man.

Louie was shocked to learn that Butch had missed the game.

He went over a friend's house and watched the game in hi-def, Butch said. Felt like he was there. He could see sweat flying off the players' faces, the picture was so clear. Every time the Eagles did something, he called his son, Brian, and daughter, Melissa. He must have called ten times, yelling into the phone, "We're gonna do it! We're gonna do it!" His daughter got very emotional and once she started she didn't stop, screaming and crying into the phone, "Dad, we're going to win, we're going to the Super Bowl!"

His son was crying, too, the victory a momentary release from the grief of these past months, losing his girlfriend to cancer. *Through the struggles of the year, something good happened.* And Butch started crying, too, sitting there at his friend's house with beer and chips and chicken wings, watching the television and his eyes welling up.

"I shed a lotta tears," Butch said. "You know how long I been waitin' for this?"

Butch stood beneath the television in the back corner of his

deli, watching highlights from Sunday, and he kept saying, "Unbelievable."

"Even the players were crying," he said. "We waited a long
time for this, a long time."

Pergolini pumped his fist as he made his own omelet of ham,
mushrooms, eggs and cheese. He wondered when his grandsons
would call, the ones who lived in Atlanta and thought the world of
Michael Vick.

"When I get them little gook kids of mine, I wanna hear their
story," he said. "Bullshit, them little mothers. You notice they don't
call. 'How they gonna catch him, Pop-Pop?' How about when they
threw him in the stands?"

"Unbelievable," Butch said again. He grabbed his life-size
cardboard cutout of Donovan McNabb and put it outside the deli
to greet the customers as they walked in.

"Whaddya think, Nance?" he said to Nancy VanTrieste.

"I'm happy it's New England," VanTrieste said. "Pittsburgh
slapped us around, Butch."

Another customer, Matt Freind, asked Butch if he was going to
the Super Bowl. Everybody wanted to know if he was going.

"If I get tickets, I don't give a damn if anybody works, I'm
going," Butch said. "I'll close the place down if I have to. I've never
been to one. I may not get to another one. I'm fifty-nine years old.
I'd love to go."

Somebody said the Eagles were lucky against Atlanta. That set
him off.

"I don't want to hear the word lucky," Butch said. "Lucky, my ass."

Gene Kelly, another customer, asked Pergolini if he thought
the Eagles could defeat New England.

"No," Pergolini said. "I'd love them to win, but these guys are
too good."

Butch stood at the grill in a black sweatshirt and jeans, singing,
"We're going to the Super Bowl, we're going to the Super Bowl."

"I'm happy they got as far as they got, but you gotta put the
icing on the cake," he said. "I think they can, honest to God. I
think they can play better."

When the season started, Kelly didn't think the Eagles could reach the Super Bowl. Hey, everybody had an opinion. His was wrong, but he was happy for the Eagles. They deserved it. It's always your Washingtons, your Giants, your Dallases, getting to the Big Dance. Now it was Philadelphia's turn. The city needed a winner after all these years of disappointment.

"Hey, how about Johnny Carson dying?" Kelly asked no one in particular. "I didn't even know the man was sick."

Then he wanted to know whether Pergolini believed that McNabb could pull out a victory in the Super Bowl.

"You think Buckwheat's going to be able to throw the ball to him?" Kelly said of McNabb and Owens.

"Don't worry about that," said Pergolini, who considered McNabb the NFL's third-best quarterback, behind Tom Brady of New England and Peyton Manning of Indianapolis. "He'll get the ball to him. He'll get a couple of interference calls with them guys."

At the least, Owens should free up the Eagles' other receivers, Kelly said.

"I change my mind," Pergolini said. "If T.O. plays, they got a shot. If he don't play, they don't have no shot at all. They lose by three touchdowns if he don't play."

"Not that much," Kelly said. "You think they're that much better than we are? No way."

If only he could get tickets, with all his son had been through, that would be great, Butch said. If he had to rent a Winnebago, he'd do it. Just to go.

"Are you kidding?" Butch said. "I'd close the store. I wouldn't give a damn. Let's face it. Who knows when this is going to happen again, you know what I mean? I waited a long time for this, boy, a long time."

At eight in the morning, Andy Reid called WIP and asked Angelo Cataldi if Shaun Young still had his face painted green. Shaun happened to be standing right there. He had met Reid a dozen times or so. At a pep rally before the season, the Eagles' coach had bear-hugged him and said, "What's going on there, crazy man?"

and had pounded on his shoulder pads. At the time, Shaun told him, "I'm telling you, this is our year." Now it was the Eagles' year, and Shaun spoke to Reid over the air and said, "Thank you, thank you, thank you."

Dave Spadaro, who ran the Eagles' website, called and said this moment was bigger than his marriage and the birth of his kids.

A seventy-four-year-old widow named Ann phoned and said, "My husband passed away nine years ago and I said the rosary and said, 'Come on Ed, this is it. Let's do it this year.' Thank you, God. I jumped up and screamed. I'm by myself. My sons were at the game, my daughters were at their houses. I said to my beagle Yogi, 'This is it, we're going baby, we're going all the way.'"

At five thirty, I met up with Shaun Young at Chickie's and Pete's, the South Philadelphia restaurant where Angelo Cataldi did his Monday night television show. "That game was the greatest moment in my life," Shaun told me. "Outside of anything to do with family, it was the greatest."

He still had not slept. "I can't," he said in a shredded voice, dressed in his shoulder pads and a black Brian Dawkins jersey. "Adrenaline is running through me. It's grand rapids right now."

If the Eagles lost the Super Bowl, it wouldn't be a successful season, Shaun said, but it wouldn't hurt as much as those three losses in the NFC championship game.

"The monkey's off our back," Shaun said. "We got one step further, but we have one more game to go. I'm not happy just to get there. I want to win it. But I won't be livid, won't be pissed off, if they lose. I mean, if they throw up a goose egg, if they went out there and crapped the bed, it would be very disappointing. It wouldn't be successful, but it wouldn't hurt as much as the last three years."

Pete Ciarrocchi, the restaurant's owner, sat at the bar in the VIP room, and said he felt an odd dislodgment. Everybody else was giddy with victory, but, to tell the truth, Pete had been happier after a few regular-season victories than he had been at the NFC championship game.

"As the game went on and got close to the end, I knew they were going to win," he said. "It was inevitable. I hadn't had a beer or anything. I was trying to get that emotion I usually have at an Eagles game. I spoke to my wife on the phone. She said, 'Are you going crazy?' I said, 'No, I'm not.' And I tried to make myself go crazy. I spoke to a couple of other people today, and they weren't going crazy either. We didn't know how to deal with it. They sent confetti up and music was playing and fireworks were going off and I didn't know what I expected. I didn't know what I wanted to feel. Wishing for something you didn't know what it was, and now you're like, 'Oh.' I couldn't be happier, I know that. I feel happy, but I'm not overwhelmed. I don't know why. I've been a season-ticket holder since 1978. I went to Super Bowl after Super Bowl. I don't know what it is. Inside, I'm happy. There's no reason not to be happy. The Eagles all come back here after games. I said to one of the executives, 'I don't know why I'm not happy.' He said, 'Maybe because there's nothing to complain about.' I said, 'No, I'm not a complainer.' The last three years were really tough, two of the last three at home, we lost. Maybe that was it. I was singing, jumping up and down. I was making myself, it wasn't natural. I wanted to give. It wasn't there. Maybe it was the snow. No hoopla for two days. Everybody was talking about the storm. Maybe you need a buildup. I was faking like I was overwhelmed. I wasn't over-whelmed. I can't put a finger on it, though."

Out in the restaurant, Ron Fasano, known as Eagle Elvis, stood in his green jumpsuit and sideburns and watched Cataldi's show. He had played college football at Kutztown University. He didn't drink or smoke. The Eagles were his vice.

"They only have to win it all once before I die," Eagle Elvis said. "I'm just looking for one. I'm not greedy. A couple'll be all right, but you know, I just want that one. I'm waiting for that euphoric high. I cried tears of joy yesterday. It's not like I was play-ing, but you got that high. Your body tingles, you get the jitters, the happiness, you're hugging everybody next to you."

The VIP room grew crowded, and Shaun stood off to the side, talk-ing with Gervase Peterson, a local guy who had been a participant on *Survivor* and knew something about squeezing a sixteenth minute from his fifteen minutes of fame. He wore a green Eagles jersey, number nine, with his first name across the back. Peterson had an idea for Shaun. Shaun had an endorsement deal with SEPTA, the local transportation authority. He wore a SEPTA patch on some of his Eagles jerseys, took the train to a couple of games. The deal was nothing to retire on, but it paid a few bills.

"You tell SEPTA you want a bus to go down to Jacksonville," Peterson told Shaun. "It's 'The Road to Jacksonville with Shaun Young.' SEPTA throws you a couple bucks, you take a bus trip down to Florida, you're there at the Super Bowl. You bring a bunch of Eagles fans with you. Who wouldn't want to go with Shaun Young, one of the Dirty Thirty, to Jacksonville to see the Eagles play in the Super Bowl?"

Peterson thought Shaun was "borderline psychotic" when he put on his shoulder pads and painted his face. He meant it in an admiring way.

"I think he pops a blood vessel every time he starts talking his talk," Peterson said. "He's one of the true, consummate fans. This guy eats and breathes Eagles. Healthy? It may not be, but here in Philly, I guess it is."

Shaun didn't know if he liked Peterson's idea. That wasn't his style, to go in and demand a city bus. He did have something in common with Peterson, though, Shaun said. He was also picked to be on *Survivor*, he said, but an injury forced him to cancel.

What happened? I asked him.

"Trash truck ran over my foot."

We spoke for a while, and then I left Shaun at the bar, talking to a woman wearing a fedora, high heels and a jersey Eagles dress. One long night was turning into another.

"I date but I don't have a steady girlfriend," Shaun had told me earlier. "I've got some dates because of this mystery-man-behind-the-makeup thing. Some interesting situations. Once, we went out to dinner and were hanging out, watching movies. Things went to a good level. As it was getting there, she saw the shoulder pads sitting up on the closet shelf. She asked me if she could wear the pads, you know what I mean? I said, 'Whatever,' and she grabbed them and threw the pads on and we did okay."

21

Tuesday, January 25

After two days, Shaun Young finally got some sleep. But he didn't win the Super Bowl lottery held for Eagles season-ticket holders. Now he had a choice to make. Stay in Philly and watch the game on television or go to Jacksonville and hope to land a ticket there.

"I'm torn," Shaun said, but added, "It's killing me to think I won't be down there."

John and Helen Kleinstuber also finished out of luck in the lottery. If somebody came through with free tickets, they'd be there. If John had to pay, he didn't see it happening. He didn't have a spare ten grand to spend on one weekend.

"But I have my Eagles shirt on, and I'm not taking it off," he said.

Wednesday, January 26

Nine days to Wing Bowl, eleven days to Super Bowl.

A page-one headline in the *Inquirer* said, "Owens May Defy Doctor." Mark Myerson, the Baltimore orthopedist who implanted two screws to stabilize the ligament damage in Terrell Owens's ankle, told the paper that T.O. was vastly improved but not fit to play in the Super Bowl. He would not give him medical clearance.

"Everybody wants him to be able to play, but in the long run it's not going to benefit him," Myerson told the *Inquirer*.

Owens had trained on a treadmill in a swimming pool, but had not tested his ankle with cutting maneuvers on a football field. Still, Myerson expected the receiver to defy his recommendation. "I'm spiritually healed," Owens told reporters at a Sixers game on Monday.

At practice today, it seemed increasingly likely that Owens would attempt to play against the Patriots, even if he had to sign some kind of liability waiver, letting the team off the financial hook if he aggravated the injury. Rick Burkholder, the Eagles' trainer, said at a news conference that the team understood Myerson's position.

"It's just that our risk-reward is different than his risk-reward," Burkholder said.

It was an archetypal clash of interests—a player's health versus his determination to play in the sport's biggest game and his team's desire to have him in the lineup.

"Are you going to put your career in jeopardy?" Brian Westbrook, the Eagles' running back said, weighing in his mind what every player would. "Is this my one shot to play in the Super Bowl? Is it worth it?"

Sonya Thomas, the reigning Wing Bowl champion, had no such distracting medical issues. A native of South Korea who lived in Alexandria, Virginia, she would return to defend her title. At ninety-nine pounds, Sonya was a gastronomic wonder. A year ago, she won by eating 167 chicken wings in thirty minutes. Now she was back, with a manager and an attitude.

"Since Wing Bowl, I destroy all food events," Sonya told Angelo Cataldi on WIP.

This was almost too much for another contestant, Hank the Tank, who had two problems with Sonya. First, she was a woman. Second, she wasn't from Philadelphia. In this parochial town, outsiders were viewed with suspicion, especially skinny outsiders who went through chicken wings the way beavers went through logs.

"This is supposed to be for fat guys," Hank the Tank told me in the WIP studio.

Still, he had learned a lesson from Sonya, who did not appear to have an ounce of flab on her body. Hank the Tank was six-foot-three and 260 pounds, a longshoreman with a goatee and a shaved head. He had lost a hundred pounds since the last Wing Bowl. With less fat pressing on his abdomen, he figured, his stomach would stretch more easily to accommodate the load of chicken wings in his belly.

His theory had been put through rigorous scientific scrutiny. A week ago, he had eaten 120 wings in fourteen minutes at a strip club, while getting a lap dance.

"Way I figure it, if I could concentrate while getting a lap dance, I'll be able to concentrate more at Wing Bowl," Hank the Tank said. "And the lap dance felt really good, so it all worked out."

Hank the Tank was on a mission, both personal and civic. He had been briefly declared the winner of Wing Bowl in 2000, then relegated to second place for not sufficiently cleaning the meat from the bone. He had violated one of the two cardinal rules of Wing Bowl: If you don't eat, you get beat.

In 2001, Hank suffered a meltdown and threw a pitcher of water in the face of Wing Bowl Commissioner Eric Gregg, a former National League umpire and a man familiar with life's weightier issues. Hank the Tank was banned for life, but the ban was later rescinded after a petition drive, and here he was, looking to claim a title he believed was rightfully his.

Sure, Sonya Thomas was a great eater, but he didn't fully trust her. She never seemed to tire. She was always hungry. "I don't know if she has a tapeworm, I don't know what she's got," Hank the Tank said. "Seriously, have you ever seen a little girl eat like that? I've seen some big girls eat, but I've never seen a little skinny girl eat. Asians, maybe they got a secret over there."

Hank had his own methods. To strengthen his jaws, he had been chewing gum six or seven hours a day. Sugarless, of course. The man was a slavish devotee of the Atkins diet. Each morning with breakfast, Hank the Tank drank a gallon of water in less than ten minutes to expand his stomach. His boss didn't like the numerous bathroom breaks Hank needed later on the docks, but he understood. At night, Hank ate three pounds of chicken and drank another gallon of water, all in noble pursuit of a cherished title. Let the Eagles dream of the Super Bowl. He would be the Henry VIII of chicken wings.

"I'm not going to lie to you," Hank the Tank said. "It's very, very painful, but to achieve a goal, sometimes you gotta go through pain, whether you want to get a doctor's degree or eat chicken wings."

Hank was tired of outsiders winning Wing Bowl. He was determined to bring the title back to Philly. Could there be a finer sports weekend, a Wing Bowl title for Philly next Friday and a Super Bowl title for the Eagles next Sunday?

"This has a little bit of it all, it has exotic dancers, and we're the second-fattest city in the country, so we got fat guys eating chicken wings," Hank the Tank said. "I'm going to bring the fame and glory back to the fat guy this year."

Then he would lend his Wing Bowl championship belt to the Eagles and let them hang it next to the Super Bowl trophy.

"It'll be known as the greatest weekend in Philadelphia sports history," Hank the Tank said. "I'll drink 'til Valentine's Day."

Another contestant, known as Sloth, phoned WIP and said he looked forward to competing against Hank the Tank. He especially looked forward to the bottle of V.O. they might drink beforehand.

Perhaps, Angelo Cataldi reminded Sloth, the whiskey had accounted for his unfortunate violation four years earlier of the second cardinal rule of Wing Bowl: If you heave, you leave.

"Is your wife aware of how you became famous in Wing Bowl?" Cataldi asked.

"Absolutely," Sloth said.

"The projectile vomit in Wing Bowl Nine?"

"Matter of fact, a couple months into dating, I showed her the video," Sloth said. "She almost dumped me."

"But she's willing to see you make a comeback four years later," Cataldi said, "even though you apparently have this unfortunate reflex?"

"You know, a good woman stands behind her man," Sloth said.

"In your case," cohost Rhea Hughes said, "I'd stand far behind."

Bob Blutinger, a referee and judge for Wing Bowl, was at WIP this morning. His favorite story happened two years ago. A pair of contestants, one named Don Lerman, the other called Coon Dog, sat discussing the eating stunts they had performed to qualify. The only thing he didn't like about Wing Bowl, Lerman said, was the sauce slathered on the wings. The sauce offended his delicate palate.

Coon Dog looked at him and said, "You ate three fucking cans of dog food to get into this contest and you're worried about the sauce?"

After his show ended, Cataldi held a staff meeting for the final planning of Wing Bowl. He wanted at least fifty Wingettes on stage to serve plates of food to contestants and provide eye candy for the audience of twenty-three thousand.

"A hundred breasts," Angelo said. "I don't go below one hundred breasts."

This would be different from the previous twelve Wing Bowls. Now that Philadelphia was in the Super Bowl, Wing Bowl would become a giant pep rally. It had great possibilities for hilarity and mayhem. Last year, Coon Dog had incited the fans, holding up two garbage can lids as shields. The lids bore the score of Carolina's victory over the Eagles in the NFC championship game. Fourteen to three. The spectators, with grief marinated in alcohol, pelted Coon Dog with a hail of cans and bottles. Never had so much beer been wasted in Philadelphia.

"I get nervous every year," Angelo told me later in his office. "We really have no idea what we're doing. We don't know how to run this event. We never have. We hold our breath for four hours and hope nobody dies. It kind of runs itself, or doesn't run itself, and we get to the end, and, well, nobody died, so it was a good Wing Bowl."

Philadelphia Magazine described Wing Bowl as the city's "grandest, goofiest spectacle," a bacchanal that consumed "every distinctive Philadelphia trait—our passion, our elevation of the lowbrow into high art, our self-loathing abandon—and hurled it back out in a gesture of vomitous, drunken love."

Or, as Hank the Tank told me, "When we get done, we go to the strip clubs, people recognize you and they buy you beer and lap dances. You're a star for a day."

WIP's celebration of the ordinary working stiff reached its apotheosis at Wing Bowl. Angelo said he began to side with the fans in 1984 when he traveled to Arizona for the *Inquirer* as Leonard Tose and his daughter, Susan Fletcher, considered moving the Eagles to Phoenix. "I still get flashbacks to '84," Angelo said. "It was like they were stealing the sport from the city. I met the people who were stealing it. They were assholes. They didn't give a shit. They had Susan Fletcher. She was ready to move the team and make all this money and nobody gave a shit about the fans in Philadelphia."

Wing Bowl also exhibited another facet of Angelo's genius. His sports talk show succeeded precisely because he didn't talk about sports. Not in the predictable, dull way of most talk shows, taking an issue and beating it all day the way Indian women did their laundry on the Ganges. What made his show work was humor, made more pungent and rhythmically knife-edged by his New England accent.

"Anybody with a limited brain can do a sports talk show," cohost Al Morganti said. "A jackass knows everything about sports. What's hard to do is mix in humor. Anything funny we do takes fifty times the work that it takes to break down a football game."

Each weekday morning, Cataldi awakened at three, arrived at WIP at three thirty or three forty-five, filling pages of a legal pad as he planned his show, which ran from five thirty to ten. In the afternoons, at home, he spent three hours on the Internet, reading voraciously, the diligent research of a reporter still in him.

His style made him a popular but polarizing figure. Even

within families, opinions of him were conflicted. Anne Clark thought Angelo "to be quite a character, very funny," while her daughter, Terry Funk, said, "He's a very intelligent guy who sold out to the entertainment business. I don't call it sports. It's chicks in bikinis, boys and their toys."

Some of his former colleagues viewed Angelo's radio career as a contradiction, even a betrayal, of his newspaper career. They doubted whether he believed much of what he said, and considered his ranting and raving to be nothing more than condescending, pot-stirring shtick.

"My sense of it is, when we covered the Eagles together, he was from out of town and he just thought Philadelphians were idiots," said Phil Sheridan, a columnist for the *Inquirer*. "When he got the radio gig, he just knew what buttons to press to get the most reaction out of people he thought were not as smart as he was. His whole career is based on getting as much reaction out of people who aren't as smart as he thinks he is."

Joe Weachter, Angelo's producer, considered this a harsh assessment. He did not see Angelo as disingenuous, but rather as someone who connected with his audience because he possessed the same sense of drama and impulsiveness that Eagles fans did.

"What he cares most about is the voice that no one else cares about—the fans," Weachter said.

Morganti, who also worked with Angelo at the *Inquirer*, said he saw no contradiction between Cataldi's newspaper and radio career. Angelo still put in the same effort and energy, Morganti said, even though his job was now to entertain more than to inform. Angelo always went nuts over nonsense, Morganti said. When they traveled together covering hockey, he said, it would take Angelo forty-five minutes to check into a hotel because he didn't like the way the pillow was fluffed.

"He sees the man on the grassy knoll, no matter what the landscape," Morganti said. "He really believes the man is there. He sees drama in everything. A referee can't just make a bad call. It has to be something in his background that made him make this bad call."

Morganti hit upon a fundamental aspect of Angelo's personality. He did not see the world as a natural evolution of events. He saw instead conspiracy and sabotage, the clandestine over the open and innocent. Once, Angelo had his neighbor Morganti hauled in by the cops. Morganti had sent a prank letter saying that radon gas had been discovered on Angelo's property. When Angelo began receiving speeding tickets from the police in Medford, New Jersey, he became convinced that this was retaliation for his treatment of Morganti. He feuded with the cops on the air.

Years ago, he also had a public blowup with the teenage boyfriend of his daughter. He didn't have a reliable edit button in his head, Angelo said. The content of his show was calculated, he said, but what came out of his mouth was not. As he saw it, his radio show was an extension of his high school days in the senior lounge in Providence, Rhode Island. He was a nerd, vice president of the chess club who could never unseat the president. He'd walk around, making critical comments about athletes, for no one's pleasure but his own.

"Screw the players," Angelo told me. "I don't care. Maybe I do envy their skill, but they should envy my ability to criticize them, because I started young."

And his on-air lechery? That also came from his days as a chess club geek, Angelo said. The idea that a younger woman would pay attention to him, even though she was only doing it to get on the radio, seemed somehow cool. Only his wife, Gail, knew how truly dull he could be, Angelo said.

"We're all dreamers," Angelo said. "It's like I'm dreaming this girl would actually give a shit about me. A part of me is really thinking she might, even though it's ridiculous."

After sixteen years on the radio, I said to him, he must have a good sense of why Eagles fans were so edgy, their ceaseless support infused with virulent negativity and animosity. Not really, he said.

"This year, at the WIP tent, it was edgier than ever," Cataldi said of his pre-game show. "It's really got a nasty, negative edge to it. I've heard many theories. That because the Eagles haven't won in forty-five years, this developed over time. That these people are beaten down by their bosses all week, and that rage pours out on

Sunday. I don't think it exists in the other three sports. You go to a baseball game, people are pretty calm. At hockey, they're downright polite. Basketball, they're fine. You go to an Eagles game, and there are many people who say, 'I'll never take my kid.' There's fights every game, nastiness. When you come in another uniform, they will beat the hell out of you. I brought my kid when he was six. I never brought him back to a game in Philadelphia. We were in the upper reaches of the stadium. All he wanted to do was watch the fights. He saw a guy topple over a landing and smash his head open. Blood was all over everything and he thought it was the coolest thing he had ever seen. He never referenced the game."

But why were the fans this way? I asked again.

"I cannot give you a good answer," Angelo said. "I guess it's part of a tradition. They love to shout 'asshole' and 'sucks' and it got to be automatic, got to be generational. But I can't say where it began."

Would it make them nicer if the Eagles won the Super Bowl?

"I doubt it," Angelo said. "I think they'd find a new way to be angry. I think they'd be just as nasty. I think there's a pride in it now. If another city gets publicity for being real nasty fans, they go, 'We are way worse.' They revel in it."

Of course, many believed talk radio could be an irresponsible enabler of obnoxious fan behavior. If he had one regret above others in his sixteen years on the air, Angelo said, it was his role in booing the selection of Donovan McNabb on draft day in 1999.

In retrospect, he called his actions stupid and reckless. Yet he also believed that Governor Rendell, who was mayor at the time, was the catalyst of the episode, providing the verbal flash powder for this incendiary moment. Rendell, on the other hand, considered Angelo the prime instigator.

"We weren't smart enough to start the whole thing," Angelo said. "The mayor started the whole thing. That was his days of being a draftnik. He thought he knew the best player to draft. He started the ball rolling, calling the show, saying, 'We gotta get 'em to draft Ricky Williams.'"

To have a little fun, Angelo said, he thought why not take a bus up to New York for the draft? It was only a couple of hours up the

Jersey turnpike. And why not bring the craziest of the crazies, the real nutcases among Eagles fans?

"I recruited them," Angelo said, "and if they came on the air and could offer a coherent thought, they were out. This had to be the nuttiest of the nutties."

He assembled a group of not-so-merry pranksters known as the Dirty Thirty. Actually, twenty-nine showed up, so Angelo recruited a homeless man, coaxing him on the bus with a promise of all the beer he could drink and donuts he could eat.

The day before, Rendell had called Angelo's show. Something had occurred to him. What if the Eagles didn't draft Williams? He urged Angelo and the Dirty Thirty not to boo anyone else who was selected. It would be embarrassing. But, it was too late.

"None of us, morons that we were, ever considered Plan B," Angelo said. Until NFL Commissioner Paul Tagliabue walked up to the podium, Angelo said, "We all honestly thought he was going to say Ricky Williams. When he said, 'Donovan McNabb,' I remember going, 'No, no,' but it was way too late."

In hindsight, it was embarrassing, a nightmare for himself and the city, Angelo said.

"The reason I regret it is, that is a huge day for a guy, and Donovan McNabb earned a better welcome than that," Angelo said. "And I would say that if the guy turned out to be a stiff. It's just the wrong thing to do."

He apologized to Donovan on television, and to McNabb's parents in person. He felt he buried the hatchet with the quarterback's mother and father, but not with McNabb himself.

"It was the wrong thing, but it was not a reaction to them selecting Donovan," Angelo said. "It was a reaction to them not selecting Ricky. That has now been completely twisted. Every time it's written, it's that they booed the idea the Eagles wanted Donovan McNabb. No. We booed the idea that they didn't get this unbelievable running back who turned out to be a wack job. I still see it and I'm embarrassed about it. It was wrong."

But, Angelo said with a sly smile about McNabb, "I think the money they gave him, he'll be okay."

22

Thursday, January 27

Eagles fever had become epidemic. Fans were getting Eagles tat-
toos, wearing Eagles contact lenses, building snow Eagles on the
lawn, putting green, white and gray rocks in their aquariums,
redecorating their basements into replicas of Veterans Stadium.
Television anchors and reporters were wearing Eagles jerseys. So
were household pets. Some guy in Havertown made a football
field in his yard out of Christmas lights. Established rules of eti-
quette for Super Bowl parties no longer applied. For once, the
football game would be more important than the commercials.
Nobody would care about the Coca-Cola dancing bears or the
Budweiser Clydesdales, Anthony Gargano said on WIP. And forget
about decorating the food. It was not necessary to serve liver paté
in the shape of a football.

"You don't want dilettantes," cohost Steve Martorano said. "All
sorts of social niceties have to go by the wayside. It's the height of
impolite behavior to get invited to a party and ask who else is
invited. You never do that, except now. Now it's okay to ask how
many small children will be running around the house."

Butch DeLuca had already made two trips to the Eagles merchan-
dise store at Lincoln Financial Field. He spent two hundred and
thirty bucks the first trip, six hundred and ten the second. He
could barely get the hats and T-shirts into his deli before customers scooped them up.

Driving down Interstate 95, he spotted a sign that said, "Please

God, one more time." Philadelphia had gone twenty-two years without a professional sports championship. Another victory by the Eagles would end the drought. Butch had to be in Jacksonville to see it. He had a line on five tickets from his connection with the Eagles. The tickets were $1250 apiece. Then he'd have to find a travel package for a flight, hotel room and rental car.

I met Butch and his wife, Sue, at their daughter Melissa Kelly's house. It was bitterly cold and a thick, crusty blanket of snow still covered the ground.

"I don't know what to do," Butch said.

One tour package, for $1150, seemed most affordable, but it required his family to stay ninety miles away, in Daytona Beach.

No problem, Melissa said.

"There's nothing to do in Jacksonville," she said.

"What the hell you gonna do in Daytona?" Butch said.

"Go to the beach."

"Weather's not warm enough to go to the beach," Sue said.

"Sixty degrees down there," Butch said.

He sat slumped on the sofa, still in his coat, tired after a long day at the deli. He wanted to go to the game, but he'd have to leave his store during a busy weekend. Plus, he'd have to leave his dog, Spunky.

"I'm more concerned about that damn dog than the business," Butch said.

Don't worry, Melissa assured her father. She'd find someone to watch his dog. Everything would work out. She worked as a supervisor at a clinic for children with developmental problems. She had a gymnast's petite effervescence.

"I may stay home," Sue DeLuca said. "I'm afraid of flying."

Tim Kelly, her son-in-law, was afraid, too. But he had a solution.

"I'll just drink before I get on the plane," he said. "We'll have three days of that anyway."

Tim worked for a company that signed people up on the Internet for dental and medical benefits. He and Melissa met in Hoboken, New Jersey, while she worked toward her master's degree in forensic psychology at the John Jay College of Criminal Justice in

Manhattan. On Sundays, they watched Eagles games on satellite television in a bar. They began dating, and eventually Tim told Melissa they would get engaged when the Eagles went to the Super Bowl. He was convinced it would happen a season ago, and he popped the question at Christmas in 2003. Then the Eagles lost to Carolina in the NFC championship game a month later and he sat at the Linc, inconsolable, until the ushers made him leave.

Tim and Melissa got married on July 24, 2004, at the Holiday Inn outside the parking lot at Lincoln Financial Field. Their wedding party was the first allowed on the playing field. Tonight, Melissa brought out her wedding album and laughed as she saw herself again, posed like a quarterback in her gown and veil and Tim in his tuxedoed three-point stance. Then she played a videotape of the reception. The Eagles pep band performed, and Tim stood there, beer in hand, so confident of the upcoming season that he announced to the wedding party, "I think there's a lot of doubters in the room. But we have all the pieces that fit the puzzle. All I have to say is, 'Book your damn tickets to fuckin' Jacksonville. We're going.'"

He had predicted sixteen victories, no defeats, during the regular season. He and Melissa sat apart at Eagles games, she with her parents, he with his brother and friends, conversing by text-message on their cell phones. Tim liked to tease her about Donovan McNabb, whom Melissa believed to have shortcomings as a passer. "Sorry, I didn't see that play," he kept messaging as the quarterback threw for four touchdowns during the season opener. "Was that McNabb on that one?"

The Eagles kept winning, and finally they broke through against Atlanta. Tim thought he had never hugged so many grown men in his life. As he and Melissa drove home from the NFC championship game, his mother, Marguerite, called. The woman never cursed, ever, but she remembered what Tim had said at the wedding reception, and she yelled into the phone, "We're going to fucking Jacksonville."

Stunned, Melissa tried to get her mother-in-law to repeat what she had said, but Marguerite Kelly demurred, saying, "If I should die right now, I'm going to hell."

As Melissa told the story in her living room, Tim said of his mother, "She's probably been to confession five times already."

For Melissa, just reaching the Super Bowl made it a satisfying season. The Eagles made it to the big game. That's all that mattered. Her father agreed. If the Eagles weren't the best team in the NFL, they would be second best. What was wrong with that?

Tim concurred, to a point. A defeat in the Super Bowl would not be as devastating as those three losses in the NFC championship game, he said. But he wanted a victory. He wanted that black cloud lifted. *If crappy places like Anaheim could win a championship, why not Philly?* He was tired of the teasing phone calls, like the ones that came after Smarty Jones lost the Belmont in the homestretch. *Even your horses can't win.* He had already planned days off to attend the Eagles victory parade.

"I want to have that one win, to be the best," Tim said. "So many years, we're the blue-collar team, which is fine, but I want to win with those qualities. For so long we've been second best with those qualities. I want to be the elite team just once. I want to be the white-collar team with the trophy. Is that too much to ask? One winner. That's all I want."

He felt Terrell Owens would play, that he would not allow himself to sit on the bench and have his team win the Super Bowl without him. T.O. would be in there. And Tim wanted to be in Jacksonville, too. The tickets were available. If only his father-in-law would make the deal with his Eagles contact.

"If I knew everything was okay and I wouldn't have any problems [at the deli]," Butch said.

"Everything's fine, you won't have any problems," Melissa assured her father.

As Butch sat on the couch, his eyes growing heavy, she said, "Don't let me down, Dad. Don't let me down."

23

Friday, January 28

The *Daily News*, seeking to get a leg up on the Terrell Owens situation, hired his fibula to write a column. This was my favorite feature since a long-ago garbage strike, when the paper offered a kind of Zagat's guide to rodent culinary preferences, rating mounting piles of refuse as a two-rat dump, a three-rat dump or a four-rat dump.

Today's column carried an editor's note, saying it was based on a source close to T.O.'s ankle:

"Oddly enough, I understand this is not the first time a star's injured body part has gotten a byline in the *Daily News*," the fibula wrote. "For many years, the People Paper had George Brett's hemorrhoid writing the gossip column."

Pressing matters of state were put on hold as the Super Bowl approached. Governor Rendell had purchased three tickets, at $540 apiece, and would be heading to Jacksonville with his wife and son next Thursday. Just in case the Eagles won, he postponed his annual budget speech from February 8 to February 9 so it wouldn't conflict with a victory parade.

"The governor didn't want to deliver a budget speech to an empty room," Kate Phillips, his press secretary, told the *Inquirer*.

A guy from Mount Ephraim, New Jersey, called Angelo Cataldi on WIP and said he had a friend go to the Wailing Wall in Jerusalem and leave a prayer for the Eagles. Then eighteen trees were planted, a winning number. The guy sang the Eagles cheer in Yiddish. Another guy called and did it in Spanish.

"Sounds like you have an upset stomach," Cataldi said.

Saturday, January 29

The *Inquirer* detected a potential softening of the country's jaundiced view of Eagles fans. A column on ESPN.com marveled that spectators had not booed when Timmy Kelly, a blind eleven-year-old suffering from cerebral palsy, had faltered in brutal weather conditions as he sang the national anthem before the NFC championship game.

The paper also cited a column by Tim Sullivan of the *San Diego Union Tribune*, who described Eagles fans as possessing a devotion that was "hypercritical and moody" but constant through decades of unrequited enthusiasm.

"When the wind feels like an icy whip, and you still can't see an empty seat," Sullivan wrote, "you have to admire the passion of these human popsicles."

Lest anyone think the fans had become warm and cuddly, though, the *Inquirer* also discovered this posting about Timmy Kelly on a fan website called 700level.com.

Dean-o: "C'mon, he's a little ten-year-old boy with physical challenges. [Who] the hell would boo him? What are we, friggin' monsters?"

Tattoo: "Dean, I know, I know . . . but I have to say it was my first thought."

On WIP, the Eagles' arrival in the Super Bowl had not cured some fans of their anxiety and insecurity. One caller to Ray Didinger and Glen Macnow said he was upset by national television commentaries and newspaper articles. The majority predicted defeat for the Eagles and detailed the familiar laundry list of boorish fan behavior.

"It seems like the whole country is against us," the caller said.

Just prepare yourself for it, Didinger said, asking the caller, "Would you rather not be in the game?"

Anyway, Didinger said, much of what was being written and said about Eagles fans was revisionist, even complimentary. Every Philadelphia cliché would be revisited during the week of Super Bowl, Macnow said. Cheesesteaks, *Rocky*, throwing snowballs at Santa.

"You gotta let it roll off your back," he said.

"Of course," Didinger said. "And you know what? It happened. You know what I mean? It happened."

"But," Macnow said, "the Santa thing is the most misrepresented, misstated story in the history of the world."

Shortly after Jeffrey Lurie bought the Eagles in May 1994, he had a luncheon meeting with Didinger, who had attended games since 1956 and had covered the team as a sportswriter since 1970. Lurie was a Bostonian who worked in Hollywood as a producer. At one point during lunch, he leaned over and said to Didinger, "I'm curious. Did they really throw snowballs at Santa?"

"Yes, they did," Didinger nodded.

Lurie seemed disappointed. He appeared to have hoped that the story was a tale that played well on the banquet circuit but wasn't true.

"His face fell," Didinger told me, "like, 'What did I just buy? I paid $180 million and I just bought the Manson family?'"

There is still debate about exactly what happened at Franklin Field on December 15, 1968, when a stand-in Santa was peppered by snowballs. While some details have grown as fuzzy as Santa's beard, the symbolism of the moment appeared irrefutable to Didinger. This was the first time that Eagles fans mobilized their frustration and anger into a kind of take-it-to-the-streets protest. And the first time the rest of the country began to consider their behavior as truculent.

Irritation had built through a season that began with eleven consecutive defeats. Just as fans consoled themselves with the idea that the Eagles would get Heisman Trophy winner O. J. Simpson in the draft, Philadelphia won games against Detroit and New Orleans. The team seemed to get everything backwards. First, it couldn't win, and, when fans came to embrace defeat, the Eagles couldn't lose.

Annoyance with Coach Joe Kuharich had coalesced in a movement to dump him. Before the 1964 season, Kuharich had traded quarterback Sonny Jurgensen to Washington for Norm Snead. Jurgensen headed to the Hall of Fame, while Snead produced one winning season out of seven in Philadelphia. By 1968, an Eagles franchise that had won the NFL championship eight seasons earlier was in tatters. A "Joe Must Go" banner trailed an airplane flying over Franklin Field and "Joe Must Go" buttons were sold outside the stadium. Some local bars even took up collections for Kuharich's ouster. Then came the fusillade of snowballs, signifying an avalanche of discontent.

On her way into Franklin Field that infamous December day, Marie Didinger, Ray's mother, stopped to buy a "Joe Must Go" button. It stunned Ray. His mother was no activist, no great joiner of causes. For her to stop and buy a button in protest showed just how deeply this frustration with Kuharich ran.

The day was miserable, snow then a sleety rain, Didinger recalled. According to Macnow and Anthony Gargano, authors of *The Great Philadelphia Fan Book*, a planned Christmas half-time extravaganza came unraveled when the day's rent-a-Santa could not get to the stadium through the snow. His elaborate sleigh, complete with fiberglass reindeer, then got stuck in the mud, much like the Eagles' offense.

This left the salvation of the Christmas pageant in the hands of a backup Saint Nick named Frank Olivo. He was twenty years old and said he was recruited out of the stands by Eagles management. He attended the game with his aunts and uncles and wore a Santa suit to the season finale as a way to bring a little merriment to a joyless season. His uncle had bought the suit for $100 several years earlier, Olivo told me. He said that he took painstaking measures to shape his cottony Santa beard and stick-on eyebrows, not wanting to destroy the illusion of children who might see him.

He said he even wore a pillow under the costume to fill out his 170-pound frame. But few others seem to remember him as a jolly old elf. And some thought his Christmas cheer was eighty-six proof.

"That was the ugliest Santa Claus," Ernie Clark, who had been attending games since 1948, told me. "It was like going to see *Phantom of the Opera*, and they pulled someone out of the audience to play the lead."

He was neither ragtag nor intoxicated, Olivo told me. The way he saw it, he bailed the Eagles out of a jam with a classic understudy adherence to the maxim that the show must go on. Except, in his case, the audience tossed more than shouts of appreciation. Some audiences wanted their stars to take a bow. Olivo's insisted that he duck.

Arriving in one end zone, he was instructed to walk the length of the field through a column formed by members of the Sound of Brass band and the Eagle-ettes, described variously as cheerleaders or a kind of color guard. Olivo said he was handed an equipment duffle to serve as a toy bag and was told to begin his march when the band played "Here Comes Santa Claus."

It was not quite clear what set the crowd off on a day when the Eagles lost, twenty-four to seventeen, to Minnesota. Olivo told me the booing began as he walked down the middle of the field. Didinger recalled Santa riding in a fire engine on the track that surrounded the field, tossing candy canes but unable to reach the stands, his arm as ineffectual as any Eagles quarterback's.

Olivo's version was that, half-time duties completed, he walked down the track, which put him in close range of fans, who showered Santa with more than milk and cookies. One or two snowballs were tossed playfully, then a barrage. Olivo said he played along, shaking his finger at offenders, telling them they wouldn't get anything for Christmas because they were being more naughty than nice. The snowballs kept coming, and the pelting even knocked his cotton-candy eyebrows off.

Ernie Clark said he did not believe he threw snowballs from the upper deck at Franklin Field, or that he could have hit Santa if he did. "But I might have," he said. "I can't say I remember declining."

When he reached his family, Olivo told me, everyone was laughing. The whole thing seemed a harmless joke. He said the Eagles even asked him if he wanted to perform again the next year. Olivo said he declined, saying, "If there's no snow, they'll be throwing beer bottles."

It was all a good laugh, according to *The Great Philadelphia Fan Book*, until that night when Howard Cosell expressed his windy displeasure on a highlights program broadcast by ABC. Philadelphia forever became the place that booed Santa and pounded him with snowballs.

There ought to be a statute of limitations on this episode, Macnow contended. What people failed to mention was that 54,530 spectators showed up in the snow that day to cheer on their team at the end of a disastrous two-and-twelve season. Where else would fans have been that loyal?

Macnow preferred a more poignant fan story, from March 2004. At his late-night urging on WIP, some three hundred fans gathered to toast Veterans Stadium less than thirty-six hours before it was imploded.

"It was a toilet, but it was our toilet," Shaun Young said.

In his adult life, Olivo, now fifty-six and living in Media, Pennsylvania, said he went through a handful of careers before health and financial issues kept him away from Eagles games. If he had any regret from that infamous day, he told me, it was over the suggestion that he was drinking or wore a raggedy costume. Neither was true, he said. Playing Santa meant so much to him that he did it for years for his nieces and nephews, he said. His Santa costume from 1968 was so durable that it lasted until five or six years ago.

In the 1980s, when he worked the craps tables at the Resorts casino in Atlantic City, he once wore the Santa outfit as a Halloween gag. His boss came up to him and said, "Is that the costume? Can I just touch it?"

So it wasn't all bad.

"I was a good Santa Claus at that game," Olivo said. "I was twenty years old. I had a little theater in me."

The Sixers invited him to a game during the 2003–2004 season, he told me. The crowd booed, then cheered. He never heard from the Eagles. As Olivo saw it, fans had a conflicted view about the snowball incident. They recoiled when they were portrayed as Visigoths and reveled in that ghastly depiction at the same time.

"During the Veterans Stadium years, that reputation became something they wanted to keep," Olivo said.

He believed that the throwing of snowballs had nothing to do with his shortcomings as Santa Claus and everything to do with frustration over a horrible season, strung together with other inept seasons like burned-out Christmas lights.

"I got it," Olivo told me. "I was a fan first. Any true fan got it. It was done to make a statement, not because they were rowdy or drunk or not into the game and looking for trouble. It was a statement: We're fed up. It's time to get it together.

"You gotta let them know where you're coming from. There's no bullshit. If you produce and do your best, you get your reward in this town. If you dog it and try to be something you're not, you're gonna hear about it."

Somebody deserved to be hit with snowballs that day, Olivo said. Not Santa. Santa was too dear to his heart. But somebody. I asked him what he would have done if he had been a regular fan instead of a stand-in Saint Nick.

"I would have thrown snowballs," Olivo said. "Probably not at Santa, but at Kuharich and the players, yes."

24

Sunday, January 30

The Eagles left for the Super Bowl, the team charter arriving in Florida on a cool, overcast afternoon. Jacksonville appeared to be incomplete, like an abandoned game of Monopoly, as if developers put up a few tall buildings then decided to move downtown to a location that remained undetermined. But what the city lacked in architectural physique, it made up for in the kind of hospitality a place exhibits when it wants, above all else, to be liked.

A few weeks earlier, Vic Ketchman, who operated the Jacksonville Jaguars' website, told me that he hoped the Steelers and the Eagles made it to the Super Bowl. Fans from Boston and other places would be too hoity-toity, he thought. "If Philadelphia and Pittsburgh play here, it'll be great," Ketchman said. "They'll sleep in their cars, eat barbecue and drink beer. They won't bitch about us." He was probably right. Eagles fans were so desperate for the Super Bowl, they were coming down here by the thousands, tickets or no tickets. They were here for football, not amenities. They had beer in Jacksonville, didn't they? Who cared about turndown service and a mint on the pillow?

As the Eagles' buses neared their hotel in Ponte Vedra Beach, outside of Jacksonville, fans began pulling their cars to the side of the road, getting out and cheering. A couple of hundred fans greeted the players upon their arrival in the lobby with the flash of cameras and the Eagles fight song. Even the Eagles Book Mobile and Eagles Eye Mobile drew applause. The players themselves carried video cameras, as if to capture a newborn's first Christmas.

"They are having the time of their life," defensive end Jevon Kearse said of the fans. "It's like a huge rock has been lifted off their shoulders. As players, we must take it upon ourselves to not be satisfied with just being here, but with going out and winning the game."

Linebacker Jeremiah Trotter appeared almost giddy with excitement. He was back with the Eagles after two forlorn seasons in Washington, and Philadelphia was in the Super Bowl. He dressed for the occasion in a tangerine suit, a color not found anywhere else except in rum drinks with parasols. He spoke fondly of the abuse Eagles fans had heaped upon him when he played for the Redskins.

"They would boo me and call me all sorts of names," Trotter said. "I knew that was out of love. Instead of 'Trotter' on the back of my jersey, they had 'Traitor.'"

At least one Eagles fan was alarmed by the team's casual arrival. Ed Bradley, the CBS correspondent and a Philadelphia native, had noticed that Tom Brady, the New England quarterback, wore a suit and a tie and carried a briefcase, while Eagles quarterback Donovan McNabb carried a video camera.

"I thought, 'Uh-oh, the Patriots have come to take care of business. The Eagles are just glad to be there,'" Bradley told the *Inquirer*. "When you're from Philadelphia, you look for things like that. If rain's going to fall, it's going to fall on you in Philly."

After the eleven o'clock news in Philadelphia, my wife, Debby, called. One of the local network stations had led with the Iraqi elections. The other two had gone with the Eagles' arrival at the Super Bowl. KYW-TV, the local CBS affiliate, put a clock on the screen, ticking down the days, hours and minutes until the game. It was still a week away, and already it was being treated like a moon landing.

Monday, January 31

Butch DeLuca got his five tickets. Sure, he worried about leaving the store. On Super Bowl Sunday, he might double his business, and with him gone, the place would be a man short. But whaddya gonna do? At least he found someone to look after his dog. He had a key made for the guy, and even the key had an Eagles logo on it. "That's all anybody's talking about, Eagles, Eagles, Eagles," Butch told me over the phone.

He and his family would be flying a charter to Daytona on Friday. Their plans weren't finalized yet. But Butch was hearing troubling things about Jacksonville. That tailgating would not be allowed in the stadium parking lot. That roads and bridges would be closed to the city on game day. It sounded more like an anthrax scare than a Super Bowl. He wanted to get to the game early and mess around. But what if he drove and couldn't find a place to park? He had never been to Florida. It didn't sound at all like Philly.

"How are the roads?" Butch said. "They got big roads?"

Under the headline "Yo, Who You Calling a Loser Now?" the *Inquirer* polled psychologists about whether an Eagles victory in the Super Bowl could cure Philadelphia of its inferiority complex.

"The Eagles are the vehicle by which Philadelphia could change its image as a second-class city on the eastern seaboard," Sally White, a sports psychologist and dean at Lehigh University, told the paper.

Others thought it would take more than a few fat guys in tights to change a city's image.

"In the short run, it will make people feel very good, and in the long run, it will have absolutely no impact at all," said Christopher Peterson, a University of Michigan psychologist who studied positive emotions.

The most interesting comment in the article came from Robert Petruzzi, a psychologist from suburban Philadelphia, who suggested that Eagles fans may not want to ditch the underdog image they have long worn, both as a badge of honor and as a security blanket.

"Nobody likes change," Petruzzi said. Even positive change, he said, was "always difficult."

This dovetailed with what I had been told by Michael Givant, an associate professor of sociology at Adelphi University who studied fan behavior. There were three major types of sports fans, he said. Ego-intensive fans who grew up with the team. Ego-deprived fans, who came from broken families or had emotionally distant fathers and viewed the team as a substitute family. And communal fans, who felt included in a larger social and moral community.

There was a function to believing in a "curse" from above, Givant said in an e-mail message. "It makes the long-suffering fan a very special kind of fan in a very special club, whose membership is sustained in the pain of a long series of heart-wrenching losses," he wrote. "Those who have suffered the most and the longest become eligible for sainthood in the church of the Eagles."

Back in Havertown, John Kleinstuber had promised himself he would not get caught up in all this pre-game hype. But now he was soaking in it like a bath. Newspapers, television, he couldn't get enough. Sure, a Super Bowl victory might change people's outlooks, he said, but not in the way psychologists were predicting.

"I'm not sure the fans won't be worse," Kleinstuber told me over the phone. "They'll be like, 'Don't mess with us.' The team will have more pressure. Now this is what we will expect. These Philly fans won't say, 'Oh, great, we're champions.' They'll be saying, 'We're gonna kick your ass. We're finally champions and screw the rest of youse.' We're gonna be really cocky and hard to handle."

According to the *Daily News*, the cantor at the Conservative synagogue Har Zion in suburban Penn Valley had chanted "Fly Eagles Fly" in Hebrew on Saturday morning. By Sunday night, a fan from Reading, Pennsylvania, had an offer of ten bucks on eBay for an Eagles logo that appeared on a piece of Apple Jacks cereal. Why not? the paper said. Some wack job had paid $28,000 for a likeness of the Virgin Mary on a grilled-cheese sandwich.

Tim Kelly, dressed in an Eagles jersey, picked up a paper at Butch's Deli in Havertown, said hello to his father-in-law, took the suburban train to the Market Street elevated line and headed into Center City. *I gotta get through four days of work,* he told himself. He had tossed and turned the night before, falling into a restive sleep after two o'clock, thinking about the game, wanting to be in Jacksonville now instead of Friday.

The national media were starting to tick him off. Especially ESPN. Nobody thought the Eagles could win. A total lack of respect. *We got as good a chance as anybody,* Tim thought. On the el, he began to get excited, nervous, almost nauseated with anticipation. A few years ago, he got so worked up before games that he almost made himself sick. He had been calmer since then, but now he felt his stomach turning. He couldn't wait to get off the train. At work, all everyone talked about was the Eagles. He found it hard to concentrate. He had to train a new employee, and he apologized for being distracted: "You have to forgive me. I just found out this weekend, I'll be going to the Super Bowl."

In Jacksonville, Freddie Mitchell had everyone atwitter. Last week, he had made an innocuous remark, saying he's "got something" for New England's all-pro safety Rodney Harrison. He also said he knew the Patriots' secondary only by numbers, not names, then proceeded to get the numbers wrong.

This is what passed for news in the vacuous two-week buildup to a Super Bowl. In retaliation, Mitchell was called an underachiever and a bust as a first-round draft pick. New England linebacker Willie McGinest said, come game time, Mitchell would have to "pay the price."

Andy Reid appeared none too happy that Mitchell had incited his opponents with bulletin board material. "We've, uh, communicated," Reid said at a news conference today, sounding like the warden in *Cool Hand Luke.*

I could understand the Patriots sniping at Mitchell in this third-grade tit for tat, and Reid's disapproval, but I couldn't understand why reporters and columnists were criticizing the Eagles' receiver and telling him to shut up. It was yet another example of the incoherent demands of sportswriting. As Randy Harvey, the sports editor of the *Baltimore Sun,* pointed out long ago, we waited our entire careers for athletes to say what was on their minds, and when they did, we hammered them for it.

Even though her husband, Butch, had secured tickets, Sue DeLuca was still nervous about flying to Jacksonville.

"She counted how many Xanax pills she had," her daughter, Melissa, told me. "She said it wasn't enough. It'll be all Eagles fans on the flight. I think that'll take the focus off her anxiety. Maybe that and a couple shots of Sambuca."

25

Tuesday, February 1

I missed the Super Bowl buildup on WIP, so I phoned the station from Jacksonville, and producer Joe Weachter let me listen to a few calls. Bill Simmons, a truck driver from south Jersey known as El Wingador, was on the line with Angelo Cataldi.

In three days, El Wingador would try to defeat the defending champion, Sonya Thomas, the "Black Widow," and win his fifth Wing Bowl title.

"When I lose like I did last year, I come back stronger," El Wingador said. "I want to wipe them out. I want to humiliate them bad."

"I hope the Eagles are as intense as you are," Cataldi said.

"I have enough energy to go down there and play that game," El Wingador said.

"You will be eating not for Bill Simmons, but for an entire city," Cataldi said.

Ron Jaworski called. He had still not watched the film from Super Bowl XV, a twenty-seven-to-ten defeat of the Eagles by Oakland. Twenty-four years had passed, and he couldn't bring himself to watch.

"Never mind winning," Jaworski said. "It's the regret of losing. No question that sits with you forever."

He had gotten as far as pre-game introductions. At that point, he turned it off. His first pass had been intercepted, and the day spiraled downhill.

"Sometimes the magnitude of the game forces you to try too hard," Jaworski said.

In the studio with Cataldi was a guy named Steve Borkowski. He was seventy-nine years old and had been a season-ticket holder for sixty-three years. He brought with him a ticket from an Eagles game against the Boston Redskins on September 20, 1936. The face value was seventy-five cents.

His daughter, Debbie Adler, said her dad was looking for a ticket to the Super Bowl. It was his lifelong dream.

"This man has to be in the stadium on Sunday," Cataldi implored his listeners. "We will accept nothing less. Sixty-three years. My guess is fifty were losing seasons. I guarantee forty were. Never did this man lose faith. This is the fan among fans. The king of the fans."

Borkowski had come to the right place. Philadelphia was in a generous mood. After a few minutes, a caller anonymously pledged a ticket for the old man to see the Super Bowl. Just when things looked bleak, someone had pulled through for him. He was on his way to Jacksonville.

"My dad was in the Navy during World War II and the Korean War," Adler told me later in the day. "Every year, he sent home money to his mother so he wouldn't lose his seat. That's dedication, you know what I'm saying?"

It was Media Day at the Super Bowl. The clock at Alltel Stadium started at sixty minutes and began to click down to zero for this hypefest. Reporters had an hour to ask questions of Eagles players who sat at podiums that resembled dunking booths at the spring fair. One interviewer from the Nickelodeon channel wore tights and a cape. Another, from a Spanish-language network, conducted his questioning with a hand puppet. A horde gathered around Terrell Owens, who sat in his uniform, a diamond earring in each ear. Looming over him was either a fuzzy boom microphone or an impaled possum.

The uncertainty had ended. Owens said he would play on Sunday, despite two surgical screws in his ankle and a lack of medical clearance from his surgeon. He knew his body better than anyone else, he said, and he would rely on faith and prayer instead of medicine.

"I got the best doctor that anyone can have," Owens said. "That's God."

He summoned Popeye the Sailor Man ("I am who I am") and he cited the Bible, saying that Sunday would bring a miracle.

A day before, Owens had worked out for the first time in six weeks with the team. In today's *Daily News*, his fibula reported in a column that it felt great. T.O.'s hands had reached for his right ankle after one reception, the fibula reported, and the Eagles went quiet, collectively thinking, *Oh my god, he hurt himself again*.

"I caught the hint and went into a slight limp," the fibula reported. "T.O.'s mouth paused a second, then broke into a grin. 'Got ya!' he laughed. Everybody cracked up."

If Owens played well on Sunday and the Eagles won, Ray Didinger told me, he might become the greatest sports hero ever in Philadelphia.

"They don't just want heroes," Didinger said. "They want bloody heroes."

After a half-hour in the Terrell Owens Chapel of Love, I meandered over to Andy Reid's podium to hear the best stories of the day. Not from Reid, but from Butch Buchanico, the Eagles' director of security and a former Philadelphia cop. Butch grew up in South Philly and liked to say that he never lived in a house that didn't have trolley tracks running past the front door. He once directed traffic at Broad Street and Pattison, outside Veterans Stadium. Bled Eagles green in those days. Still did.

Wistfully, Butch recalled the ingenious ways fans sneaked alcohol into games. Vodka poured in baby bottles or shot with hypodermic needles into juice cartons or smuggled in baggies under brassieres. Guys in wheelchairs fitted with kegs. People hiding cans of beer in hoagie wrappers and rolls.

"God bless 'em," Butch said, emotion in his voice.

He had silver hair and a mustache and talked with the humorous informality of a man whose career had left him with endless stories to tell on the banquet circuit. He was so disarming that he could get away with saying that Reid learned to coach at "Tight Ass University."

Philly ate, breathed and slept Eagles, Butch said. Domestic violence went up and productivity went down when the Eagles lost. When you lose, everybody hates you, he said. They curse every member of your family. When you win, the same people want to hand you a beer and take you home for dinner.

All over the country people said Eagles fans were bad, Butch continued. It can be ugly anywhere, he said. Name a city, and he could give me a bad experience. Anyway, in his mind, Eagles fans used to be a lot tougher physically than they were now.

"We used to call it the head-bustin' detail in them days," Butch said. "You only got called when security couldn't handle it. I used to wear the old police pants, the high boots. I used to tape my knees, you know, with the Ace bandages. I always had gloves, even when it was warm. When you went into the stands, you were going to fight. You were going to roll down them steps with some-body. They were a lot tougher in them days. Today they're more vocal, more abusive, language-wise. But you go to a movie or got HBO, you gonna hear that, you know what I mean?"

On September 16, 2002, near the end of a thirty-seven-to-seven victory by the Eagles at Washington, police used pepper spray to calm drunken fighting in the stands.

"You use gas in Philly?" one of the cops asked Butch.

"Naw, you insult our people," he replied. "They'd rather get hit with a stick. It's a badge of honor."

He had been a cop for three decades, and he had been around the Eagles, on the inside and the outside, and he knew more than most how it felt to have hope slashed and victory deprived.

Maybe this week would be different. Butch remembered how it was when the Flyers won their second consecutive Stanley Cup in 1975. He was a mounted policeman that day, making an excited, exhausting trip down Broad Street to JFK Stadium.

"My horse was straight up in the air, that's how we went down the street," Butch said. "We got to JFK Stadium—my horse was a brown horse—it was totally lathered up white, foaming at the mouth. My arms, I couldn't hold 'em anymore. When I got in the stadium, a hundred thousand people. I still get chills. Greatest thing I've ever seen. They made us go around twice. When I got off my horse, I went right to the ground, because I was so fatigued, but I felt so good. This is going to top that."

In late afternoon, I got a call from John Kleinstuber in Havertown.

"I'm getting itchy," he said. "Really itchy."

John was mainlining all the Super Bowl coverage he could find on television and in the newspapers. Today's *Daily News* spent three pages on such pressing items as a list of best- and worst-dressed players and their astrological signs. A cheerleader diary took up another column. Two pages were devoted to the Eagles Book Mobile and Eye Mobile. No word on the Ingrown Toenail Mobile. Now John was going through withdrawal. He needed another fix from me in Jacksonville.

Philadelphia was going nuts, he said. A guy who sat two rows in front of him at Eagles games was in the *Inquirer* this morning. Kevin P. O'Donoghue, of Glen Mills, Pennsylvania, had taken out a second mortgage on his house to buy a Super Bowl package worth $4000.

"Sometimes, the cards are maxed out, you got to do what you got to do," O'Donoghue told the paper.

KYW-TV, Philadelphia's CBS affiliate that billed itself as the official Eagles channel, had Dr. Phil on to discuss whether Owens should play, John told me. If Owens wasn't 100 percent recovered, he shouldn't play, Dr. Phil recommended.

"I mean, they've got Dr. Phil on live," John said. "What the hell does Dr. Phil know about this?"

I called Shaun Young, and he was down. His ride to Jacksonville had fallen through. He wouldn't be going to the Super Bowl. He got a call at five o'clock, and it sucker-punched him. He turned his television off and sat there in his Eagles basketball jersey, deflated. *Damn. I was set, ready to roll.*

"I always dreamed of being there," he said. "It was like somebody pulled the rug from under my feet."

26

Wednesday, February 2

Governor Rendell led an Eagles pep rally in the Capitol Rotunda in Harrisburg. He held an Eagles flag aloft like a high school drum major, while the Eagles pep band played on the Rotunda steps.

At City Hall in Philadelphia, city officials spoke gingerly about plans for a Super Bowl parade next Tuesday, fearing that they would jinx the Eagles.

"We don't say 'parade' around here," Dan Fee, a mayoral spokesman told the *Inquirer*. "We say, 'a procession to mark an amazing achievement.'"

A case of influenza had caused Pope John Paul II, already frail and eighty-four, to cancel audiences at the Vatican. This led to a discussion among the top editors at the *Daily News*. If the Pope died, who would get more prominent display in the paper, John Paul II or the Eagles? It was not a frivolous question in a city with a huge Catholic population and a tabloid newspaper whose circulation could increase 10 to 15 percent the day after Eagles' games. In December, the death of Reggie White had received more visible placement than the Asian tsunami.

"Not our finest day," Pat McLoone, the assistant managing editor, told me in Jacksonville.

After a discussion, it was decided that a special section on the Pope would be wrapped outside of a special section on the Eagles.

"Cooler heads prevailed," McLoone later said. "But it wasn't a slam dunk."

• • •

Shaun Young called in midmorning. His mood had rebounded.

"I guess I'm back on," he said.

Scott Teller, a marketing agent for several Eagles, had found a ride for Shaun. They would be leaving tonight with a group of fans in a thirty-two-foot recreational vehicle painted Eagles green.

"I can't picture the Eagles in the Super Bowl and Shaun not being part of it," Teller told me. "It's like eating cheesesteaks without cheese."

They had met at an autograph session on December 18, the day before Terrell Owens got hurt. Brian Dawkins, the Eagles' safety, was one of Teller's clients. Shaun was there in his face paint and jersey and shoulder pads.

"There must have been a thousand people in line to get autographs," Teller said. "I realized there was this one signature on almost all the memorabilia. I didn't know whose it was. We looked over and Shaun was posing for pictures, people were asking for his autograph. It was the greatest thing. Some people think he's just a fan. Guys on the team feel Shaun is part of the team. When I look at Shaun, I just see green. First time I saw him out of his makeup, I didn't know it was Shaun until he walked up to me."

It would be tough finding a ticket for him. Shaun didn't have a lot of money to spend. Teller would see what he could do. Maybe he could pull some strings and get a freebie.

"First one I get goes to Shaun," Teller said.

In midafternoon, I spoke to Shaun again. He had his shoulder pads and five jerseys packed.

"It's my American Express card," he said. "I don't leave home without it."

By nine p.m., the RV was headed through Maryland on Interstate 95, driving through the night toward Jacksonville. Ten Eagles fans were on board. The driver and owner, John Tirpak, was from Allentown. The RV had been custom-painted with Eagles wings. Its awning was made from the same material that formed a chute for players to run onto the field at the Linc.

Inside, the RV was outfitted with green carpet, gray linoleum,

customized Eagles blinds, photographs and newspaper clippings
from the 1981 Super Bowl. The bathroom was decorated with an
Eagles tissue box. The bed was fitted with an Eagles bedspread
and Eagles pillows and sat beneath a banner that said, "You're in
Eagles country."

Just before I called, the theme from *Rocky* played over the
stereo system and Shaun entertained the group with one-arm
push-ups as they rolled down the Interstate.

"I'm so amped up," he told me over the phone. He could feel the
hair standing up on his arms. And, in this excited state, he said, he
could almost feel his hair growing through his shaved head.

"I'm like a friggin' Chia pet," he said.

Thursday, February 3

Chris Clark was on a train to Philadelphia from Washington. He
and his father were flying out to Jacksonville tonight. Chris
received his game tickets on Monday and fretted ever since what
to do with them. If he lost them, they could never be replaced. The
first day, he took them home, left them in his bedroom. That didn't
work. *I'm going to forget them.* On Tuesday, he brought them to his
office. That didn't calm him, either. *Suppose the cleaning crew finds
them and steals them.* On Wednesday, he took the tickets with him
to Washington. He kept them in his suitcase and kept the suitcase
in his sight all day. At night, he and his associates went to dinner,
and as soon as they returned to the hotel for a drink, Chris
excused himself. He ran up to his room first and opened the suitcase. The tickets were still there.

"I'll be paranoid 'til Sunday," he said.

The *Daily News* announced the winner of its Super Bowl contest.
Frank Trout, who had broken his hand fighting off burglars, lost his
job a week before Christmas and had his television set repossessed
right before the NFC championship game, was awarded a new fifty-
six-inch high-definition TV and enough food for a football feast.

Nearly a thousand fans had written to the paper, pleading to be given a free party. "My friends think I deserve to win because my wife cheated on me and threw me out of my house," one of the entrants wrote. "Now I live on my brother's couch watching the Eagles on a twenty-seven-inch TV while my cheating wife and [her] boyfriend have my Eagles basement."

And the Eagles thought they were on a losing streak.

In midafternoon, I drove out to the Jacksonville airport. I was flying home tonight for the Wing Bowl tomorrow morning. Shaun Young and his RV crew had arrived a couple of hours earlier. They were staying at a campground near the airport. The trip had been uneventful, except for a stop at a strip club in South Carolina at three thirty in the morning.

"One billboard advertised for the club and the next one said, 'Jesus Christ, Savior of the World,'" Shaun said. "I know I'm in the South."

We met at the ticket counter at the Jacksonville airport. Since I was headed to Philly, my hotel room was available for a night. I gave Shaun my key so he could get some rest.

A Boston television crew approached Shaun, who was still dressed in his Eagles basketball jersey, and asked, "Can you get fired up?"

"You don't know who you're dealing with!" he screamed into the camera on cue. "Welcome to Phillyville. E-A-G-L-E-S, Eagles! Believe it, yeah."

The reporter looked amused and shocked by Shaun's vehemence, flipped like a switch.

"Have you ever thought of getting into professional wrestling?" he asked.

At work in Center City, Tim Kelly had a restless day, thinking about his trip to Jacksonville tomorrow. At lunchtime, he and others worked off some energy by throwing a football at a cardboard cutout of Patriots quarterback Tom Brady.

"Brady is no longer standing," Kelly said. "He's broken."

Tonight, his wife, Melissa, packed for the Super Bowl. She packed nothing red and blue. No socks, no underwear, nothing that came in the colors of the New England Patriots. Everything in her suitcase was green, white and gray—Eagles colors.

Tim had peaks and valleys of emotion all week. He tried not to get caught up in the Super Bowl, but sometimes he couldn't contain himself. Tonight, he took Tylenol P.M. and tried to force himself to sleep, finally dozing off at three, with his alarm set for six.

27

Friday, February 4

At three thirty in the morning, I headed out the door for Wing Bowl. By four, I pulled into a parking lot near the Wachovia Center in South Philadelphia. Thousands of people had already arrived. Some had partied all night in U-Haul trailers. Most had breakfast in a bottle.

Outside the basketball arena, someone dribbled an empty keg in the parking lot. The lines were long and impatient. As I headed for the media entrance, bottles whizzed nearby and plinked as they crashed on the sidewalk.

"This shit is crazy," a security guard said.

"They're throwing bottles," another guard warned. "Don't antagonize them."

Inside the arena, I seemed to have stepped into a *Girls Gone Wild* video. Women were flashing their breasts to raucous applause. A promoter named Shawn Palmer stood on the infield, where the basketball court was usually situated, and held a camera.

"It's four thirty in the morning, we're drunk and there's titties everywhere," he said.

Later, a woman held up a sign that said, "Forget the Boobs. Show us your Birds."

With the Eagles in the Super Bowl, this year's Wing Bowl would serve as a boisterous and soused pep rally. By five o'clock, twenty-three thousand spectators had squeezed and staggered into the building. People still in line were advised to leave, with an estimated ten thousand waiting to get into this annual gustatory challenge, described by Al Morganti, its founder, as "Fellini meets the Hell's Angels at a family picnic."

The cops were so officious in bracing for rowdy behavior that the WIP hosts and some of the contestants had trouble getting into the arena. Pat Palmer, a correspondent for *Barhopper* magazine, said he had seen only one other event reach such boozy anticipation—Mardi Gras.

"I've been to Daytona for Bike Week," Palmer said. "It's nothing like this."

By five o'clock, Angelo Cataldi arrived wearing a white-and-green WIP jersey. Thirteen years ago, Morganti and Cataldi started Wing Bowl in a local hotel lobby with two contestants. Now a basketball arena could barely contain the event. This frat-party crowd seemed particularly young to Cataldi.

"I feel like I'm in *The Twilight Zone*, and I keep looking for Rod Serling," he said. "What scares me is, they're so drunk."

Automatic entry had been extended to gastronomic superstars like Sonya "Black Widow" Thomas and Bill "El Wingador" Simmons. Lesser contestants had been required to perform feats of alimentary extreme to qualify. One swallowed six pounds of spinach in seventy-nine seconds. Another, Uncle Buc, ate a one-and-a-half-pound Yankee Candle, which was essentially Ex-Lax with a wick. Once, a character named Slushy Shelly ate the snow and street crust from the wheel well of a car.

Obi Wing Kanobi, a physics student at Villanova whose real name was Doug Petock, had munched on eight Madagascar hissing cockroaches before the Eagles-Dallas game in December. Later, he said, he trained at altitude for Wing Bowl to improve his oxygen-carrying capacity but avoided the temptation of steroids.

"I want to do it right, for the kids," Obi Wing said backstage.

Wing Bowl was begun in homage to fans of the Buffalo Bills, who always celebrated the coming of the Super Bowl even though the team lost four consecutive times in the 1990s. In Philadelphia, the end of an Eagles season brought unfailing gloom. Wing Bowl was meant to lift the sagging community spirit.

"It was like an Irish wake," Morganti said. "Now it's an Irish wake where the corpse woke up."

Backstage, Uncle Buc planned another provocative entrance. His real name was Eugene Rawlings, a thirty-four-year-old contractor, who had been a boy of ten when the Eagles last played in the Super Bowl. "Cried like a baby" when the Eagles lost, he said. The team had broken his heart too many times since. Now, he pulled for the Eagles' opponents in the playoffs.

"I jumped ship," he said. "I'm a winner every time."

Two years ago at Wing Bowl, he had reenacted the interception by Tampa Bay cornerback Ronde Barber that sealed Philadelphia's doom in the 2003 NFC championship game. Uncle Buc tried to dodge a hail of beer and hot sauce, but a cup of cheese fries exploded on his head like a grenade. He looked down and even saw a pair of false teeth in the muck.

"I need an exit strategy," Uncle Buc said this morning as his entourage planned their latest confrontational scheme.

In a tiny dressing room, Sonya Thomas relaxed in a T-shirt and jeans, her hair in a ponytail, certain of repeat victory. She was thirty-seven, a resident of Alexandria, Virginia, who worked at Burger King at Andrews Air Force Base. Ten years ago, she had emigrated from South Korea. Daily, Sonya dined on a chicken Whopper, fries and a gallon of diet soda.

"I eat at work," she said. "Soda is free."

Her previous feats of culinary stardom included eating six pounds of asparagus in ten minutes, an eleven-pound cheesecake in nine minutes, four hundred thirty-two oysters in ten minutes and sixty-five hard-boiled eggs in six minutes, forty seconds. A year ago at Wing Bowl, Sonya had consumed one hundred sixty-seven chicken wings in thirty minutes. This year, she trained by eating a nine-pound cheeseburger in forty-eight minutes, all the more remarkable considering that she weighed only ninety-nine pounds.

"I don't like to lose," Sonya said. "I get so upset."

Victory would be hers again today, she said.

"No doubt about it."

Across the hallway, El Wingador wore white basketball shorts and a white sleeveless T-shirt. He was a truck driver from Woodbury Heights, New Jersey, who tipped the scales at three-hundred-plus pounds. A popular four-time champion at age forty-three, El Wingador felt he had been robbed in a second-place finish last year. Over the past two weeks, he had attempted to strengthen his jaw muscles by eating seven pounds of frozen Tootsie Rolls. He vowed to regain his crown, which he would proudly place over his peroxide mullet and retire.

"I'm too old for this," he said.

On stage, the twenty-nine contestants would be surrounded by Wingettes, who would provide the chicken wings in oval plates. Many Wingettes were strippers, their most frequent dance partners a pole. A couple seemed to be wearing little more than strategically placed Eagles logos.

Others had loftier ambitions. A Temple University student and Miss Black Pennsylvania, Kimberly Whittaker dreamed of becoming the first African American woman on the Supreme Court. But she was willing to start a few rungs down on the judicial ladder as a Wingette. Two weeks earlier, she arrived at WIP wearing a low-cut dress and what appeared to a push-up bra that did not come from the Sandra Day O'Connor collection. Producer Joe Weachter cautioned Whittaker that Cataldi was always leering at women. He was a harmless lech, but a lech nevertheless.

"That's okay," the statuesque, six-foot Whittaker said. "People don't talk to me. They talk to my chest."

Where others might have been impressed with Whittaker's business-law major, Cataldi was more taken with her skills as a belly dancer. "I just died and went to heaven," he said.

And then there was Jennifer Drumgoole, a graduate art student at Yale. She was serving as a Wingette for Sonya Thomas as part of a photography project. At Wing Bowl, she could ignore the objectification of women, the strippers in thongs, the spectators flashing their breasts. She found Thomas fascinating. So Drumgoole dressed for the event in a leopard-print unitard and the hidden girding of adhesives.

"I duct-taped my boobs," she said. "Sometimes you've got to take one for the team."

Before the eating of chicken wings began around eight o'clock, the contestants made grand entrances with their entourages, as if this were a prize fight. The favorites were introduced as "The Three Horsemen of the Esophagus."

An undercurrent of xenophobia was evident in this provincial city. Thomas was a woman and an outsider while, as many saw it, Wing Bowl was a local event made for hometown guys. As Thomas made her entrance as her nom de wing, the Black Widow, carried on a minifloat with a spider-web backdrop, she and her entourage were pelted with beer and other flying objects.

"I got hit with four beer cans," Drumgoole said. "The other Wingette got it with a block of cheese. I don't know what that was about."

Uncle Buc invited a caustic response. He and his entourage dressed in New England jerseys and held up a sign that said "Patriots 30, Eagles 0," drawing a fusillade of beer, hot sauce, Cheese Whiz and other projectiles. It could have been worse.

"No one threw false teeth this time," said George Sarkis, a member of the Uncle Buc entourage.

In time-honored Philadelphia style, a fight in the stands stopped for the national anthem, then started again. Miss Wing Bowl burst from a giant replica of the Vince Lombardi Trophy, flapping six-foot Eagles wings and wielding an axe to ceremonially smite New England's chances against Philadelphia in the Super Bowl.

Although Miss Wing Bowl swung the axe with great purpose and accuracy, she wore stiletto heels, fishnet stockings and a G-string not found in the average lumberjack wardrobe, hinting at her dual careers as an exotic dancer and master mechanic.

"She can build a Harley from the ground up," Morganti said with fond admiration.

Attention turned to the eating, which was held in three periods lasting fourteen, fourteen and two minutes. Hank the Tank, a hundred pounds slimmer and battle-trained with lap dances to sharpen his concentration, was shockingly eliminated in the first round. Damaging Doug, apparently finding chicken wings more palatable than state-issued bread and water, made the top ten. But it was clear from the start that El Wingador was on his game.

"There is a physical poetry there," George Shea, chairman of the International Federation of Competitive Eating, said in his play-by-play voice. "He's eating with an intuitive understanding of the wing that I've not seen before."

At halftime, a character named Mize slammed beer cans against his head as great fizzing streams geysered forth and his forehead turned scarlet.

Before the two-minute lightning round, Shea stood in his suit and straw boater and summoned his best oratorical bombast, saying, "Competitive eating is the battleground upon which God and Lucifer wage war for men's souls."

After thirty minutes of peristaltic vigor, the Black Widow and El Wingador were tied at 147 wings apiece. A new car awaited the winner. Just before the two-minute overtime began, El Wingador sent back his plate. Confetti had fallen into the wings. In the overtime, both ate ravenously, their Wingettes offering bosomy encouragement, but when the final buzzer sounded, El Wingador had consumed 162 wings and the Black Widow had swallowed but 161. El Wingador was the five-time champion, and the Wing Bowl title had been dutifully returned to a resident of the Philadelphia region.

Only in Philadelphia could twenty thousand fans cheer for a three-hundred-pound truck driver, said Marc Rayfield, general manager of WIP. "El Wingador went beyond competitive eating into an area of pure emotion," Shea said. "He separated himself from the rules of physics and was able to do something science can't explain."

And that was it. By ten in the morning, El Wingador had retired from competitive eating, his face, T-shirt and pants smudged with sauce. He wanted to lose fifty pounds, he said, and didn't want to die of a heart attack while his daughters were young. But he had one more immediate stop on this blustery morning.

"Breakfast buffet," he said.

As I walked to my car through a parking lot strewn with alcoholic refuse, someone kicked a beer can behind me. It was Ron Aukamp of Pottstown, Pennsylvania. He had to pick up his car and drive back to the Wachovia Center. And he wasn't happy about it.

"This is a damn good time if your friend doesn't pass out ten minutes into it," he said.

28

Saturday, February 5

The best day of the week in Jacksonville. It was sunny and breezy along the Riverwalk, and the wind brushed the St. Johns River like suede. Eagles fans began to gather at a huge white hospitality tent christened the Eagles Nest. Inside, Ray Didinger and Glen Macnow did their Saturday radio show on WIP. Ray and Glen sat at a table, cordoned from the crowd with yellow tape that said, "Caution Wet Paint."

Fans wore Eagles jerseys, smoked cigars and drank beer. One guy had his beard painted kelly green. Somebody called and chanted "E-A-G-L-E-S" in Russian. A few men leaned in close so they could hear Didinger's prediction for the Super Bowl. Both he and Macnow had picked identical scores: Eagles twenty-three, Patriots twenty.

The Eagles were the hungrier team, Didinger reasoned, a legal pad full of notes to ratify his position. New England was playing for its third Super Bowl title in four years, while the Eagles hadn't reached the Super Bowl for twenty-four years. Philadelphia could pressure and unnerve New England quarterback Tom Brady. The Eagles' run defense would stop Patriots' running back Corey Dillon from dominating. Donovan McNabb wasn't as predictable and sedentary as the Patriots had found Peyton Manning earlier in the playoffs. McNabb could destroy a game plan. He could take short drops, deep drops, roll out, play-fake, move the pocket, run. He was cool and confident, having thrown not a single interception in the playoffs. He understood the pressure on his shoulders and accepted it.

"I think McNabb is going to go out and play a whale of a football game," Didinger said as the fans erupted in applause.

John Kleinstuber gave me a call from Havertown. He had pulled a trick on a guy from the pro shop at his golf club, a New England fan. He put food coloring in the guy's turkey club sandwich, turning his lips and his tongue and his teeth green.

"He might be up here shortly looking for me," John said.

He just wanted tomorrow to get here. The club was closing for a month and he just wanted to finish up at work and get home. He'd have dinner at five or six and then go to bed. Shut it down. Super Bowl Sunday couldn't get here fast enough. He'd go in for a few hours on Sunday, too, just to keep his mind off the game.

"If I start crackin' beers, I'll be unconscious by game time," John said.

He was invited to a million parties, but he turned them all down. This was a game he had to watch with no distractions.

"Depending on the outcome, my TV and me are going to be in love," he said.

At one o'clock, I met up with Shaun Young and his new friends aboard the Eagles RV that had traveled to Jacksonville from Philly. They had come armed with six hundred beers and two thousand cigarettes. One essential item was left behind. Bill Byrnes, a retired civil engineer from the Philadelphia suburb of Norristown, was known as Arrow Man. He sat in the end zone holding up three laminated arrows, which pointed downward when the opponent attempted a field goal or extra point and upward when the Eagles kicked the ball. Arrow Man had forgotten his arrows. His wife had found them behind a bureau in the bedroom.

"Make some new ones," his wife suggested.

"No way," Bill told her. "These have been through wars."

So she had them FedExed to Jacksonville, with 150 hot dogs.

Bill didn't have Super Bowl tickets, but that hardly mattered. He would watch on television at an RV park and hold up the arrows anyway, hoping his mojo worked from long distance.

Bill had been a season-ticket holder for forty-two of his sixty-three years. He could take losing season after losing season, but he could never take the price of beer at Veterans Stadium. So his father used to carry a case beneath his wheelchair, and they would push him into the bathroom and dispense the brews from beneath this rolling beverator. His mother, Edith, used to carry beer into the stadium in her purse.

"But with the sixteen-ouncers, they got heavier and she got older and walked kind of stooped," Bill said. "Security knew something was wrong. I used to let her follow me in to protect her, but they said, 'Lady, we gotta look in your purse.' She was seventy-seven then. She's eighty-nine now. They caught her and she said, 'My sons are alcoholics. They need this.'"

Actually, two RVs had made the trip from the Philly area in this convoy, eighteen people in all. There were a dozen aboard today, including a Patriots fan named Scott Berk, an Air Force pilot from Bear, Delaware. His neighbor, Pat Oakes, was an Eagles fan. If Philadelphia won the Super Bowl, Berk would paint an Eagles logo on the side of his house. If New England won, Oakes would paint his lawn mower red, white and blue and cut his neighbor's yard for the summer.

"But only at night," Oakes said.

Berk wore a New England jersey. And he gave as good as he got from the Eagles fans in the RV. To do any less would be like a wildebeest surrendering to a pride of lions.

"I doubled the IQ of this RV just by getting on," he said.

Shaun wore his face paint and shoulder pads and a black Terrell Owens jersey. The theme from *Rocky* was piped over the speakers and Shaun jogged in front of the bus as we rolled through downtown. He kept going straight as the bus turned left, and the others shouted for him to make a U-turn.

Shaun had been doing this for two days now, running ahead of the RV, or shouting with his hoarse voice out of the window to stunned onlookers: "You are no longer in the world you woke up in! This is my world! I will never stop! My head will explode, but I will grow a new head! I am the only one who realizes if I am stable or unstable and even I can't tell you!"

He climbed back in, panting slightly. The theme song of the day was played next, a football version of Jimmy Buffett's "Margaritaville," sung cannily by Philly comedian Joe Conklin.

> *I don't know the reason*
> *Suffered so many seasons*
> *Nothing to do but just sit there and boo.*
> *After years of frustration*
> *There's now jubilation*
> *It's time to crack open another cold brew.*
> *Eagles fans are takin' over Jacksonville*
> *Gonna win our first Super Bowl*
> *Some people claim we're satisfied just to be here*
> *I say, no*
> *Hell, let's win it all.*

"It's been a hell of a season, no question," Shaun said. "But we can't be satisfied with just getting there. Bottom line is, we need to win the Bowl. You don't want to end the season in second place. The first loser, nobody remembers that."

Our first stop of the afternoon was the Mayport Naval Station. Randall Cunningham and other retired Eagles were playing in a flag-football game. Shaun was revved up. The night before, a woman had posed for a photograph with him and placed his hand on her breast.

"I've signed a few bare ones," he said.

As we neared the naval station, Berk, the Air Force pilot, pointed out the three giveaways to every base—pawn shops, strip clips and a trailer park at the end of the runway.

"Hide the beers," he cautioned as we went through a security checkpoint.

We parked on a sandy road outside the makeshift football field, and Shaun autographed the shirts of a few kids.

"You playing in the Super Bowl tomorrow?" a girl asked.

"I'm not, but I wish I was," he said.

We watched for a half as Cunningham, still possessing a languorous whip of an arm, passed the retired Eagles to a three-touchdown lead over an eager but overmatched team from the base.

At halftime, players signed autographs. Shaun shook hands with several of the former Eagles who said hello and slapped at his shoulder pads. One of them, Marc Woodard, a linebacker in the mid-1990s, had once told Shaun, "You're more famous than I am."

Kenny Jackson, a former Eagles receiver, noticed the green RV with wings painted on the side and said, "Somebody's smokin' something up in there."

'Can you imagine the party in there?" Jackson said. "That's true Eagles football. It's not a limousine, it's not New York. That's the Eagles. A Winnebago. And it ain't one of them fancy ones, either."

There was an Eagles pep rally at Jacksonville Landing later in the afternoon, so we headed back toward downtown. The theme from *Rocky* was cranked up again. Shaun jogged in front of the RV, then bent down and did one-armed push-ups. Jackson looked over from the sideline and his hand flashed V for victory. Ted Washington, a gargantuan defensive lineman for the Oakland Raiders, gave a more quizzical look. He appeared puzzled why a man would be wearing shoulder pads and grease paint on a Saturday afternoon at a naval base, and even more bewildered why the guy would be performing calisthenics in front of a moving recreational vehicle.

Back on board, Shaun spotted a woman wearing a Tom Brady jersey. "You are out of your mind!" he screamed at her in scratchy theatricality. "Go back to Foxboro, you pansies! You have no idea who you are messing with! You are going to play by my rules! You will see me somewhere close to you on a Post Office wall! I will be there, I will be everywhere! Don't you forget it!"

On the ride to Jacksonville Landing, a retail center full of shops and restaurants, the talk turned to the primacy of Eagles fans.

"The fans are deserving," said Paul Natarcola, an Eagles supporter from Delaware. "That's what the whole sport is about, the fans."

"I'm not going to look at it as being owed anything," Shaun said. "But we, as a city, need a championship, just to solidify the city as a winning city. We know we have winners in the city. It just always seems like every time we're gonna make a move, something happens. We just need it. People will feel a lot better about themselves as a whole."

One of the guys on board, Bob Stahl, learned from a phone call that his grandson had won free tickets. He would be arriving tomorrow. Brian Statare, a news anchor at WIP, arrived today, fell into a conversation with a guy on a water taxi, and bought a ticket for $1900.

"Unless you're Shirley MacLaine, you only do this once," Statare said.

Shaun and the rest of the guys in the RV appeared out of luck.

"A guy called me Friday and had tickets and wanted three grand," Oakes said. "I ain't payin' that kinda money."

At the Jacksonville Landing, we pulled in behind a fire truck painted Eagles green. Shaun and I followed a phalanx of cheerleaders to a stage in the center of a plaza. Thousands of Eagles fans were jammed tight into this retail amphitheater for the pep rally. Governor Rendell was there, dressed in khakis and a blue blazer.

"I haven't seen a Patriots fan since I've been down here and I've been here since Thursday night," Rendell told me, surveying the fuel-injected crowd, his shouting voice barely audible. "There are fifteen thousand people down here, Eagles fans, and I'd say about a hundred have tickets."

Not just with his heart, but with his head, Rendell said, he thought the Eagles would win.

"I think their intensity level is going to be higher, they're going to care more about winning," he told me. "They don't make any mistakes, they win."

Presciently, he added, "Nothing can compensate for turnovers."

On stage, the governor asked, "Who needs tickets?"

Tomorrow, the outcome would be up to the fans, he said. If the fans did their job, the players would be ready to do their jobs. "We have to make this an Eagles home game, right?" he said. The players had to hear the fans cheering from the opening kickoff to the final gun. If they did, he would see everybody back in Philly at the victory parade on Tuesday, and at next year's Super Bowl in Detroit.

John Street, Philadelphia's mayor, also spoke and got booed. Shaun took the stage to a smattering of jeers, too, remnant catcalls from the harsh treatment of McNabb nearly six years earlier on draft day.

"Welcome to Phillyville!" Shaun said, his voice a torn shriek. "Nobody, I mean nobody, is going to disrespect this team after tomorrow, when we are Super Bowl XXXIX champions! We are the greatest, I mean absolutely fantastic best, fans in the country!"

After the pep rally, we had a *Spinal Tap* moment. The RV had disappeared, apparently ordered away by the cops. The Eagles' unofficial official mascot was left in downtown Jacksonville without a ride home—Batman without his Batmobile.

"Un-fucking-believable," Shaun said as he dialed his cell phone.

While we waited for his friend, Scott Teller, to pick us up, it became clear exactly where Shaun's star fit into the constellation of Eagles fans. Other Philadelphia fans urged him on, almost as if he were a player, as if he had a hand in the outcome, while New England fans mocked him in his shoulder pads and Terrell Owens jersey.

"Hey, T.O., how's your ankle feel?" one group of Patriots fans said tauntingly. "It ain't going to feel good tomorrow."

"Come over here, I'll show you how it feels, bro'," Shaun said.

A guy walked up to Shaun, pulled a can of Bud Light out of his pocket and handed it to him.

"You deserve it, baby," the Eagles fan said.

"I don't drink," Shaun said, declining.

A group of hip-hoppers walked by, and one turned and looked and said, "That's one of them for-real fans right there. Diehard."

A guy asked Shaun to pose for a picture.

"You're the fuckin' man, dude."

"Shaun, you got a ticket? No? Why don't you talk to [Jeffrey] Lurie, get a ticket?"

Steve Castellano, a Navy cook, said his companion had sent him videotapes of the Eagles when he was stationed in the Persian Gulf. It had been uplifting to see Shaun on the tapes, he said.

"You're the outstanding number one fan, hands down," Castellano told Shaun. "The governor, he's number two. To come down here to Jacksonville and represent the way you do, you got to be number one."

A guy with a giant foam hand slapped high-fives with Shaun. "Yo, Shaun," someone else shouted. "Tomorrow's the day. We're gonna do it."

It was getting cold. Shaun's friend was having trouble finding us. Back home, the Philadelphia skyline was decked out in green. Here we were in Florida, shivering on a street corner. A group of Patriots fans crossed the street in front of us.

"Hey, T.O., the doctor says you can't play," one of them teased.

"I do what I want to do," Shaun growled.

29

Sunday, February 6

Super Bowl Sunday. By eight thirty in the morning, Shaun Young and the Eagles RV had moved from Pecan Park near the Jacksonville airport to the corner of Talleyrand and Swift, a ten-minute walk to Alltel Stadium. There must have been three dozen RVs squeezed into a lot with two power boxes. Almost no one had tickets to the game. It was enough just to be close by. Shaun wore a black Brian Dawkins jersey over his shoulder pads. Another guy walked around in a green cape with a hood. The back of the cape read "G. Reaper" and bore the numerals 0:00, as if to say the clock had run out on New England's football dynasty. In a tree, someone hung a Patriots player in effigy.

"I have no idea what time it is," Shaun said before noon, appearing outwardly calm with the kickoff six hours away. "I can just tell it's getting closer and closer. My blood and my mind are going two hundred miles an hour. I'm just trying to chill my body out."

Down the street, a Patriots fan had attached a dollar bill to a line from a Popeil Pocket Fisherman. He let the dollar bill sit on the sidewalk and yanked it away every time an Eagles fan bent over to retrieve it. A couple of hours later, I saw the same guy raising a white wooden chair over his head and smashing it on the ground, apparently having lost both his dollar and his sobriety.

Limousines drove down the narrow street in front of the RV park, which interfered with touch football games. Scott Berk, the lone Patriots fan among the Philadelphia tailgaters, barked, "Eagles fans get back on the sidewalk and take your Geritol. I know you been waiting since 1960 for this."

A guy walking down the street in a Donovan McNabb jersey overturned his ice chest and beer spilled onto the pavement. "Asshole," the crowd chanted playfully in unison, then helped him pick up the cans.

Ernie and Chris Clark showed up at the Eagles RV, Chris in an Eagles pullover, Ernie in a Super Bowl windbreaker and khakis. Father and son had spent every moment together for the last three days. It had been great, Ernie said, except that Chris "learned that his father snores a lot when he drinks."

They had shared a room in a local home, and Chris had slept fitfully last night, thinking about the game, getting up at five thirty this morning, flipping on the NFL Channel.

"I slept four hours all weekend," Chris said.

He went on a scouting mission for a Catholic church, telling his father, "This is not the day to miss." The priest at ten o'clock mass had walked to the pulpit and said, "In our position, we're supposed to remain somewhat partial, but originally I'm from outside Philly."

He let it go at that and everyone laughed.

Ernie had a good feeling about the game. He had seen the Eagles win NFL titles in 1948 and 1960 and, after forty-four seasons, he thought he might hit a delayed trifecta today.

"I think Donovan's got to have a big game, but we can get it done," Ernie said. "For right or wrong, it's kinda on his shoulders, really. I hope T.O. runs out in the starting lineup, I can tell you that."

Chris felt more uncertainty.

"I'm not really sure what kind of animal we're dealing with here," he said. "I have tremendous respect for the Patriots. I'm trying to determine if we've got the stuff to deal with it. We'll see."

Pat O'Brien, a quarterback at Villanova in the late 1970s and early 1980s who now lived in Clearwater, Florida, joined the tailgating. He said he had never seen fans from one city take over a Super Bowl town the way Eagles fans had taken over Jacksonville.

He had a hard-core New York Giants fan from Brooklyn living across from him in Clearwater. When the Giants came to Tampa to play in the Super Bowl in 1991, it was nothing like this. Nothing.

"Guys in Philly make thirty thousand a year and they take their money aside to go to Eagles' games," O'Brien said. "My father was a season-ticket holder back at Franklin Field. He went with all his cronies. They were all cops, union guys, blue-collar guys. My father raised eleven kids as a cop and took his money aside. He went to Eagles games every year for thirty-eight years. Bill O'Brien. Reds O'Brien. That's what he did. He also worked two other jobs. He drove a truck. He worked in a liquor store, whatever. He raised eleven kids and every Sunday, we never saw him. He left at seven in the morning and went down the old Franklin Field, then the Vet. One o'clock games he'd come home around nine, ten o'clock at night, you know. Stumblin', bumblin', you know. But he had a good time. He had a good time."

Plastic hard hats had been set on a table outside the Eagles RV. When the players went to work, so would the fans. Three television sets were going. A grill sizzled with ribs and hot dogs. Three and a half hours before game time, Rich Edwards, an Eagles fan, and Scott Berk, the Patriots fan, stood by the grill in hard hats and began to heat-butt each other like bighorn sheep. I think Berk's jabbing humor was wearing thin. They banged heads and Berk's hat slid down on his eyes and he took it off and there was a mark on his forehead as if he had just returned from Mass on Ash Wednesday.

"We'll duct-tape you to the back of the RV on the way home," Edwards said. "I was nice all the time, but it's over."

On the Comcast SportsNet pre-game show, Governor Rendell admonished Eagles fans to be enthusiastic but not destructive, win or lose. No destroying property or setting fires, he pleaded gently.

"We don't want to mar a great victory, or if we lose, a great season," Rendell said.

•   •   •

Outside the stadium, I met up with Butch and Sue DeLuca, who were dressed in Eagles jerseys. They had warmed up for the game at Hooters and they were ready to take their seats. "Unbelievable," Butch kept saying. "Unbelievable."

They had driven in from Daytona, instead of taking a bus with their tour group, because Tim Kelly, Butch's son-in-law, did not want to mingle with New England fans. It would be especially hard on the way back if the Eagles lost. Tim hardly said a word the entire drive to Jacksonville.

"I'm a little tense," he told me at the stadium. "I hope the team's not tense. I'm so nervous, but I'm optimistic. We got a shot, a realistic shot. I guaranteed a victory to my mother."

Just before I headed up to the auxiliary press box, I ran into a friend, Jill Lieber, from *USA Today*. She was with Lesslee Kay Fitzmorris, president of a company that choreographed Super Bowl half-time shows. We didn't know each other, but we had been at LSU at the same time in the 1970s. Fitzmorris had been a member of the Golden Girls, the dance team of the LSU band.

Earlier in the afternoon, Fitzmorris told me, she saw an Eagles fan climb out of a limousine and throw up. Then his friends jumped out and took pictures.

"Only Eagles fans would jump out and take pictures," she said.

And LSU fans, we agreed.

Inside, Alltel Stadium did not seem so different from Lincoln Financial Field. It resembled a concrete accordion and was loud and packed with Eagles fans clumped in their green jerseys, and their white-and-black jerseys like numbered salt and pepper shakers, greatly outnumbering Patriots fans in sunburned anticipation. Many had been drinking all day, massing outside the stadium, carrying beer in plastic mugs shaped like footballs, their pasty bodies blotchy in the sun. They were not here for ceremony. They cared little about the fireworks and military flyovers and movable sound stages with the Black Eyed Peas and Charlie Daniels and the NFL's flailing attempt at safe, lowest-common-denominator hipness after

Janet Jackson's nipple-ring affront. They flew from Philly on chartered planes and drove their cars and piloted their recreational
vehicles to be present for a kind of boozy pigskin exorcism. They
wanted to win, sure, but most of all they wanted to purge the losing that came with calendar precision, with Gregorian certainty,
for forty-four barren seasons since the Eagles last won a championship, for twenty-two fallow years since any professional team in
Philadelphia had won a title. One fan, in a green Brian Dawkins
jersey, held up a sign that said, "Dear God, Please Complete My
Life." He appeared to be about twenty-five.

These fans did not want to lose, but the most perceptive of
them must have wondered what they would have without the losing. Some might have feared victory as much as defeat. Defeat, or
at least its anticipation, had shaped their civic identity. It brought
them to Jacksonville in nervous desire. It put them on common
ground with their anguished fathers and grandfathers and made
them suffering saints in the communal church of the Eagles. It
gave desperate spice to life's Cream of Wheat blandness and provided irritable comfort, each season ripped and torn like a pair of
favorite jeans. Victory carried emotional risk and responsibility
and expectation. Championships brought fleeting satisfaction but
ended when the next season began, while defeat could be soaked
and wallowed in with the solacing envelop of a hot bath.

As it turned out, the auxiliary press box was nothing but a couple of tables laid over the top rows of seats, high above the Eagles
bench. The Philadelphia fans in front of us never sat down, and it
would have been foolhardy to ask them. One guy held up the
unfolded carrying case of a Miller twenty-four pack. On the cardboard he had written "700 Level."

As darkness fell, players from both teams strolled toward the
field's tunneled entrances, some walking abreast with the slew-
footed confidence of gunfighters, others fidgeting with their gloves
like anxious debutantes. And then the smoky, fog-machine sprint
onto the field beneath giant inflatable helmets. Brian Dawkins
flexed with the pose of a professional wrestler. During warm-ups,
others lay in calm repose on the field or knelt at the bench in

prayer or slam-danced in the end zone or banged helmets to summon courage and invincibility, the evening's pressure and fear and determination evident in red, raw, teary eyes.

Before kickoff, Ernie Clark called back to Philadelphia on his cell phone. He and Chris had great seats, thirty-yard line on the Eagles side of the field. Better than their seats at the Linc. The rest of the family was gathered in Bucks County at the home of his daughter, Sue Harrigan. They talked for a couple of minutes—it was hard to hear in the rising din—and at the end, the Clarks said what they always said before an Eagles game, "Let's get it done."

Inside, Chris's emotions paddled like a Ping-Pong ball. *Man, they could get blown out. Just let them be okay. I know we're good enough to play with these guys. Don't let them be freaked out.*

Father and son thinking the same thing.

Just give us a good game. Don't embarrass us. Don't come up with a clunker.

Philadelphia won the toss and elected to receive, and the opening kickoff summoned a firefly flash of cameras. Terrell Owens jogged back into the lineup, seven weeks after breaking a bone in his right leg and tearing ligaments in the ankle. He wore thin white sweatbands above his elbows, like garter belts on a Wild West saloonkeeper. He split left on first down, but immediately the Eagles faced a tactical surprise.

Given two weeks to prepare, New England did some portly chessboard rearranging, switching from three defensive linemen to four, and the Eagles seemed confused, uncertain in their blocking assignments. McNabb took the opening snap and was pressured to the sideline. With no place to run, he threw an incompletion. On third down, linebacker Tedy Bruschi pounced on a blitz and McNabb turned to absorb the blow and ducked away, but he lost the ball in a jolting blur of blue and silver. New England recovered at the Philadelphia thirty-six-yard line. Fortunately for the Eagles, McNabb's knee had touched the ground before the ball came loose. But the game had just started and already Philadelphia appeared nervous, rushed, unsettled.

Midway through the first quarter, the Eagles' flat-lining offense finally began to resuscitate. Owens loped across the middle on a short crossing route, leapt and reached over his head to make a balletic catch. His doctor had not cleared him to play, and he risked breaking the surgical screws in his ankle, but he showed no flinch of injury. He gloved the ball in one hand, then cradled it against his forearm, his eyes locking on the defensive back, his knees pumping high in elegant speed, cleats flashing silver in the light, his left shoulder dipping slightly, his left leg offered in a slight bounding stutter-step, his all-pro deceptiveness calculated in feints and angles and sideline geometry.

He was pushed out of bounds after thirty yards, and a penalty against New England for unnecessary roughness put the ball at the Patriots' eight-yard line. Owens stood on the sideline and flapped his arms. Surely, the Eagles were about to take flight.

But Philadelphia was still jittery, unsure, in the face of New England's shifting defense. McNabb was sacked for a loss of sixteen yards. *If you're gonna take a hit, get rid of the ball*, Butch DeLuca thought to himself, sitting in the corner of the end zone, the Eagles coming right at him. *How do you get sacked like that without throwing the ball out of bounds? Get rid of it. Do something.*

McNabb's next pass was tipped and intercepted, but a penalty nullified the mistake. On first and ten at the New England nineteen, McNabb threw for the left corner of the end zone, but his pass seemed wounded. The ball wobbled and hovered for anyone to catch. When his passing was ineffective, McNabb often threw at the feet of his receivers, but he seemed overly excited tonight, and in the adrenaline rush the ball sailed on him. *One of them lollipop jobs*, Butch DeLuca thought as safety Rodney Harrison intercepted at the Patriots' four-yard line.

As he released the ball, McNabb's mouth formed a perfect O in anticipation, then flattened into a smile of regret. "Noooo," Chris Clark screamed from his seat. *Damn, he can't get it done.*

At the RV park near Alltel Stadium, Shaun Young screamed, too, then put his hands on his head in bewilderment. This season, McNabb had become the first NFL quarterback to throw more than thirty touchdown passes and fewer than ten interceptions. *Not one turnover in the red zone.* Now he had been picked off twice in two plays. *Why is this happening?*

"Did it slip out of your hand?" Coach Andy Reid asked on the sideline in a conversation caught by NFL Films.

"No, it got caught in the wind," McNabb said, his breath visible in the cool evening air.

Reid stared ahead in his reading glasses, a curl of his mustache betraying his exasperation.

On the next Philadelphia drive, tight end L. J. Smith caught a pass, but was wrangled and calf-roped during a rodeo tackle. The ball was punched away. Four drives in the first quarter, two turnovers. Nobody wasted these kinds of chances and beat New England. Back in Havertown, watching in his living room, John Kleinstuber thought despondently, *Here we go again. It's going to be another twenty years.*

Still, nobody had scored. And New England had managed only one first down in the opening quarter against Philadelphia's punishing blitz. The Eagles' defense was playing with haughty confidence. Chris Clark took a deep breath. *Okay, this is going to be a game. Back and forth. The defense is playing well enough. We'll at least be okay. The offense has to figure a way to get it done.*

Early in the second quarter, Philadelphia began to move the ball again. Todd Pinkston, questioned about his heart, reluctant to catch the ball over the middle, jabbed into New England's defense for seventeen yards then vaulted for another catch of forty yards. Jeffrey Lurie, the Eagles owner, stood and cheered. Brian Westbrook brushed off left tackle for eleven yards to the Patriots' six-yard line. On third and goal, McNabb looked toward Owens, who got shoved to the ground. McNabb pumped his arm, and his pass protection held and he had time to look elsewhere. Smith, the tight end, muscled his way past a linebacker, made a diving catch and redeemed his earlier fumble with a touchdown. With nine minutes, fifty-five seconds remaining in the first half, the Eagles had scored first to take a seven-zero lead.

Tim Kelly began to get text messages on his cell phone: *We're going to win this game*. Shaun Young jumped up and hugged and high-fived everyone around him in the Eagles RV. Ernie and Chris Clark called home and the voices on the other end began to sing the Eagles fight song and Chris screamed through the tumult, "We're feelin' it down here, we're feelin' it."

But New England had one more strategic trump card to play. To counter Philadelphia's blitz, the Patriots began stretching the Eagles' defense with four wide receivers, then tossing screen passes to running back Corey Dillon. Late in the second quarter, the Eagles punted from their twelve-yard line, and the ball skidded off Dirk Johnson's foot and traveled only twenty-nine yards.

With an opening at the Philadelphia thirty-seven, New England finally gathered its composure and resolve. Again, the Patriots distended the Eagles' defense with four and five receivers and punched the ball across the goal line in seven plays. On second and goal at the four-yard line, Brady patiently found receiver David Givens alone in the right corner of the end zone, throwing the ball sharply across the field. Lito Sheppard, the Eagles' cornerback, seemed frozen with uncertainty. Givens placed a foot on the ball and flapped his arms and flexed his muscles in mimicry of Owens. The game was tied at seven to seven.

Seventy seconds remained until halftime. The momentum seemed to be changing to Chris Clark, tilting away from the Eagles. He had an animated discussion with his father.

"Let's just get the hell out of here seven-seven," Chris said.

"Screw that," Ernie Clark said. "You gotta go for it here."

Pinkston caught a pass for ten yards, then another for fifteen to the Philadelphia forty-one, but the clock expired. At halftime, the game had been sloppy but the score was even. Still, Chris Clark felt a sense of opportunity missed. *Geez, we had our chances.*

During intermission, he ran into Chris Berman, the ESPN personality. They chatted briefly.

"Whaddya think?" Clark asked.

"You played terrible and its seven-seven," Berman replied. "You have a chance."

Yeah, but I'm not comfortable with this, Clark thought to himself. Brady had hit nine of his last ten passes. *The Patriots seem to have their legs under them a little bit.*

Still, he believed, the game was winnable.

It's right here in our grasp. If we can just play one good half of football, this can be ours.

The game was halfway over, but it wasn't too late for bargain viewing and unisex fashion statements. Martin Kane of Admore, Pennsylvania, was drinking outside a bar near the stadium, when two Super Bowl vendors showed up. They appeared to be high school girls, who said they were exhausted after the week's festivities and had walked off the job. They offered to sell their uniform shirts and credentials for sixty bucks each. Deal. Wearing bright-orange shirts, ladies' medium, Kane and a buddy arrived just in time to watch Paul McCartney perform his half-time show.

"I knew a couple other dudes who tried to get in in old Pepsi jumpsuits, acting like they were delivering soda," Kane said. "They didn't have the right credentials. It works every time at Eagles games."

New England received the second-half kickoff, and Chris Clark's fears became justified. The Patriots moved the ball sixty-nine yards in nine plays, spotting vulnerability in the Eagles' secondary. Cornerback Matt Ware was a rookie and Patriots' receiver Deion Branch challenged his inexperience with three receptions to the Eagles' two-yard line. Linebacker Mike Vrabel then lined up as a tight end for New England and swatted at a pass in his unfamiliarity as a receiver. He appeared to be wrestling a badger. But Vrabel finally clutched the ball in the end zone, and New England went ahead fourteen to seven. This was Vrabel's fifth career reception, and his fifth touchdown.

"Dad, we can't stop them," Chris Clark told his father.

We gotta get this back, Ernie Clark thought to himself, growing concerned. *Donovan doesn't seem to play well from behind. He's had a great year, but it was almost always from in front.*

But Philadelphia's defense stiffened and the offense found an inventive rhythm. Westbrook glided furtively out of the backfield and turned a short pass into fifteen yards. He swept left for one first down and shimmied off tackle for another. He lined up wide and reached back for a one-handed catch, then sprinted across the middle from the slot. McNabb threaded the ball between two defenders for a ten-yard touchdown pass. With three minutes, thirty-five seconds remaining in the third quarter, the Eagles had tied the game at fourteen to fourteen.

McNabb pounded on his chest. Shaun Young ran outside the Eagles RV and began pounding his chest, too. He ran into a Patriots fan from Connecticut, and the guy asked him, "Do you think you have us?"

"This is our year, our game," Shaun said in his raspy voice. "The trophy is coming back to the City of Brotherly Love."

At the stadium, Chris Clark told his father, "I just want the ball once with the score tied. Just get us the ball once."

An odd thought crept into the head of his sister, Terry Funk, who was watching back in suburban Philadelphia. She felt sad. No matter how it ended, in victory or defeat, the game and the season would be over in less than an hour. *You wait so long and it consumes your life from August to now and it's going to be over.*

"Hey," Terrell Owens screamed on the sideline, pounding his chest, exhorting the Eagles' defense. "I need the ball back. I need it back."

For the first time, a Super Bowl remained tied after three quarters. But Philadelphia would never get the ball back with a level score. Inexorably, New England began to pull ahead as the third quarter became the fourth. Corey Dillon shouldered into the end zone from two yards, running behind a guard lined up at fullback. New England went ahead to stay, twenty-one to fourteen.

In Havertown, the game became a blur for John Kleinstuber. It had been torture, pure torture, waiting six hours for kickoff. He partied too hard and now he could tell the game was slipping away and the rest became a vague shape, a smudge. A switch went off in his head. *This is over. They weren't the Birds. They weren't even there. They weren't fired up, crackin' people's asses. Played the whole game on their heels.*

New England scored again on a twenty-two-yard field goal by

Adam Vinatieri to extend its lead to twenty-four to fourteen. On Philadelphia's next possession, there was more frantic emotion than accuracy in McNabb's arm, and Tedy Bruschi intercepted for New England.

"They're not going to get it done," Chris Clark said in resignation to his father.

But the Eagles would not go meekly. The defense held and Philadelphia retrieved the ball at its twenty-one-yard line. Five minutes, forty seconds remained. It was a long shot—the Eagles needed two scores to win or force overtime—but there was still time for a comeback if they hurried.

Wait. . . . What the hell? Why were they taking so much time? Where was the two-minute drill? The no-huddle offense?

Fans inside and outside the stadium began screaming, at the players, at their television screens.

Come on.

What the fuck?

What are these guys doing?

Get up to the line. Call a fuckin' play.

Fans became apoplectic, but the Eagles felt there was no need to rush. Needless hurry would cause mistakes. But the clock was draining toward zero.

Back in Philadelphia, Jennifer Clark, put her hand on her chest and said, "My heart can't stand it." All evening, her sister, Terry Funk, kept looking over, and Jen kept saying, "I don't know if I can stand this. My heart is racing." *You know what drives me crazy. If the Eagles weren't in this game, I'd be enjoying the Super Bowl.* Jen was a nervous wreck.

The Eagles moved assuredly, if glacially, downfield. Greg Lewis scooped a low pass. Owens made his ninth reception, a fingertip catch, and got both feet down near the sideline. First and ten at the Philadelphia forty-six. Three minutes, thirty-six seconds left.

McNabb faked a handoff to Westbrook, rolled away from pressure and threw low for Owens over the middle. Just as McNabb released the ball, he was jackhammered by defensive end Jarvis Green. On the next play, either center Hank Fraley snapped the ball prematurely or McNabb was not ready for it. He looked for an opening then went to the ground and took a hard shoulder in the back from Bruschi. McNabb appeared to walk slowly and awkwardly back to the huddle.

The clock ticked below three minutes. Third and ten, still at the Philadelphia forty-six. A half-minute elapsed before the next play.

They're taking too much time.

Get up there.

Hurry the fuck up.

McNabb gathered himself and threw over the middle for eleven yards to Freddie Mitchell. His only catch of the game gave Philadelphia a first down at the New England forty-three. But the clock was expiring. The Eagles needed ten points just to reach overtime. Reid stood and watched, his play chart tucked under his arm.

McNabb seemed to try to call a play at the line of scrimmage, but apparently could not. Then the Eagles gathered in a huddle, as McNabb appeared to be coughing or trying to catch his breath. What happened to him fell into the ambiguous gray of a team that was frequently not forthcoming with black-and-white explanations.

Fraley would later say on Angelo Cataldi's television program that McNabb soldiered on despite appearing exhausted and on the verge of vomiting. McNabb would say he wasn't sick or exhausted, only winded on a day in which he threw fifty-one passes and took a pounding. The Eagles would tell the *Inquirer* that Bruschi's hit left McNabb gasping for air. The quarterback had thrown up at a game in Jacksonville during the 2002 season. And he had been known to vomit while playing at the University of Syracuse. The pressure and fatigue of these moments of intense physical exertion could be overwhelming. The dehydration and weariness and shouting to be heard and knowing that a whole country was watching and any mistake would cost the game.

Why are they huddling?

We ain't got all day.

This is inexcusable.

Show some goddamn urgency.

Still first down at the New England forty-three. With the 40-second clock receding, McNabb threw over the middle to Westbrook, who dropped the ball in the wide open. More precious time wasted. Two fourteen left. Then McNabb found Westbrook out of the backfield for a first down at the New England thirty. Two-minute warning. On the sideline, safety Brian Dawkins held up two fingers that either signaled the time remaining or a desperate V for victory.

On first down at the thirty, McNabb took a short drop, but his pass was batted away. One fifty-five left. Second and ten. The Eagles had to hurry now. McNabb stood in the shotgun and threw over the middle in a feathery arc to Greg Lewis, who had lined up in the wrong spot at receiver, inside instead of outside. But Lewis ran a post pattern, sprinted past a rookie safety and made a great leaping catch in the end zone. Patriots twenty-four, Eagles twenty-one. One forty-eight left.

The Eagles still had a chance. In suburban Philadelphia, the Clark family had split into separate rooms at Sue Harrigan's house, some impatient with McNabb, others jarred by the short delay on the high-definition television. Now they gathered again, sang the Eagles fight song, then went back to separate televisions. There was hope, but it was slim. The touchdown drive had eaten nearly four minutes.

What do we do now?

Onside kick?

Kick away?

We still have two timeouts.

Even if we don't recover the kick, maybe we get the ball back at the fifteen or twenty.

The Eagles bunched seven players near the left sideline for an onside kick, but David Akers blooped the ball beyond his coverage. Christian Fauria, a tight end, easily fielded the kick for New England at the Philadelphia forty-one yard line. *I think I could have caught that ball,* Ernie Clark thought dismissively. One forty-seven remaining. The Patriots played conservatively, willing to run the ball and force Philadelphia to expend its final two timeouts. Then

New England punted and the ball rolled to the Eagles' four-yard line.

Why the hell didn't they have anybody back to field the punt?

Forty-six seconds on the clock. No timeouts. On first down, McNabb was pressured. He flicked a pass to Westbrook, who unwisely caught it for a meager one-yard gain. The clock kept running.

"What's he doing?" Ernie Clark said, exasperated. "He's gotta drop that."

Second and nine at the five-yard line. Twenty-two seconds left. The Eagles anxious now. McNabb looked for Owens, but threw it short at the twenty-five. It was too late. The Eagles missed their chances in the first quarter and became desperate in the fourth. On third and nine, McNabb retreated in the shotgun, one last frenetic hope, but the ball sailed high and off the fingers of L. J. Smith and into the hands of Rodney Harrison, the Patriots' safety. New England had won its third Super Bowl in four years, by a cumulative nine points. The Patriots had prevailed with a maddening style. They had played just well enough to win, and to leave the Eagles believing they had beaten themselves. Philadelphia would ache through an off-season with the bitter taste of missed opportunity.

Reid explained what needed no explanation: Three interceptions, one lost fumble, four turnovers.

"When you have two good football teams playing each other, you can't turn the ball over," he said. "That's the name of the game."

Governor Rendell, on *Post Game Live* at the stadium, said that, on balance, McNabb had done "some good things" by throwing for three touchdowns and 357 yards. But, as for the Eagles' time management, Rendell said, "There was no excuse for that."

Several viewers e-mailed the panel, complaining that McNabb was overrated, that he could never deliver a Super Bowl win, that he choked at the slightest pressure.

These assertions made Ray Didinger angry.

"Anybody who watched what this guy accomplished this year and could say he's a choker and you're never going to win a Super Bowl with him, they don't have a clue," Didinger said.

Only four quarterbacks in the Super Bowl era had a winning percentage above 70 percent, Didinger said—Tom Brady, Roger Staubach, Joe Montana and McNabb.

"I think any other fan base in the National Football League would get down on their knees and thank God they have this guy as their quarterback," Didinger said. "Donovan McNabb didn't play his last Super Bowl tonight. He will be back here with the Eagles. Before his career is over with, he will win one."

Having established a football dynasty in the era of free agency, New England allowed itself to gloat. Freddie Mitchell had promised "something" for Rodney Harrison, but Harrison caught more passes from McNabb at safety (two) than Mitchell did at receiver (one).

"All he does is talk," Coach Bill Belichick told *Sports Illustrated*. "He's terrible, and you can print that. I was happy when he was in the game."

In the stands, a couple of New England fans started giving it to Chris and Ernie Clark, holding up three fingers, saying, "That's number three," bragging about the Patriots' supremacy. Angry, disappointed, Ernie Clark started to jaw back at them, but Chris put his hand on his father's shoulder and said, "Dad, when you win, that's what you get to do."

The best team won, Chris thought to himself, and then he said aloud, "Why can't we be the best just once?"

All week, Jacksonville seemed to be a suburb of Philadelphia. But as Chris and his father left Alltel Stadium, in eerie quiet, they seemed to be nearly alone in a swarm of Patriots fans. In victory, the New Englanders seemed to have multiplied.

As Butch DeLuca drove his family back to Daytona, Tim Kelly, his son-in-law, sat in the back of the minivan, silent, deadened. Not really angry or depressed, not yet. Mostly void of all feeling. You get hit in the face so many times, it goes numb. Tim couldn't believe it. This was the Eagles' shot. If you can't go into a hurry-up offense with five, six minutes left, that's inexcusable. People said the Eagles were built to last, but how long had fans heard that? *Why are we so happy being second best? I'm sick of being second best. Absolutely sick of it.* He was as happy as the next guy for the great season the Eagles gave him, but pissed because they didn't win it all. Sure, they were pro athletes, but Tim wondered if they felt the pain that the fans felt. *God, at least show some urgency.* Now he had to go through an entire season just to get back to the playoffs. A fifth straight NFC championship game? That was unheard of. Tim didn't think it had ever been done. The Eagles could end up being a better team next season and not get as far. *Let's be realistic.*

As they drove to the house where they were staying in Jacksonville, Ernie and Chris Clark talked about how the outcome of the Super Bowl should not ruin a whole season. The Eagles had kept their fans entertained until the final play of the final minute of the final game. What more could you ask for? Ernie and Chris had spent four days together, a father and his son at a ballgame. Isn't that what every son wanted? To be with his dad at a game? To laugh and shout and nudge and argue and hope for the shared joy of history overcome? It had been a once-in-a-lifetime experience. Chris wanted to remember it as a great thing. But he was an Eagles fan and there was a gnaw in his heart.

If only.

At the RV park near Alltel Stadium, Scott Berk, the Patriots fan in Shaun Young's group, climbed atop the Eagles RV. He started taunting the dejected Eagles supporters, pointing to his Patriots jersey and derisively singing, "Fly Eagles Fly." This did not go over well with the boys from Philly and Delaware and Allentown.

"You wanna fight? I'll fight you right now."

"Get off my RV or I'll throw you off."

Everybody was upset, and when Berk tried to stick out his hand, Shaun was in no mood to be congratulatory.

"Dude, chill out, or you gonna get your ass whipped."

It was a scattershot anger, at Berk, at the Eagles in those final minutes. Clock management was brutal. For the life of him, Shaun couldn't understand what happened to the Eagles in those last six, seven, eight minutes. They had no fire in their belly. They needed a couple of first downs, and they ran the ball and threw dink passes. *What the fuck?* They're better than what they put on the field. They played lousy for the most part and barely got beat. That's what really stung. They could have won without their best game, but still they lost, unable to prevail even by mediocrity's adequate obligation.

Shaun's group had planned to party near the stadium if the Eagles won, but they were in no mood after this kind of defeat, so they packed up and headed back to Pecan Park near the airport. Shaun removed his face paint and his shoulder pads. He lay on the floor of the RV and tried to sleep but couldn't. The space around him seemed cramped, confining, defeat pressing in on him. He got thirty-eight phone calls, but ignored all of them. The game kept playing in his head—*Why this? Why that?*—a fan's unanswered questions slapping back and forth like windshield wipers. He tossed and turned, finally nodding off for maybe ten minutes before the sun came up on an empty morning, the wait of forty-four seasons without a championship extending to forty-five.

30

Monday, February 7

John Kleinstuber couldn't bring himself to turn on the television in Havertown. It was the first thing he did on Monday morning after an Eagles game, but he couldn't bear to see Tom Brady and Tedy Bruschi holding up that Super Bowl trophy.

"Fuck 'em."

John woke up and he wanted to sell his boat and his Eagles tickets. He had a thirty-foot Bayliner. All the boat did was break. All the Eagles did was lose. Get rid of both of them, he told his wife, Helen. But of course he wouldn't do it. Not a chance. Eagles fans always said they were leaving, and they always came back. The first invoice for season tickets would be arriving any day.

"I'm not going to let it ruin my life," John said.

The Eagles went conservative. *It friggin' killed them. God-damnit, they were right there*. They had it. But he had to move on, to do whatever else there was in life until training camp began in August. All of next season wouldn't mean a damn thing until the playoffs and the Super Bowl. Four months of foreplay. All that waiting, just to get back to this point. The Eagles seemed ready to get back again, but it would be a long, painful wait.

Twenty-two years without a professional championship in the city, going on twenty-three.

"Are we ever going to get over this?" John said. "Just some-body. Phillies, Flyers, Sixers. Can't somebody do this?"

He got out of bed, but he wouldn't put on his Eagles fleece. And he was mad at Donovan McNabb. He didn't want to be. He had played football, and he knew how difficult it was. But three interceptions? The game could have been a lot more lopsided than it was. One of the guys on WIP said he had a love-hate relationship with McNabb. John understood. *Brady had been on the sideline, talking over the next play, and Donovan had a Gatorade towel over his head.* Maybe he could have taken it a little more seriously. Maybe he was too loosey-goosey. But John didn't want to be mad. The Eagles had given him a great season. Still, why couldn't it happen?

Helen said, why don't we find out what time the team is coming back and go down and see them? John didn't want to. It was over.

"Dude, I'm three hundred pounds of hollow," he said.

One of these years, Washington and the Giants and Dallas would get better. Still, the Eagles seemed lined up to get back to the big game. But that's what sucked. A whole season asking, can we win the Super Bowl? It would be torture. He wouldn't listen to WIP any more until training camp. The Flyers were canceled and he didn't want to hear about the Sixers. He would wait patiently until August. He'd find another outlet. He didn't know what it would be, but he would find something.

His golf club was closing up for a month. He went in to work this morning, just for something to do, and he didn't turn his computer on, or the radio. Everyone was standoffish. They knew he could be a sore loser. His mother called, left a message. *I hope everything is okay.* He could tell by her voice that she was afraid to call. But he was doing better than he had after those losses in the NFC championship game. Much better. He hadn't torn down the wooden eagle head in his yard. The season was over. No sense in being a crybaby about it.

"I'm trying not to let it ruin my life," John said.

Still, he was down.

"I'm talking to myself not to be, it's just football, but I'm cloudy," John said. "Here we go again. I might be divorced if we have to go through much more of this. I think I'd divorce me if I had to put up with me."

The next couple of days would be tough, but he'd get over it. It might take until August, but he'd be okay. The Eagles were such a good team. They could be right back there again. But it seemed like such a long trek. Today was not easy.

"I can't let it ruin my life," John said. "The cat woke me up. I was sitting in bed, saying, 'Sell the boat, sell the tickets.' But it's a football game. I don't know where to detach. Where's football and where's life? But we move on."

It was three thirty in the afternoon and still John had not turned on the television. He bought the paper and read a few stories, but the TV stayed off. He didn't want to see Tom Brady and Tedy Bruschi showing off that trophy.

"It sounds spiteful, but you know what?" John said. "Fuck 'em."

We talked by phone. I had flown from Jacksonville to Port of Spain, Trinidad, to cover a soccer match. It was the height of Carnival season. Sound trucks and glittery steel-drum strutting in the streets, party girls in their beads and bikinis. But it seemed vacant somehow, compared to what might have been in Philadelphia. There would have been a hell of a parade in Philadelphia.

"Damn!" said the front-page headline in the *Daily News*.

Shaun Young and his crew began the long trip home in the Eagles RV. Another RV traveling with them blew a tire on a trailer somewhere in South Carolina. Shaun felt horrible, empty, angry, sick to his stomach. His throat was sore from yelling and his body was cramped from all the straining and gyrating. It was an ugly feeling, but a familiar one.

"This is rough, this sucked, this was a winnable game," Shaun said. "It just seems every time things are going to happen, something comes up. We falter. It's going to take a while to get through it. I don't believe in that curse stuff. But something goofy is going on. It just wasn't our time. People say, 'When is our time?' I wish I could say. I wish I had an answer. Sooner or later this has to come to an end. I'm not going to die until it does. I refuse to die until it happens. I'm trying to make a deal with someone to make sure I don't go anywhere until it happens. People are so hungry. Why can't we win once? I have no doubt it's going to happen, but I'm getting tired of saying, 'Next year, next year.'"

Ray Didinger drove from Jacksonville to Sarasota, Florida, to see his parents. His father, also named Ray, was eighty-two now. Ray the elder had spent so many hopeful vacations at the Eagles training camp in Hershey, watching practice during the day, sitting and planning his roster cuts in the hotel room at night. He had seen the Eagles win a championship in 1960, but now his hope had flickered on seeing another one. He was eighty-two. How many more chances did he have to say "Wait 'til next year"?

"I've finally come to the conclusion that I'll never live to see the Eagles win the Super Bowl," Ray the elder told his son.

His voice seemed anguished.

Ernie and Chris Clark drove to Orlando to catch their flight back to Philadelphia. Chris hoped they could do this again next year, when the Super Bowl was in Detroit. The Eagles seemed well positioned, but he had a new appreciation for how difficult it was to maintain greatness, especially in the era of free agency. Players were getting older. All it took was one key injury—heaven forbid something happened to McNabb—and a season could be ruined in a heartbeat. It seemed impossible to stay on top forever. Maybe this was the end of the Eagles' run. Maybe that's the best he and his father would get out of it, four NFC championship games and a trip to the Super Bowl. He hoped not, but if it was, then, hey, that wasn't a bad deal. He was in better spirits than a year ago, when the Eagles faltered against Carolina and he snarled, "That's it, I can't take it anymore," and said he was never coming back. He had a little more distance now. His three young children were at home and they didn't care much whether the Eagles won or lost, and he couldn't be moping around all the time, thinking, *Woe is me*. He still rooted his heart out, he still wanted them to win as much, but he was forty-one now and he could take it a little more in stride. The past four years had not given him any championships, but they had given him perspective.

Chris had spent every waking minute over the last five days with his father. Who gets to do that anymore, a grown son alone with his dad for five days? *At his age.* Ernie Clark was seventy now. Chris spent a lot of time thinking about that. The clock was running. He brought his father to the Super Bowl and they had a great time, and now they were heading home.

"Dad, it's a weekend I'll never forget," Chris told his father when they reached Philadelphia. "I hope you know how much it meant to me."

Ernie Clark smiled and gave his son a hug.

"There's always next year," he said.

Epilogue

Four days after the Super Bowl, Ernie and Anne Clark visited friends in Palm Springs, California. For the most part, the game was out of Ernie's system. He had followed the Eagles since the 1940s, and a half-century had taught him to loosen the grip or it could be strangling. The sun still came up. He had to move on. His daughter, Terry, was expecting twins. That was more important than any football game.

"Although it didn't seem that way at the time," Ernie laughed.

He talked about perspective. The Eagles' record could match anyone's over the past five years. At least they hadn't embarrassed themselves or their fans against New England. That wasn't much solace, but it was better than getting beat forty-six to ten. There was always next year. And then Ernie thought for a second. The hell with perspective. He was an Eagles fan. Perspective was over-rated.

"Can we trade that good perspective for a championship, just once?" he said.

With no Eagles victory parade to distract him, Governor Rendell gave his annual Pennsylvania budget speech three days after the Super Bowl. A copy of the text made no mention of the Eagles. After a bone spur in his heel cleared, Shaun Young went back to work hauling trash in Springfield, Delaware County. Ray Didinger took a short leave of absence from NFL Films to finish writing an Eagles encyclopedia. John Kleinstuber left his golf club job. He and his wife, Helen, opened a restaurant in Havertown, and John wondered whether he should close on Sundays during football season.

Andy Reid and his wife, Tammy, went on vacation to Peter Island, a secluded spot without cars or television in the British Virgin Islands. At least the Reids thought it was secluded. During lunch at a beachfront restaurant, as Reid said to his wife, "We're away from the world," a catamaran pulled up and deposited its guests in a dinghy for the shore.

The beachcombers recognized Reid, just as he realized who they were and thought, "Oh, no, Elvis sighting."

And then he heard a familiar chant. "E-A-G-L-E-S, Eagles!"

"It was classic," Reid told the Philadelphia newspapers. "They were out of control. They were crazy. We were taking pictures. We were best friends. They wanted me to get on that yacht and go back with them."

Five days after the Super Bowl, I caught up with Butch DeLuca at his deli in Havertown. He was removing his neon Eagles helmet from the front window, storing it until next season. The Eagles streamers were gone, too, and the life-size cardboard cutout of Donovan McNabb.

He shook his head.

"They had the game in the bag," he said from behind the counter. "They had it in the bag. Old Donovan couldn't come through again. He choked. Four turnovers killed 'em. Killed 'em."

How come nobody on New England got sick or tired or whatever happened to McNabb? Butch wanted to know.

"I don't know, he just can't win the big game," Butch said. "You put the rush on him, you blitz him, he gets wacky back there."

What was he doing throwing the ball down the middle of the field with fifty-five seconds left and no timeouts? Butch asked. Everybody knows you throw to the sideline and try to get the guy out of bounds.

"He takes the lump," Butch said. "I don't know. He chokes, that's my gut feeling."

Should the Eagles get rid of him?

"Oh, no, you can't do that," Butch said. "Can't get rid of the guy. You keep hopin' and hopin' and hopin'. He didn't play his game. Two games before that, he was fine. This one, I don't understand. I don't know. Why can't they win? The Philly jinx."

What did he have to look forward to until next summer? Butch didn't follow the Sixers, and the Phillies were sure to stink. Five days after the Super Bowl and he still wasn't over it. He stood at the grill and burned a muffin and a bagel.

"Look at what the hell I did," Butch said.

Gene Kelly, another regular, came in.

"I told you they weren't going to get there with a black quarterback," Kelly said.

He liked McNabb well enough, Kelly said, thought he was a really good quarterback, but not great. Maybe he could be if he had a line to protect him.

"He got us there," Kelly said. "Can he get us back? I think so. Can he win the big one? That's the question."

A guy ordered French toast and Butch made eggs.

"He's all shook up," said the customer, Bob Hunsberger.

McNabb's all right, Butch said. But how long did it take the guy? He's here, what, five, six years?

"I don't know what the answer is," Butch said. "Everybody in that stadium thought they were going to win. Everybody thought they had a shot. I'm figuring this'll be the second black quarterback to ever win the Super Bowl. Everything's pointed his way, and he didn't get the job done."

He had that Gatorade towel on his head, Butch said. Made it seem like he didn't care. That's one thing Philly wouldn't tolerate. Not caring. It's a shame. Very depressing. Of course McNabb cared. "He's, he's, he's just not consistent," Butch said. "Throwin' them lollipop passes and stuff like 'at. How do you get sacked in the red zone without throwing the ball away? You gotta throw it away."

"You hate to start with this black-white stuff," Butch said, "but I don't know if McNabb's smart enough. I just don't know. Like he's not into the game. And the play-calling's horrible. How do you run the ball with fifty-five seconds to go. Whaddya think, someone's going to break it for ninety-five yards? Unbelievable, unbelievable."

He didn't mean this racial stuff, Butch said. It was just his emotion and disappointment coming out.

"Just a crazy speech, frustration," Butch said.

Chick Currie, a customer, approached Butch at the cash register and said he needed his address.

"I'll send you a get-well card," Currie said, and laughed.

McNabb was the key to next season, Butch said. He wasn't giving up on him. He even had a spare McNabb cardboard cutout in the back room. Saving it for next year.

"Oh God," Butch said, whisking eggs for an omelet. "They'll be there. I think they'll be there again."

They got one step farther this year, you know. What the hell. Next year's Super Bowl was in Detroit. Butch had a friend who lived forty-five minutes away. Already offered him a place to stay.

"I don't know, I don't know," Butch said. "How many years does it take to do this? I don't know. We can't win the big game. They have the players. Why can't they win? Why can't they win?"

He'd still follow them. Of course he would. He enjoyed it. Thirteen picks in the draft. Maybe a couple of free agents. There'd be some new faces.

"I don't have much more time left, you know what I mean?" Butch said. "Once in a lifetime. Just one. Just win one. They get so close. So close. They can do it."

Shaun Young didn't want to hear racial talk about McNabb. He was sick and tired of it.

"Of course he's smart enough," Shaun said. "If he wasn't smart enough, he wouldn't have made it this far in the first place."

Shaun gave so much of himself to the Eagles. Did he ever think he gave too much? Not at all, Shaun said. That's who he was. He couldn't yank the reins on his emotions. He was always competitive and animated. He wore his heart on his sleeve. He couldn't be any other way. He loved the team. Not so much the players—don't get him wrong, many of them were nice guys—but it was the team he loved above all. And he would keep coming back. Always.

"I jump off the bandwagon, and then they win the whole thing," Shaun said. "I don't want to be left off of that. You need to go through turmoil to get to the other side of the rainbow. You need to hit a few bumps. We've hit quite a few."

Detroit for the Super Bowl would be a hell of a lot colder than Jacksonville, nothing like Miami or New Orleans, but hey, if the Eagles were there, Shaun would be there, too.

"I'd go to Anchorage, Alaska, if it meant getting a ring on the players' hands," Shaun said.

Winter thawed and so did heartbreak over the Super Bowl. By mid-April, Philadelphia had returned to its fractious normalcy. The 2005 season schedule made the front page of the *Daily News* and earned a banner headline above the masthead in the *Inquirer*. Again Philly began reveling in its three favorite sports: rooting for the Eagles, worrying about the Eagles and complaining about the Eagles.

Tim Kelly gathered with friends to watch videotape highlights of their tailgating parties. Butch DeLuca bought a deli in Delaware for his son, Brian, who was still grieving over the death of his girl-friend. This would be a chance for Brian to start over, get his mind on other things. He'd make a go of it. He'd been around the deli business his whole life. Brian was still deciding whether to stay open year-round or just from Memorial Day to Labor Day.

"He wants to come home for the Eagles," Butch said.

Terrell Owens wanted to renegotiate his contract, saying he "wasn't the guy who got tired in the Super Bowl," a cutting refer-ence to McNabb. Owens skipped a minicamp and threatened to miss training camp. McNabb fired back, saying that if anyone had a problem with him, he should settle it like a man. Anybody look-ing for an excuse for the Super Bowl loss, McNabb said, should "pretty much just keep my name out your mouth."

On WIP, Howard Eskin started a food drive in case Owens couldn't live on his scheduled salary of $3.5 million dollars.

Freddie Mitchell went to a business seminar at Harvard, said that McNabb lacked confidence in him. He also complained that his teammates were too scared of New England to support him after he incited safety Rodney Harrison. Andy Reid had heard enough. He told Mitchell not to come to minicamp and, a week later, cut him.

Was this the first sign of implosion or just the normal restlessness of a team that had reached the Super Bowl? Losers in the Super Bowl had a history of nose-diving the next season. But questions about the Eagles could not be answered for months. Already, though, Ray Didinger sensed that these Eagles players and the coach and owner didn't possess the same endearing qualities of the 1981 Super Bowl team. Dick Vermeil's face was still on billboards around town two decades later. But this was a different era. The people who ran and coached and played for the team now represented Philadelphia but were not of Philadelphia. They seemed somehow less accessible. There was a kind of detachment. Would Reid and McNabb and others stay in the area, making their lives here after football, as many from that previous team did? Didinger wondered.

"I think this team will be judged strictly on whether it wins the Super Bowl or not," he said.

A week into baseball season, the Phillies flirted with irrelevance, before a brief June recovery. Still, they had been bumped by their flagship radio station on Friday nights for Frank Sinatra music. As the NBA regular season wound down, Chris Webber, the Sixers' latest acquisition, played indolently against the Celtics after returning from injury and the crowd booed lustily. Allen Iverson said he loved Philadelphia, but added, "I don't know how good you can play when your home crowd boos you."

By chance, that same night I went to see a one-man play, *The Philly Fan*, a funny and plaintive tribute to the city's unreciprocated love for its sports teams. Near the end of the play, the Fan said, "When we like ya we cheer ya. When we don't like ya we boo ya. And if you can't take it, get the hell outta Philly."

In an elegiac soliloquy, the Fan made a desperate plea for Philadelphia's sporting hunger to be sated after twenty-two years with no championship, forty-four years if you were talking Eagles. LSU had finally won a national title after forty-five seasons. Maybe the Eagles would also get lucky in the forty-fifth year. "When's our turn?" the Fan asked.

> That's all we want. Guys from around here, ya know, we just— we go to work, raise the family—nothin' fancy. But there's a whole generation of kids 'round here don't know what it's like to have a winner. And now these prick owners pricin' us out and, it's like, like, I don't know, like they're . . . they're all so fuckin' greedy. They're takin' somethin' away from us. And trust me, we ain't got that much to start with. All we wanta do is watch the game. We buy tickets. We stick by ya. How many cities would come all these years for this string'a losers? Just . . . throw us a bone every once in a while. Give us a champ.

After the show, playwright Bruce Graham sat with the star and director for a question-and-answer session. If the Eagles ever did win the Super Bowl, Graham said, his play would become obsolete.

"I don't care," he said. "I want the Lombardi Trophy."

Acknowledgments

I would like to thank the core characters in this book for their patient indulgence—Shaun Young, the Clark family, the DeLucas and the Kellys, John and Helen Kleinstuber, Ray Didinger, Angelo Cataldi and Governor Edward G. Rendell. If I couldn't be a fan, it was great fun to be among the devoted. Special thanks to Ray Didinger for his unmatched knowledge of the Eagles and his gracious willingness to share it.

Thanks to Rich Hofmann of the *Philadelphia Daily News* for introducing me to the Clark family. And to all the other sportswriters and broadcasters and editors who traveled in the Eagles' orbit through the years and lent their friendship and stories and advice and encouragement and expertise: Bob Ford, Bill Lyon, Gordon Forbes, Jay Searcy, Phil Anastasia, Angelo Cataldi, Al Morganti, Glen Macnow, Phil Sheridan, Sal Paolantonio, Ron Reid, Stan Hochman, Kevin Noonan, Jack McCaffery, Bob Brookover, Bob Grotz, Merrill Reese, Mike Quick, Stan Walters, Ron Jaworski, Howard Eskin, Gene Collier, Paul Domowitch, Les Bowen, Pat McLoone, Bill Conlin, Rhea Hughes, Stephen A. Smith, Sam Donnellon, John Smallwood, Dave Spadaro, Anthony Gargano, Steve Martorano, Michael Barkann, Ed Hilt, Reuben Frank and Mark Eckel.

I'd like to thank my editors at the *New York Times,* Tom Jolly and Kristin Huckshorn, for assigning me to cover the Eagles through their playoff run last season, which made the book possible, and for their understanding while I wrote it.

Thanks to David Hirshey, my editor at HarperCollins, for his trust, candor, direction and his way with titles. And to his assistant, Miles Doyle, for looking after all the details. And to my agent, David Black, for smooth sailing.

At WIP, I'd like to thank producer Joe Weachter for access to the station, and Jill Speckman for providing audiotapes. At Comcast SportsNet, I'd like to thank Maureen Quilter for access to *Post Game Live* and for the load of videotapes.

I'd like to thank the Eagles' public relations staff, present and past, especially the retired Jim Gallagher, a human Rolodex of numbers and stories. Thanks in particular for that film of the 1944 Orange Bowl.

I would also like to thank Bruce Graham for his time and permission to quote from his play, *The Philly Fan.*

As always, this would not have been possible without my wife, Debby, who freed up everything so I could write and who spent hours taping programs and sifting through newspapers and whose love is matched only by her intelligence. Thanks, too, to my daughter Julie-Ann, who kept her Eagles radar alert at school and allowed me on the computer long enough to get the book written.

And thanks to my parents for their remembrances and for making sport fun and funny.

BOOKS